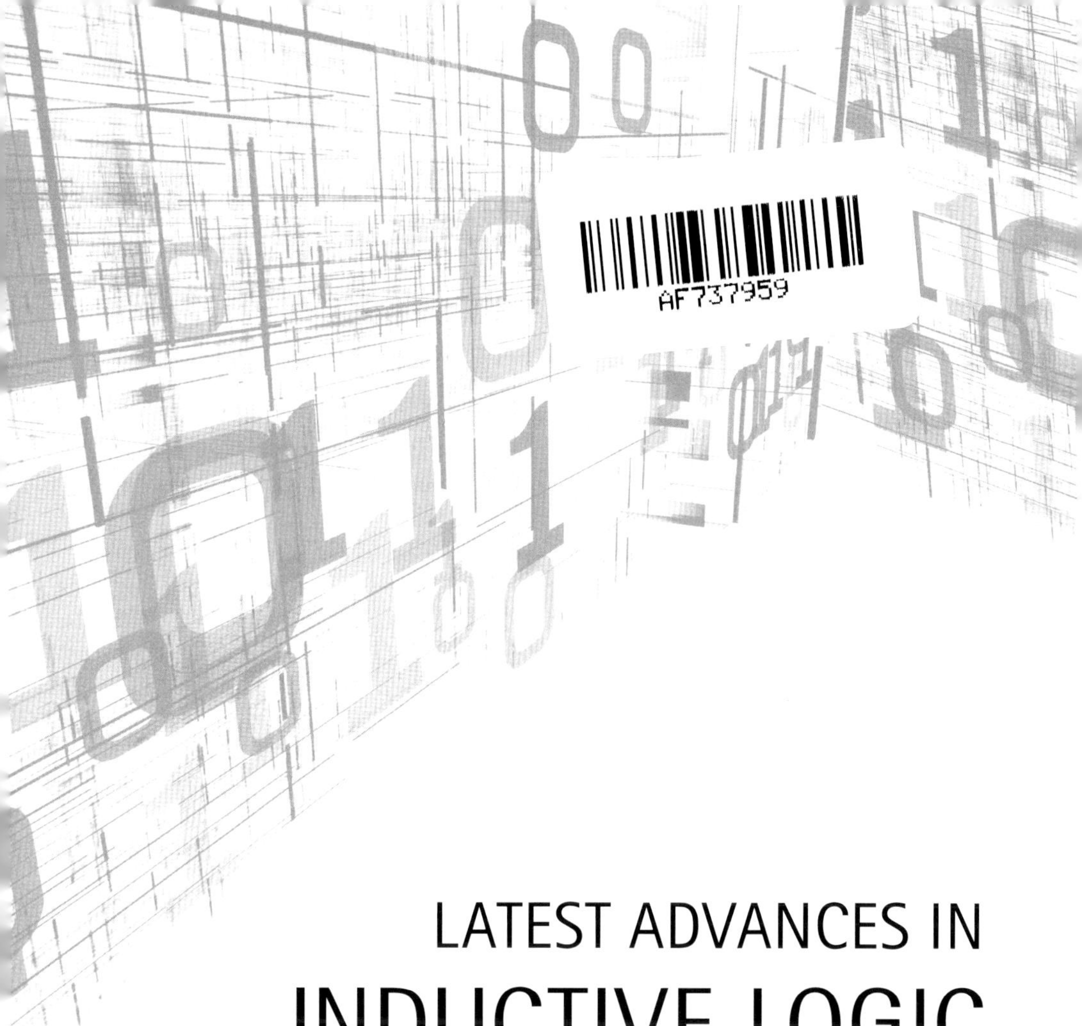

AF737959

LATEST ADVANCES IN INDUCTIVE LOGIC PROGRAMMING

Stephen H. Muggleton & Hiroaki Watanabe
Imperial College London, UK

ICP
Imperial College Press

Site HE | MIDDLESEX UNIVERSITY LIBRARY
Accession No. 73664448
Class No.
Special Collection ✓

Published by

Imperial College Press
57 Shelton Street
Covent Garden
London WC2H 9HE

Distributed by

World Scientific Publishing Co. Pte. Ltd.
5 Toh Tuck Link, Singapore 596224
USA office: 27 Warren Street, Suite 401-402, Hackensack, NJ 07601
UK office: 57 Shelton Street, Covent Garden, London WC2H 9HE

Library of Congress Cataloging-in-Publication Data
Muggleton, Stephen, author.
Latest advances in inductive logic programming / Stephen Muggleton, Imperial College London, UK, Hiroaki Watanabe, Imperial College London, UK.
pages cm
Includes bibliographical references and index.
ISBN 978-1-78326-508-4 (hardcover : alk. paper)
1. Logic programming. 2. Induction (Logic) 3. Machine learning. I. Watanabe, Hiroaki, 1969– author. II. Title.
QA76.63.M84 2014
006.3'1--dc23

2014033096

British Library Cataloguing-in-Publication Data
A catalogue record for this book is available from the British Library.

Copyright © 2015 by Imperial College Press

All rights reserved. This book, or parts thereof, may not be reproduced in any form or by any means, electronic or mechanical, including photocopying, recording or any information storage and retrieval system now known or to be invented, without written permission from the Publisher.

For photocopying of material in this volume, please pay a copying fee through the Copyright Clearance Center, Inc., 222 Rosewood Drive, Danvers, MA 01923, USA. In this case permission to photocopy is not required from the publisher.

Typeset by Stallion Press
Email: enquiries@stallionpress.com

Printed in Singapore by FuIsland Offset Printing (S) Pte Ltd

LATEST ADVANCES IN

INDUCTIVE LOGIC PROGRAMMING

Preface

This book represents late-breaking papers associated with the 21st International Conference of Inductive Logic Programming (ILP 2011) which was held in Cumberland Lodge, Great Windsor Park and marked 20 years since the first ILP workshop in 1991. During this period the conference has developed into the premier forum for work on logic-based machine learning. The submission procedure for the conference followed a similar format to that of previous conferences, and was particularly close to that used in ILP 2006. Submissions were requested in two phases. The first phase involved submission of short papers (six pages) which were then presented at the conference and posted on the conference website prior to the conference itself. In the second phase, reviewers selected papers for long paper submission (15 pages maximum). These were assessed by the same reviewers, who then decided which papers to include in the Machine Learning Journal Special Issue and Proceedings. The post-conference proceedings of ILP 2011 has been published as Volume 7207 in the Springer Lecture Notes in Artificial Intelligence.

An overview of this book is as follows. Part 1 contains *Applications* of ILP in the domains of Game Theory, Robotics, Data Mining, Search Engine, Cosmetic Product Selection, Mobile Phone, Biology, and Ecology. This wide variety of applications characterises the diversity of real-world applications of ILP.

In Part 2, attempts for extending ILP to *Probabilistic Logical Learning* are presented. Probabilistic extensions of ILP have been extensively studied over the last decade. These five papers indicate some of the latest developments in this sub-area.

Part 3 covers novel *Implementations* in ILP. This part starts from a paper on a customisable multi-processor architecture and its application to hardware-supported search within ILP. The strong speed-up results in the paper indicate that such special-purpose hardware is a promising and exciting new avenue of development within the area, and an indication of the maturity of the field. The second paper proposes Multivalue Learning which makes hypothesis search more expressive by analysing statistical aspects of the background knowledge. The third paper studies the learning of dependent concepts in order to induce model-transformation rules in the automation of model-driven data warehouses. The last paper is on Graph Contraction Pattern Matching problems in a domain of graph mining. This paper combines Information Theory tools with relational learning.

We turn to *Theory* papers in Part 4, in which a novel method to machine learn patterns in formal proofs is discussed, using statistical machine learning methods. The second paper investigates the issue of whether ILP can deal with incomplete and vague structured knowledge.

In Part 5, two attempts at *Logical Learning* are reported. The first attempt concerns efficient higher-order logical learning. The authors empirically show that the proposed class of higher-order logic outperforms the existing higher-order machine learning system, λ-Progol. The second paper studies automatic invention of functional abstractions. The authors' approach is implemented in the KANDINSKY system using an algorithm that searches for common subterms over sets of functional programs.

Part 6 contains a single paper on *Constraints* in learning roster problems. Finally, relational learning for football-related predictions is reported from a *Spacial and Temporal* learning point of view in Part 7. Relational data is derived from match statistics.

The variety of approaches and applications within the book gives an insight into the vibrancy and maturity of the field.

S. H. Muggleton and Hiroaki Watanabe

Acknowledgments

The 21st International Conference of Inductive Logic Programming 2011 was held at Cumberland Lodge in the UK from 31st July to 3rd August 2011 under the auspices of the Department of Computing, Imperial College London. In addition to the many technical paper presentations, the invited talks this year were given by a distinguished group of Artificial Intelligence researchers, namely Hector Geffner, Toby Walsh and Richard Sutton.

We gratefully acknowledge Syngenta Ltd for supporting the applications prize, and the Machine Learning Journal for supporting the theory prize.

Contents

PART 1

Applications

Chapter 1

Can ILP Learn Complete and Correct Game Strategies?

Stephen H. Muggleton and Changze Xu

Computing Department, Imperial College London, UK

While there has been a long history of applying machine learning to game playing, our approach differs by attempting to provide a general approach to learn complete winning strategies for a group of combinatorial games and the first time to apply ILP (inductive logic programming) to learn complete and correct game strategies. Instead of learning the winning moves under different game states, the learning problem we propose is to learn a classifier for P-positions, in which the next player has at least one minimax winning move. Combining such a classifier with a move generator produces a winning strategy. We report the predictive accuracy curves of learning the positions for winning strategies of a range of combinatorial games. In each of the six combinatorial games 100% accurate prediction is achieved after presenting, at most, 26 randomly sampled examples of play. These results were averaged over ten independently sampled trials. We also report the predictive accuracy curves of learning the positions for the winning strategy of Nim using artificial neural network (ANN), support vector machine (SVM) and case-based reasoning (CBR). Even with 200 randomly sample examples, 100% predictive accuracy is not achieved in any case by ANNs, SVMs and CBRs.

1.1 Introduction

Automated Game Playing, Machine Learning and Logical Reasoning are each important sub-areas of research within Artificial Intelligence (AI) [Russell and Norvig (2010)]. This chapter combines these three aspects of AI. In combinatorial game theory [Berlekamp *et al.* (2001)], an impartial game is a game in which the allowable moves depend only on the position and not on which of the two players is currently moving. Nim is an impartial game in which two players take turns removing objects from different heaps. On

Table 1.1 A 3-Heap Nim game starting with 1, 2, 4 objects.

Heap1	Heap2	Heap3	Moves
1	2	4	Player1 removes one object from Heap 3
1	2	3	Player2 removes two object from Heap 2
1	0	3	Player1 removes two object from Heap 3
1	0	1	Player2 removes one object from Heap 1
0	0	1	Player1 removes the last object and wins

each turn, a player must remove at least one object, and may remove any number of objects provided they all come from the same heap. The player to take the last object wins. Table 1.1 shows an example of a 3-heap Nim. The winning strategy of Nim is based on computing the xor sum of the number of objects in each pile [Bouton (1902)] and was extended to impartial games by Sprague and Grundy [Sprague (1936); Grundy (1939)]. The Sprague–Grundy theory [Berlekamp *et al.* (2001)] shows that any impartial game is isomorphic to a Nim game; in other words, despite appearances, all impartial games are mathematically equivalent to Nim. Later, Guy and Smith [Guy and Smith (1956)] applied this theory to obtain complete, closed-form solutions to a wide variety of impartial games. However, it is still non-trivial for humans to manually find an accurate mapping from an impartial game to a Nim game. It is well known [Berlekamp *et al.* (2001); Gardner (1988)] that each state of an impartial game must be classified to one of two types of positions: P-positions and N-positions and there are three theorems [Berlekamp (1988)] which form the basis of winning strategies of impartial games: any move applied to a P-position turns the game into an N-position; there is at least one move that turns the game from an N-position into a P-position; the final position (when the game is over) is a P-position. Our aim is to use the ILP system Progol 4.5 [Muggleton and Firth (2001)] to learn the classifier for N-P positions of impartial games. Then we use the learned N-P classifier to construct the winning move generator of these games. This approach can be easily extended for partisan games (non-impartial combinatorial games) whose winning strategies are based on N-P positions such as Northcott's game [Berlekamp *et al.* (2001)].

1.2 ILP Representation of Games

An impartial game in a P-position is a positive example. An impartial game in an N-position is a negative example. There is a set of mathematical operations {xor, mod, ×, /, +, −} regarded as general background knowledge. There is some specific background knowledge that encodes the game states. A classifier for N-P positions (target hypothesis) H which entails all the positive and none of the negative examples. A winning strategy is a function that takes as input the current state of the game, player (for partisan games), AND outputs a winning move that the current player can play.

1.2.1 *Learning schema*

Given
A set I^+ of P-positions and A set I^- of N-positions
General background knowledge (a set of mathematical functions) **GB**
Specific background knowledge for each impartial game **SB**
A space of N-P classifiers **H**
Find an N-P classifier p-Pos ∈ **H** such that
$\forall\, i^+ \in I^+, \mathbf{GB} \cup \mathbf{SB} \cup$ p-Pos $\models i^+$ and $\forall\, i^- \in I^-, \mathbf{GB} \cup \mathbf{SB} \cup$ p-Pos $\not\models i^-$
Construct the winning move generator
Input : CState-current game state Player-current player
Output : Action-winning move AState-the game state after taking the action
If p-Pos(CState)
Return an Action ∈ LegalActions(Player) with the least change to CState.
Else
  Forall Action ∈ LegalActions(Player)
   If play(Player,CState,Action)
    ←updateState(Player,CState,Action,AState),p-Pos(AState)
   Return Action and AState.

1.3 Experiments

Experiments for learning the N-P classifier for the winning strategies of six different combinatorial games are performed in this section. We will analyse the relationships between sample size and predictive accuracy of each game.

1.3.1 *Learning N-P position of impartial games by ILP*

We use Progol 4.5 [Muggleton (1995); Muggleton and Firth (2001)], as the reference system. We use the minimax algorithm to generate examples assuming that both players are playing winning strategies. We fix the sample size to 50 where 32 of them are positive examples and 18 of them are negative examples. We use the qsample program in Progol 4.5 which is based on the sampling algorithm [Knuth (1997)] to randomly generate training and testing examples. If N examples are chosen from the total sample dataset as training examples, then the remaining 50-N examples are test examples. For each game, we conduct experiments by sampling 1 to 27 training examples and repeat the same experiment 10 times for each size of training examples and calculate the mean predictive accuracy and the standard deviation. For all impartial games, we use the same set of math functions $\{xor, mod, \times, /, +, -\}$ as general background knowledge. Figure 1.1 shows the relationships between sample size and predictive accuracy of games: TakeAway, Nim, Turning Turtle, Nimble, Northcott's, and Green Hackenbush, respectively. For more details of the game rules see [Berlekamp (1988)]. In general the predictive accuracy increases with the increase of sample size for each of the six games. As we can see from the six graphs, 26 examples at most are required for a predictive accuracy of 100% in each case.

1.3.2 *Experiment to determine performance on Nim of ANNs, SVMs and CBRs*

We use MATLAB 2011B as the reference system, and the ANN toolbox (contains the ANN method) and the Bioinformatics Toolbox (contains the SVM method) in MATLAB, and implement a CBR system by MATLAB to learn the N-P classifier of a 3-heap Nim. We use 200 randomly generated examples (100 positive and 100 negative) as the total sample dataset. Examples are represented in two forms: Decimal Form and Binary Form. An example "3 4 5 1" in the Decimal Form, which means a positive example of a 3-heap Nim with $3, 4, 5$ objects, is represented as "00011 00100 00101 1" in the Binary Form (the last digit represents the class of the example: 1≡Positive and 0≡Negative). We randomly choose 20,40,60,80,100,120,140,160,180,200 examples (half positive and half negative) from the total sample dataset as the subsample and use 10-fold cross validation to find the average predictive accuracy for each size of subsample.

Figure 1.2 shows the relationships between sample size and predictive accuracy of Nim games under six different kinds of configurations. In general, SVM has higher predictive accuracy than ANN under each sample form, and for each machine learning technique, learning under Binary Form has higher predictive accuracy. CBR has extremely high predictive accuracy under Binary Form but extremely low predictive accuracy under Decimal

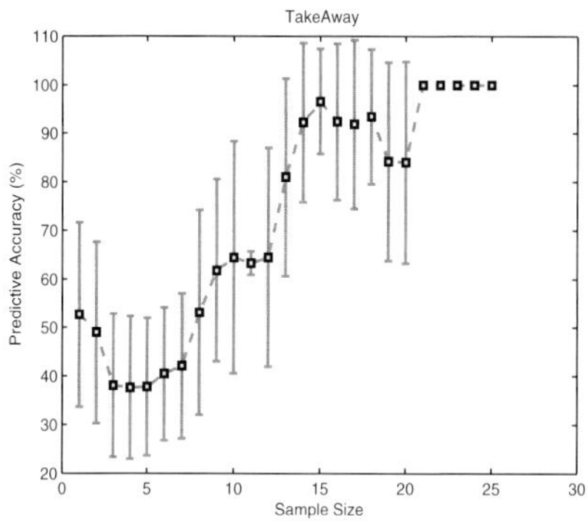

(a) Take Away

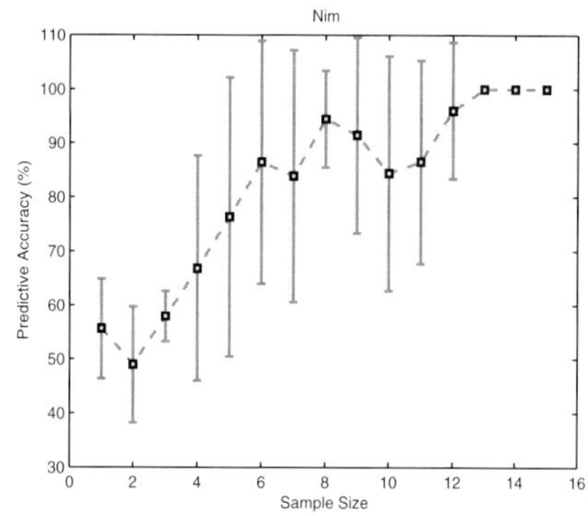

(b) Nim

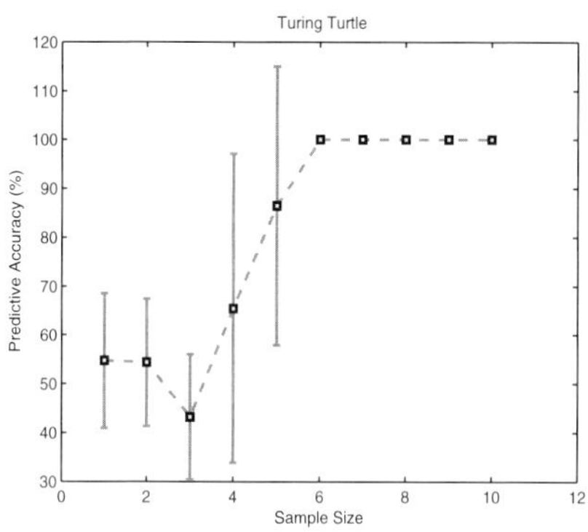

(c) Turning Turtle

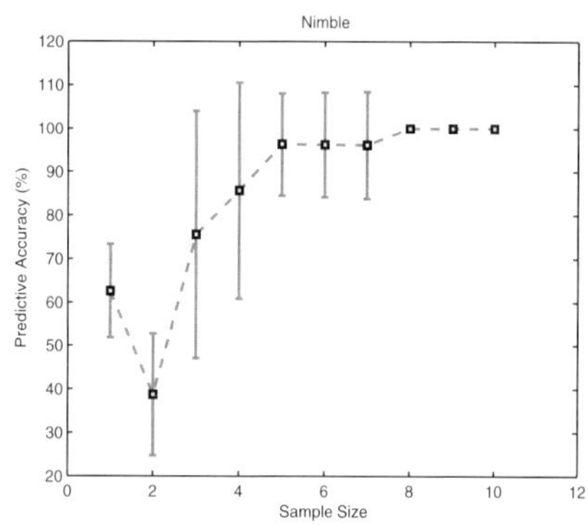

(d) Nimble

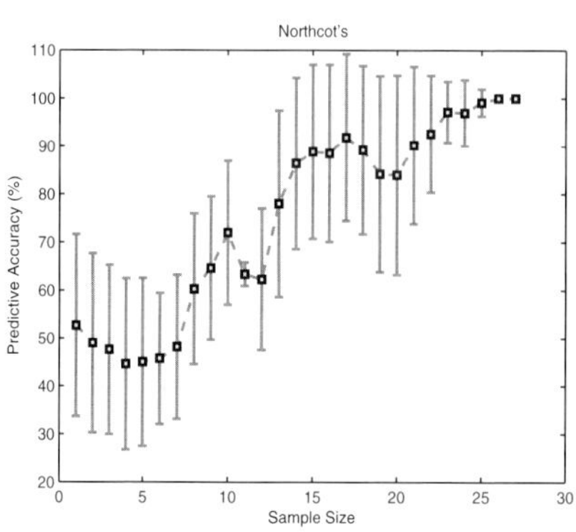

(e) Northcott's

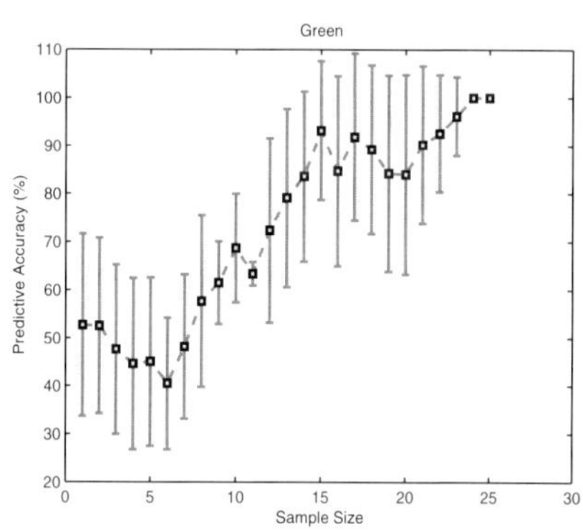

(f) Green Hachenbush

Fig. 1.1

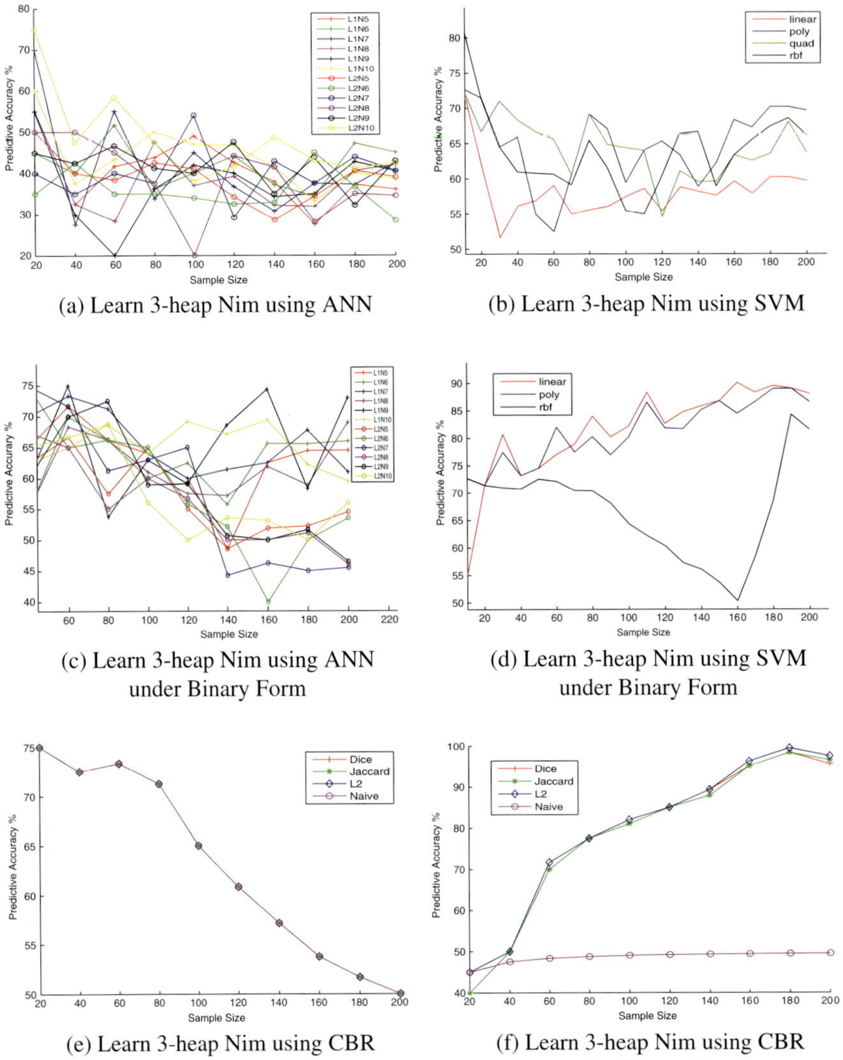

(a) Learn 3-heap Nim using ANN

(b) Learn 3-heap Nim using SVM

(c) Learn 3-heap Nim using ANN under Binary Form

(d) Learn 3-heap Nim using SVM under Binary Form

(e) Learn 3-heap Nim using CBR

(f) Learn 3-heap Nim using CBR under Binary Form

Fig. 1.2

Form. According to Fig. 1.2 the best results are achieved with SVMs using kernel functions 'linear' and 'poly' (with max exponent 3) under Binary Form which makes the predictive accuracy tend to 90% and with the CBR using similarity measure 'L2' under Binary Form which makes the predictive

Table 1.2 L means Layers, N means Neuron, Train means Training Function, Transfer means Transfer Function, R means the Learning Rate and more detail about the meaning of the ANN Values at www.mathworks.com/help/toolbox/bioinfo/ref/svmtrain and the SVM Values at www.mathworks.com/help/toolbox/nnet/ and the CBR Values at [Liao *et al.* (1998)].

Fig.	System	Sample Form	Parameter	Value
1.2(a)	ANN	Decimal	L/N/Train/ Transfer/R	2...3/5...10/ trainscg/tansig/e-4
1.2(b)	ANN	Decimal	L/N/Train/ Transfer	2...3/5...10/ trainscg/tansig/e-4
1.2(c)	SVM	Binary	Kernel	linear/poly/quad/rbf
1.2(d)	SVM	Binary	Kernel	linear/poly/rbf
1.2(e)	CBR	Decimal	Similarity Measure	dice‖ jaccard‖ naive‖ L2
1.2(f)	CBR	Binary	Similarity Measure	dice‖ jaccard‖ naive‖ L2

accuracy up to 98%. Even though the predictive accuracies in these cases are very high, they still cannot reach 100% which is the basis to construct a winning-move generator. The settings of the experiments are shown in Table 1.2.

1.4 Related Work, Conclusions and Future Work

In this chapter, four machine learning approaches (ILP, ANN, SVM and CBR) for learning N-P positions of combinatorial games have been demonstrated. Experiments have shown that ILP is able to learn the N-P classifier for the winning strategy of each of 6 different combinatorial games given with up to 26 examples and sufficient background knowledge. Even with 200 randomly sampled examples, 100% predictive accuracy is not achieved in any case by ANNs, SVMs or CBRs. Another disadvantage of ANNs, SVMs and CBRs compared with ILP systems is that they are unable to give the players useful hints to play the Nim game as the learned N-P classifier is not human readable. The proposed method can be applied for any partisan games whose winning strategies are based on P and N-positions. Mihai Oltean uses the Multi-Expression Programming — a genetic programming variant to compute the winning strategy for Nim [Oltean (2004)]. The idea is to read the game tree, check N and P-positions during the traversing of the game tree and count the number of configurations that violates the rules of the winning strategy. However, the Genetic Programming is not guaranteed to converge and the approach is only tested on a single game. By contrast, our approach has been demonstrated to produce correct solutions across a variety of combinatorial games. Bain and Muggleton [Bain and Muggleton (1994)] applied the ILP system Golem to learn the optimal strategies of certain the Chess endgame King-and-Rook-against-King but were only able to learn a complete strategy for depths 0,1 and 2. Future work will aim to extend our ILP approach to learn strategies across a broader range of combinatorial games, including impartial games under Misre play (the player that is forced to take the last stone loses) and complex partisan games. Future work will also apply multi-clause learning to learn game strategies.

Bibliography

M. Bain and S. H. Muggleton. *Learning Optimal Chess Strategies.* Oxford University Press, Oxford. 1994.

E. R. Berlekamp. Blockbusting and domineering. *J. Comb. Theory Ser. A*, **49(1)**, 67116. 1988.

E. R. Berlekamp, J. H. Conway and R. K. Guy. *Winning Ways for your Mathematical Plays, Volume 1.* A K Peters/CRC Press, London. 2001.

C. L. Bouton. Nim, a game with a complete mathematical theory. *Ann. Math.*, **2**, 35–39. 1902.

M. Gardner. *Hexaflexagons and Other Mathematical Diversions: The First Scientific American Book of Puzzles and Games.* University of Chicago Press, Chicago. 1988.

P. M. Grundy. Mathematics and games. *Eureka*, **2**, 6–8. 1939.

R. K. Guy and C. A. B. Smith. The g-values of various games. *Proc. Camb. Phi. Soc.*, **52**, 514–526. 1956.

D. E. Knuth. *The Art of Computer Programming, Volume 1.* Addison-Wesley, Boston. 1997.

T. W. Liao, Z. Zhang and C. R Mount. Similarity measures for retrieval in case-based reasoning systems. *Applied Artificial Intelligence*, **12**, 267–288. 1998.

S. H. Muggleton. Inverse entailment and Progol. *New Generation Computing*, **13**, 245–286. 1995.

S. H. Muggleton and J. Firth. CProgol4.4: a tutorial introduction. In S. Dzeroski and N. Lavrac (eds). *Relational Data Mining*, Springer-Verlag, Berlin, pp. 160–188. 2001.

M. Oltean. Evolving winning strategies for nim-like games. *World Computer Congress*, **9(2)**, 353–364. 2004.

S. J. Russell and P. Norvig. *Artificial Intelligence: A Modern Approach (Third Edition).* Pearson, New Jersey. 2010.

R. P. Sprague. Über mathematische kampfspiele. *Tohoku Mathematical Journal*, **41**, 438–444. 1936.

Chapter 2

Induction in Nonmonotonic Causal Theories for a Domestic Service Robot

Jianmin Ji

Department of CSE, The Hong Kong University of Science and Technology, Hong Kong

Xiaoping Chen

School of CS, University of Science and Technology of China, China

It is always possible to encounter an unexpected scenario which has not been covered by a certain theory for an action domain. This chapter proposes an approach to treating this problem. We reduce this learning task to the problem of modifying a causal theory such that the interpretations corresponding to new scenarios become a model of the updated theory, while all the original models remain unchanged. We illustrate our approach through a case study based on a domestic service robot, KeJia.

2.1 Introduction

Nonmonotonic causal theories [Giunchiglia *et al.* (2004)] are designed to be a nonmonotonic formalism for representing causal knowledge, which can be used to formalize action domains, including indirect effects of actions, implied action preconditions, concurrent actions, nondeterministic actions, ramification and qualification constraints. However, in practice, it is hard to model a complicated action domain completely and there always exist unexpected scenarios which are not covered by a specific theory. An important problem for developing an intelligent agent is how to automatically modify a causal theory for an action domain so that the updated theory can cover a new scenario once it is encountered during the agent's exploration of the real world.

In this chapter, we attack the inductive learning problem in nonmonotonic causal theories. We take domestic service robots as the setting, though the results apply to other applications. Our robot is initially equipped with a causal theory as the model of its environment, with which it provides services for its users. In order to get more complete causal theories, we assume the robot gets one or more new scenarios through learning from demonstration [Argall *et al.* (2009)], for each of which the robot recognizes and remembers the entire history of its behaviors and relevant fluents of the environment. Formally, this history is an interpretation of the causal theory, but not a model of it. Therefore, we reduce the learning task into the problem of modifying the causal theory such that this interpretation becomes a model of the updated theory, while all the models of original theory are still models of the updated theory. We illustrate our approach through a case study based on a domestic service robot, KeJia [Chen *et al.* (2009, 2010)]. Only the core part of this work will be described in this short chapter.

2.2 Nonmonotonic Causal Theories

The language of nonmonotonic causal theories [Giunchiglia *et al.* (2004)] is based on a propositional language with two zero-place logical connectives: $\top$ for tautology and $\bot$ for contradiction. We denote by *Atom* the set of atoms, and *Lit* the set of literals: $Lit = Atom \cup \{\neg a \mid a \in Atom\}$. Given a literal l, the *complement* of l, denoted by $\bar{l}$, is $\neg a$ if l is a and a if l is $\neg a$, where a is an atom. A set I of literals is called *complete* if for each atom a, exactly one of $\{a, \neg a\}$ is in I. In this chapter we identify an interpretation with a complete set of literals.

A *causal theory* is a set of *causal rules* of the form: $\phi \Rightarrow \psi$, where ϕ and ψ are propositional formulas. For a causal rule r of such form, we let $head(r)$ be its head ψ and $body(r)$ its body ϕ. Intuitively, the causal rule reads as "ψ is caused if ϕ is true."

Let T be a causal theory and I an interpretation. The *reduction* T^I of T w.r.t. I is defined as $T^I = \{\psi \mid \text{for some } \phi \Rightarrow \psi \in T \text{ and } I \models \phi\}$. T^I is a propositional theory. We say that I is a *model* of T if I is the unique model of T^I.

For example, given $T_1 = \{p \Rightarrow p,\ q \Rightarrow q,\ \neg q \Rightarrow \neg q\}$ whose signature is $\{p, q\}$. Let $I_1 = \{p, q\}$, $T_1^{I_1} = \{p, q\}$ and I_1 is the unique model of $T_1^{I_1}$, then

I_1 is a model of T_1. Let $I_2 = \{\neg p, q\}$, $T_1^{I_2} = \{q\}$, both I_1 and I_2 are models of $T_1^{I_2}$, then I_2 is not a model of T_1. We can see that T_1 has two models $\{p, q\}$ and $\{p, \neg q\}$.

As a syntax sugar, a causal rule with variables is viewed as shorthand for the set of its ground instances, that is, for the result of substituting corresponding variable-free terms for variables in all possible ways.

2.3 Induction in Causal Theories

The induction problem considered in this chapter is defined as follows. Given a causal theory T and an interpretation I, I is not a model of T, we need to modify T to a new causal theory T' such that I is a model of T' and each model of T is still a model of T'.

Before proposing one such modification, we consider the notion of *relevance*. Following the intuition behind the work of Galles and Pearl [Galles and Pearl (1997)], relevance is concerned with statements of the form "Changing X will alter the value of Y, if Z is fixed." In the setting of nonmonotonic causal theories, the world is specified by a set of models, an atom a is related to another atom b under a set S of literals, if changing the value of a will alter possible evaluations of b given S.

Specifically, given a set M of models and a set S of literals, an atom a is *semantically related* to another atom b under S w.r.t. M, if:

- there exists two models $I_1, I_2 \in M$ s.t. $S \cup \{l_a, l_b\} \subseteq I_1$ and $S \cup \{\bar{l}_a, \bar{l}_b\} \subseteq I_2$,
- there does not exist a model $I' \in M$ s.t. $S \cup \{\bar{l}_a, l_b\} \subseteq I'$,

where $l_a \in \{a, \neg a\}$ and $l_b \in \{b, \neg b\}$. Note that given M and S, the defined relevance relation is reflexive, symmetric and transitive.

Given a causal theory T, an atom a is *semantically related* to an atom b in T, if there exists a set S of literals such that a is semantically related to b under S w.r.t. the set of models of T. However, it is NP-hard to decide where two atoms are semantically related in a causal theory. Now, based on syntactic properties, we propose a relaxed definition of relevance which can be computed easily.

Given a causal theory T, an atom a is *syntactically related* to an atom b in T if (1) $a = b$, (2) both a and b occurs in a causal rule of T, or (3) both a and b are syntactically related to another atom c. Note that the syntactical relevance relation is also reflexive, symmetric and transitive.

Proposition 2.1. *Given a causal theory T and two atoms a and b. If a is semantically related to b in T, then a is syntactically related to b.*

Now, based on syntactical relevance, we propose an approach for the induction problem. Given a causal theory T and an interpretation I which is not a model of T, let $tr(T, I)$ be the causal theory obtained from T by:

(1) modifying each causal rule $r \in T$ to $body(r) \wedge head(r) \Rightarrow head(r)$, if $I \models body(r)$ and $I \not\models head(r)$; and
(2) adding a causal rule $L \Rightarrow l$, for each literal $l \in I$ such that $T^I \not\models l$, where L is the conjunction of literals which belong to I and in which occurred atoms, are syntactically related to the atom which occurred in l.

The number of causal rules generated by the conversion is polynomial for an interpretation in the number of literals.

Proposition 2.2. *Given a causal theory T and an interpretation I which is not a model of T, I is a model of $tr(T, I)$ and every model of T is a model of $tr(T, I)$.*

Note that we assume that the relevance relation in the domain has been revealed by the original causal theory. With the help of such relevance relation, not limited to I, some other interpretations might become the models of $tr(T, I)$. Consider the causal theory T_1 in Section 2.2, $I_2 = \{\neg p, q\}$ is not a model of T_1, p is not related to q, then $tr(T_1, I_2) = T_1 \cup \{\neg p \Rightarrow \neg p\}$. In addition to I_2, $tr(T_1, I_2)$ has another new model $\{\neg p, \neg q\}$.

Every new causal rule $L \Rightarrow l$ added in $tr(T, I)$ can be generalized by substituting variables for some constants occurring in the rule. Note that every model of T is still a model of the new theory. Generally, the robot can be taught with multiple examples, which leads to some common inductive learning issues investigated in the literature.

2.4 A Case Study in a Domestic Service Robot's Domain

In this section, we demonstrate the inductive approach by a case study in a domestic service robot's domain.

As shown in Fig. 2.1, there is a board on the edge of a table, with one end sticking out. There is also a can on each end of the board, keeping it balanced. The task is to pick up the can on the inside end. Note that the outside can may fall if the robot picks up the inside-end can.

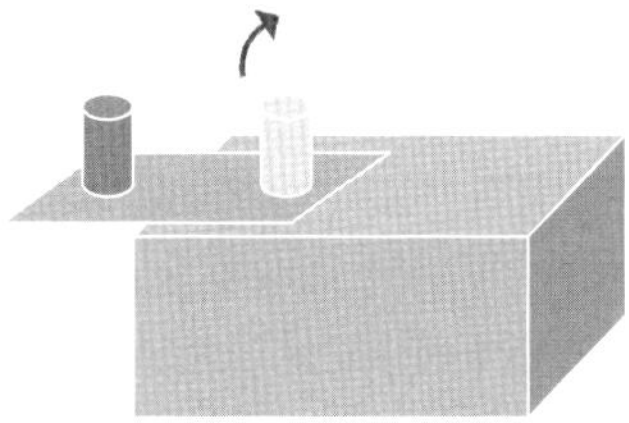

Fig. 2.1 Setting of the case study.

First, following the approach in [Giunchiglia *et al.* (2004)], we use causal rules to formalize the action domain. The atoms are expressions of the form a_t and f_t, where a, f, and t are action, fluent, and time names, respectively. Intuitively, a_t is true if and only if the action a occurs at time t, and f_t is true if and only if the fluent f holds at t.

In this setting, we focus on the robot's ability of "grasp" and the corresponding properties of the environment. The action names and fluent names used in the specification follow, where X and Y are variables ranging over possible objects in the environment:

- $grasp(X)$: the action of gripping object X and picking it up.
- $holding(X)$: the fluent that object X is held in, in the grip of the robot.
- $on(X,Y)$: the fluent that object X has on object Y.
- $falling(X)$: the fluent that object X is falling on the floor.

In addition, σ is a meta-variable ranging over $\{on(X,Y), \neg on(X,Y), holding(X), \neg holding(X), falling(X), \neg falling(X)\}$.

The effect of executing the action $grasp(X)$ is described as follows:

$$grasp(X)_t \Rightarrow holding(X)_{t+1} \tag{2.1}$$

$$grasp(X)_t \wedge on(X,Y)_t \Rightarrow \neg on(X,Y)_{t+1} \tag{2.2}$$

The precondition of grasping requires the grip holds nothing:

$$grasp(X)_t \wedge holding(Y)_t \Rightarrow \bot \tag{2.3}$$

The occurrence of the action is exogenous to the causal theory:

$$grasp(X)_t \Rightarrow grasp(X)_t \tag{2.4}$$

$$\neg grasp(X)_t \Rightarrow \neg grasp(X)_t \tag{2.5}$$

The initial state (at time 0) can be arbitrary:

$$\sigma_0 \Rightarrow \sigma_0 \tag{2.6}$$

There are some restrictions among these fluents:

$$holding(X)_t \wedge falling(X)_t \Rightarrow \bot \tag{2.7}$$

$$on(X, Y)_t \wedge falling(Y)_t \Rightarrow falling(X)_t \tag{2.8}$$

Rule (2.8) specifies that $falling(X)$ is an indirect effect of some action that causes $falling(Y)$ while X is on Y. The frame problem is overcome by the following "inertia" rules:

$$\sigma_t \wedge \sigma_{t+1} \Rightarrow \sigma_{t+1} \tag{2.9}$$

The causal theory formed by rules (2.1)–(2.9) represents the action domain for the robot's ability of "grasp." Let $0 \leq t \leq m$, the models of such causal theory correspond to the histories of the action domain whose length is m. In particular, an interpretation I is a model if and only if the state s_{i+1} is a successor state of the state s_i after the concurrent execution of actions A_i, where $s_i = \{f_i \in I \mid f \text{ is a fluent name}\}$ and $A_i = \{a_i \in I \mid a \text{ is an action name}\}$.

During the development of our robot, there are some real scenarios that have not been captured by a certain version of the causal theory. Particularly, in one execution the robot recognizes that s_1 is a successor state of an initial state s_0 after the occurrence of an action a_0, but the interpretation $I = s_0 \cup \{a_0\} \cup \{\neg a'_0 \mid \text{action name } a' \text{ different from } a\} \cup s_1$ is not a model of the causal theory with $0 \leq t \leq 1$. In this case, we can use our inductive approach to modify the causal theory so that I becomes its model and all other models remain unchanged.

In the setting, with the current causal theory, the robot cannot predict the end state in that the outside will fall after the action "grasp the inside can" is executed. This new scenario is formally represented by the interpretation I:

$$\{on(a, bd)_0, on(b, bd)_0, \neg holding(a)_0, \neg holding(b)_0, \neg falling(a)_0,$$
$$\neg falling(b)_0, \neg falling(bd)_0, grasp(b)_0, \neg grasp(a)_0, falling(bd)_1,$$
$$on(a, bd)_1, \neg on(b, bd)_1, \neg holding(a)_1, holding(b)_1, falling(a)_1,$$
$$\neg falling(b)_1\}$$

which is not a model of the causal theory T with two objects a, b, time names 0, 1, and the constant bd standing for the board. The interpretation I also expresses the knowledge that a and bd will fall after the action $grasp(b)$ occurs in the setting.

Using our inductive approach, the robot obtains a new causal theory $tr(T, I)$, which contains all causal rules in T and the new rule: $\bigwedge_{l \in I} l \Rightarrow$

$falling(bd)_1$. Note that every atom occurred in I is syntactically related to $falling(bd)_1$. Letting M be the set of models of T, we can see that none of interpretations in M satisfy $falling(bd)_1$ and $falling(bd)_1 \in I$, then every atom is semantically related to $falling(bd)_1$ under some set of literals w.r.t. $M \cup \{I\}$.

The learned rule can be further generalized by changing 0 to t, 1 to $t+1$, and some constants like a, b, and bd can be replaced by variables.

According to Proposition 2.2, I is a model of $tr(T, I)$ and every model of T is still a model of $tr(T, I)$. Then the robot uses $tr(T, I)$ as the new model of the action domain and is aware that if it picks up b in the setting then a has a possibility to fall. Thus, to accomplish the task, the robot would compute a more cautious plan in which it removes a from the sticking-out end of the board first before grasping b.[1]

2.5 Discussion and Conclusion

We use nonmonotonic causal theories to model the action domains of the robot, mainly because:

- They are convenient to formalize action domains, including the frame problem, indirect effects of actions, concurrent actions, nondeterministic actions, ramification and qualification constraints.
- They can be easily computed by existing sophisticated solvers. The problem of computing models of a causal theory can be equivalently translated to computing answer sets of a logic program with negative as failure [Lee (2004)] and solved by ASP solvers. The causal theory can also be converted to a propositional theory, whose models can be computed by SAT solvers [Lee (2004); Giunchiglia *et al.* (2004)].
- More importantly, this effort provides evidence that the modification of a theory for an action domain is convenient by using nonmonotonic causal theories. Intuitively, an enlarged causal theory most likely covers new interpretations and original models as its models this way: If no abnormal features related to the service task are observed, then the original knowledge still works. Otherwise, the newly generated knowledge from the new scenario should be used. Both the original and the new knowledge

[1] A similar case study is featured in the video demo "Towards Robot Learning from Comparative Demonstration" at `http://ai.ustc.edu.cn/en/demo/`, where the robot is taught with a positive and a negative example in the same setting.

are integrated conveniently into the enlarged theory as a whole due to the nonmonotonicity of causal theories.

However, there is not much work on inductive learning in nonmonotonic causal theories. But the problem can be closely related to the context of Nonmonotonic Inductive Logic Programming [Sakama (2001)]. Sakama [Sakama (2005)] proposed an inductive learning approach in nonmonotonic logic programs. Our approach differs from Sakama's approach in that we may need to modify rules in the original causal theory while Sakama keeps the rules in the original program unchanged.

Bibliography

B. D. Argall, S. Chernova, M. Veloso and B. Browning. A survey of robot learning from demonstration. *Robot. Auton. Syst.*, **57**, 469–483. 2009.

X. Chen, J. Jiang, J. Ji, G. Jin and F. Wang. Integrating NLP with reasoning about actions for autonomous agents communicating with humans. *Proceedings of IAT-09*, **2**, 137–140. 2009.

X. Chen, J. Ji, J. Jiang, G. Jin, F. Wang and J. Xie. Developing high-level cognitive functions for service robots. In W. van der Hoek, G. Kaminka, Y. Lesperance, M. Luck and S. Sen (eds). *Proceedings of AAMAS-10*, 989–996. 2010.

D. Galles and J. Pearl. Axioms of causal relevance. *Artif. Intell.*, **97**, 9–43. 1997.

E. Giunchiglia, J. Lee, V. Lifschitz, N. McCain and H. Turner. Nonmonotonic causal theories. *Artif. Intell.*, **153**, 49–104. 2004.

J. Lee. Nondefinite vs. Definite Causal Theories. *Proceedings of LPNMR-04*, 141–153. 2004.

C. Sakama. Nonmonotonic Inductive Logic Programming. *Proceedings of LPNMR-01*, 62–80. 2001.

C. Sakama. Induction from answer sets in nonmonotonic logic programs. *ACM T. Comput. Log.*, **6**, 2, 203–231. 2005.

Chapter 3

Using Ontologies in Semantic Data Mining with g-SEGS and Aleph

Anže Vavpetič and Nada Lavrač
Department of Knowledge Technologies,
Jožef Stefan Institute, Slovenia

This chapter describes a prototype semantic data mining system called g-SEGS, which uses ontologies as background knowledge in the learning process. The system is a generalization of an existing system SEGS, which is limited just to the field of functional genomics. Also, the chapter describes how to formulate the problem of semantic data mining in the inductive logic programming system Aleph. Both approaches are experimentally evaluated on two real-life biological domains.

3.1 Introduction

The knowledge discovery process can significantly benefit from the domain (background) knowledge, as successfully exploited in relational data mining and Inductive Logic Programming (ILP). Additional means of providing more information to the learner is by providing semantic descriptors to the data.

Usually, there is abundant empirical data, while the background knowledge is scarce. However, with the expanding of the Semantic Web and the availability of numerous ontologies which provide domain background knowledge and semantic descriptors to the data, the amount of *semantic data* (e.g. ontologies and annotated data collections) is rapidly growing.[1] The data mining community is now faced with a paradigm shift: instead of mining the abundance of empirical data supported by the background knowledge, the new challenge is to mine the abundance of knowledge

[1]See the Linked Data site `http://linkeddata.org/`

encoded in domain ontologies, constrained by the heuristics computed from the empirical data collection. This paper uses the term *semantic data mining* to denote this new data mining challenge and approaches in which semantic data are mined.

As a step towards the described paradigm shift, we have developed g-SEGS, which still focuses on exploiting ontologies as background knowledge, using them to form a language bias. System g-SEGS is a successor of SEGS, a system for Searching of Enriched Gene Sets [Trajkovski *et al.* (2008)] designed specifically for functional genomics tasks. While SEGS is a special purpose system for analysing microarray data with biological ontologies as background knowledge, g-SEGS is a general purpose semantic data mining system.

The described semantic data mining task requires a level of expressiveness that cannot be adequately represented in propositional logic. The reason is that ontologies can encode extremely complex relations. Since this clearly becomes a relational data mining problem, we find it useful to employ an inductive logic programming system Aleph to this task as well.[2] In this paper we describe the procedure to formulate the semantic data mining task in Aleph.

In order to empirically compare both approaches we evaluated them on two real-life problems from the field of functional genomics.

The paper is organized as follows. We describe the related work in Section 3.2. In Section 3.3 we present the prototype system g-SEGS. Section 3.4 describes the problem formulation in Aleph. In Section 3.5 we present the experimental results. Section 3.6 concludes the chapter and gives some ideas for further work.

3.2 Related Work

The idea of using hierarchies is not new. It was proposed by Michalski in 1983 [Michalski (1980)], where a methodology which enables the use of hierarchies for generalizing terms in inductive rule learning is described. In [Garriga *et al.* (2008)], the use of taxonomies (where the leaves of the taxonomy correspond to attributes of the input data) on paleontological data is studied.

In [Aronis *et al.* (1996)], background knowledge is presented in the standard inheritance network notation and the KBRL algorithm performs a general-to-specific heuristic search for a set of conjunctive rules that satisfy

[2] `http://www.cs.ox.ac.uk/activities/machinelearning/Aleph/aleph.html`

user-defined rule evaluation criteria. A domain-specific system that uses ontologies and other hierarchies as background knowledge for data mining is SEGS [Trajkovski *et al.* (2008)]. Given ranked gene expression data and several biomedical ontologies as input, the SEGS system finds groups of differentially expressed genes, called *enriched gene sets.*[3]

The main differences of system g-SEGS, described in this paper, compared to the related approaches is that these (1) use non-standard ontology formats [Garriga *et al.* (2008); Trajkovski *et al.* (2008)], (2) are domain specific [Garriga *et al.* (2008); Trajkovski *et al.* (2008)] and (3) perform non-symbolic classification tasks [Garriga *et al.* (2008)].

3.3 g-SEGS

This section describes a prototypical semantic data mining system, called g-SEGS, which can be used to discover subgroup descriptions both for labelled or ranked data with the use of input OWL ontologies as background knowledge. The ontologies are exploited in a similar manner as in SEGS (i.e. ontological concepts are used as terms that form rule conjuncts), with the important difference that they can be (1) from any domain and (2) in a standard OWL format.

Input. Apart from various parameters (e.g. for controlling the minimum support criterion and maximum rule length) the main inputs are: (1) *background knowledge* in the form of ontologies in OWL or in the legacy SEGS format, (2) *training data*, which is a list of class-labelled or ranked examples (each example has a numeric value associated to it) and (3) an *example-to-ontology map* which associates each example with one or more concepts from the given ontologies. We say that an example is *annotated* with these concepts.

Hypothesis language. The hypothesis language consists of rules $class(X) \leftarrow Conditions$, where $Conditions$ is a logical conjunction of terms which represent ontological concepts. If we put this into a more illustrative context, a possible rule could have the following form: $class(X) \leftarrow doctor(X) \wedge germany(X)$. Both *doctor* and *germany* are terms which represent the ontological concepts *doctor* and *germany*. If our input

[3]A gene set is enriched if the genes that are members of this gene set are statistically significantly differentially expressed compared to the rest of the genes.

examples are people, we can say that this rule describes a subgroup of people who are doctors and live in Germany.

Rule construction. A set of rules which satisfies the size constraints (minimum support and maximum number of rule terms) is constructed using a top-down bounded *exhaustive* search algorithm, which enumerates all such possible rules by taking one term from each ontology. Due to the properties of the *subClassOf* relation between concepts in the ontologies, the algorithm can employ an efficient pruning strategy. If the currently evaluated rule does not satisfy the size constraints, the algorithm can prune all the rules which would be generated if this rule was further specialized.

Additionally, the user can specify another relation between the input examples — the *interacts* relation. Two examples are in this relation if they interact in some way. For each concept that the algorithm tries to conjunctively add to the rule, it also tries to add its interacting counterpart. For example, the antecedent of the rule of the form $class(X) \leftarrow c_1(X) \wedge interacts(X, Y) \wedge c_2(Y)$ can be interpreted as: all the examples which are annotated by concept c_1 and interact with examples annotated by concept c_2.

Rule selection. As the number of generated rules can be large, uninteresting and overlapping rules have to be filtered out. In g-SEGS, rule filtering is performed using *wWRAcc* (Weighted Relative Accuracy with example weights) [Lavrač *et al.* (2004)], which uses example weights as means for considering different parts of the example space when selecting the best rules during rules post-processing by a weighted covering algorithm used for rule selection.

Implementation. g-SEGS is implemented as a web service in the Orange4WS environment which upgrades the freely available Orange [Demšar *et al.* (2004)] data mining environment. Additionally, we developed an easy-to-use user interface for our system in Orange, allowing simple experimentation with g-SEGS by using it in workflows together with the existing Orange widgets.

3.4 Problem Formulation in Aleph

In order to solve similar semantic data mining tasks in Aleph as with g-SEGS, we need to encode (1) the ontologies, (2) the given examples and (3) the example-to-ontology map (annotations).

In Aleph, each ontological concept `c`, with child concepts `c1,c2,..,cm`, is encoded as a unary predicate `c/1`:

```
c(X) :- c1(X) ; c2(X) ; ... ; cm(X).
```

Each child concept is defined in the same way. To encode the whole ontology, we need to start this procedure at the root concept. All these predicates are allowed to be used in the rule body and are tabled for faster execution.

If the k-th example is annotated by concepts `c1,c2,..,cm` (defined by the example-to-ontology map), we encode it as a set of ground facts:

```
instance(ik). c1(ik). c2(ik). ... cm(ik).
```

Additional relations (if available) can also be trivially added to the background knowledge.

In order to encode the input examples, we transform the ranked or labelled problem into a two-class problem (the positive class is the class which interests the user) and split the examples accordingly.

3.5 Experimental Results

We tested both approaches on two publicly available[4] biological microarray datasets: *acute lymphoblastic leukemia* (ALL) [Chiaretti *et al.* (2004)] and *human mesenchymal stem cells* (hMSC) [Wagner *et al.* (2008)]. Both datasets encode gene expression data for two classes. The challenge is to produce descriptions of sets of differentially expressed genes involved in the process of each domain.

First, we preprocessed the datasets by following the SegMine [Podpečan *et al.* (2011)] methodology. Genes were first ranked using the ReliefF [Robnik-Šikonja and Kononenko (2003)] algorithm and then filtered using the logarithm of expression fold change (logFC). All genes g with $|logFC(g)| < 0.3$ were removed from the set, resulting in 8,952 genes in the ALL domain and 11,389 genes in the hMSC domain.

The ranked genes were annotated by Gene Ontology[5] (GO) and Kyoto Encyclopedia of Genes and Genomes[6] (KEGG) concepts by using the Entrez database[7] to map between gene identifiers and the ontology concepts. The top 300 were used as the positive class examples and from the

[4] `http://segmine.ijs.si`
[5] `http://www.geneontology.org/`
[6] `http://www.genome.jp/kegg/`
[7] `http://www.ncbi.nlm.nih.gov/sites/gquery`

remaining examples we randomly selected 300 examples, which we labelled as negative.

Experiments on both datasets were repeated 20 times. Both systems were applied on the same sets of positive/negative examples. Finally we selected the top 20 rules produced by each algorithm, calculated the selected measures and statistically validated the results. We applied the Wilcoxon test [Wilcoxon (1945)] using significance level $\alpha = 0.05$ for each measure separately. This approach is proposed as an alternative to the paired t-test, which proves to be less appropriate for such a comparison [Demšar (2006)].

Table 3.1 presents the performance of both approaches on the two domains. The discovered rule sets were evaluated using the descriptive measures of rule interestingness as proposed in [Lavrač *et al.* (2004)]: the average rule coverage ($AvgCov$), the overall support ($OvSup$), the average significance ($AvgSig$), the average unusualness ($AvgWRAcc$) and the area under the convex hull (AUC). Additionally, we also measured the execution time (t).

The results show that g-SEGS produces more significant rules, with statistically significantly higher $WRAcc$ (interestingness) and AUC scores and in much less time. Other measures indicate that a rule discovered by Aleph (on average) covers more examples and that the rule set covers a higher percentage of all positive examples. An interesting fact is also that g-SEGS produces the resulting rule set approximately 20–30 times faster than Aleph, which is due to the fact that g-SEGS exploits the hierarchical

Table 3.1 Experimental results. Values in bold represent statistically significantly better performance.

			ALL			
System	$AvgCov$	$OvSup$	$AvgSig$	$AvgWRAcc$	AUC	t[s]
g-SEGS	0.094	0.532	**17.371**	**0.023**	**0.587**	**10.700**
Aleph	**0.110**	**0.727**	9.792	0.020	0.575	230.550
			hMSC			
System	$AvgCov$	$OvSup$	$AvgSig$	$AvgWRAcc$	AUC	t[s]
g-SEGS	0.060	0.542	**9.772**	**0.015**	**0.569**	**7.750**
Aleph	**0.092**	**0.646**	2.577	0.008	0.535	232.050

properties of the ontologies. Of course we need to take into account that it is not necessary that these measures reflect a better rule set, which would in fact provide novel and interesting knowledge for the domain expert. Such an analysis by the domain expert is planned in future work.

3.6 Conclusion

This paper presented g-SEGS, a general-purpose semantic data mining system, based on the successful system SEGS, which was designed exclusively for functional genomics. The paper also shows how to solve a similar task with the general purpose ILP system Aleph. Both approaches were experimentally evaluated on two real-life biological domains. The evaluation shows that, although g-SEGS produces more significant rules with higher interestingness and AUC, Aleph can also be successful in this type of task and its potential should necessarily be further exploited in building of the system for semantic data mining of linked data, whose development is planned in our future work.

Acknowledgments

The research presented in this paper was supported by the Slovenian Ministry of Higher Education, Science and Technology (grant no. P-103) and the EU-FP7 projects e-LICO and BISON.

Bibliography

J. M. Aronis, F. J. Provost, and B. G. Buchanan. Exploiting background knowledge in automated discovery. *Proceedings of the 2nd International Conference on Knowledge Discovery and Data Mining*, pp. 355–358. AAAI Press, Menlo Park, California, 1996. KDD 1996: Portland, Oregon, 2–4 August 1996.

S. Chiaretti, X. Li, R. Gentleman, A. Vitale, M. Vignetti, F. Mandelli, J. Ritz and R. Foa. Gene expression profile of adult t-cell acute lymphocytic leukemia identifies distinct subsets of patients with different response to therapy and survival. *Blood*, **103**, 2771–2778. 2004.

J. Demšar. Statistical comparison of classifiers over multiple data sets. *J. Mach. Learn. Res.*, **7**, 1–30. 2006.

J. Demšar, B. Zupan and G. Leban. Orange: From experimental machine learning to interactive data mining, white paper. Faculty of Computer and Information Science, University of Ljubljana, 2004. Available online: www.ailab.si/orange. Accessed 8 August 2014.

G. C. Garriga, A. Ukkonen and H. Mannila. Feature selection in taxonomies with applications to paleontology. *Proceedings of the 11th International Conference on Discovery Science*, pp. 112–123. Springer-Verlag, Berlin, 2008. DS 2008: Budapest, Hungary, 13–16 October 2008.

N. Lavrač, B. Kavšek, P. A. Flach and L. Todorovski. Subgroup discovery with CN2-SD *J. Mach. Learn. Res.*, **5**, 153–188. 2004.

R. S. Michalski. Pattern recognition as rule-guided inductive inference. *IEEE T. Pattern Anal.*, **2(4)**, 349–361. 1980.

V. Podpečan, N. Lavrač, Igor Mozetič, P. K. Novak, I. Trajkovski, L. Langohr, K. Kulovesi, H. Toivonen, M. Petek, H. Motaln and K. Gruden. SegMine workflows for semantic microarray data analysis in Orange4WS. *BMC Bioinformatics*, **12**. 2011.

M. Robnik-Šikonja and I. Kononenko. Theoretical and empirical analysis of ReliefF and RReliefF. *Mach. Learn.*, **53**, 23–69. 2003.

I. Trajkovski, N. Lavrač and J. Tolar. SEGS: Search for enriched gene sets in microarray data. *J Biomed. Inform.*, **41(4)**, 588–601. 2008.

W. Wagner, P. Horn, M. Castoldi, A. Diehlmann, S. Bork, R. Saffrich, V. Benes, J. Blake, S. Pfister, V. Eckstein and A. D. Ho. Replicative senescence of mesenchymal stem cells: A continuous and organized process. *PLoS ONE*, **3(5)**, e2213. 2008.

F. Wilcoxon. Individual comparisons by ranking methods. *Biometrics*, **1**, 80–83. 1945

Chapter 4

Improving Search Engine Query Expansion Techniques with ILP

José Carlos Almeida Santos and Manuel Fonseca de Sam Bento Ribeiro

Microsoft Language Development Center
Tagus Park, Portugal
and
ISCTE-Lisbon University Institute, Portugal

Query expansion is the process in which a query is augmented so that it matches more documents, thus potentially increasing the number of relevant results. This is frequently done by spell correcting the query and adding synonyms, morphological variations or other type of relevant data. Query expansion would, for example, expand "automobile" with "car" or "car" with "cars".

Given a concrete set of queries and particular words within these queries, it is relatively simple to generate lists of candidates that would later reflect as good or bad alterations. However, generalizing from a ground truth set, which is a list of alterations considered to be good, to a model which allows the generation of good alterations to an unseen set of words is a challenging task.

In the present work we provide such a model for the English language, discovered with Inductive Logic Programming (ILP). The model induced by ILP is a set of Prolog rules. An important aspect of having the model as rules in Prolog is that, instead of merely being able to classify a given pair $\langle term, candidate \rangle$ as good or bad, we are now able to generate good alterations for a given word, which is the main goal of this investigation.

4.1 Introduction and Motivation

Having a search engine return relevant links for an arbitrary query is a complex task involving the work of several components, most importantly: indexing, query expansion, matching and ranking.

The indexing component crawls the web, updating and annotating a database of valid URLs. The query expansion component focuses on spell correcting and augmenting the query with synonyms, morphological variations and other related terms. The matching component is given an augmented query and has to find all the documents in the index that match at least one of the query words. Finally, the ranking component is given a list of documents that match the query and ranks them according to their relevance, trying to maximize the Normalized Discounted Cumulative Gain (NDCG) [Järvelin and Kekäläinen (2002)] of the results list.

Since matching only returns documents that match the tokens in the query, query expansion attempts to intelligently add elements that return more relevant documents. For instance, the query "used automobiles" may be expanded to "used word:(automobiles cars)", meaning that the words "automobiles" and "cars" are equivalent when returning documents to the ranker.

In this paper we consider *Term* to be a token which may be extended with another token. *Candidate* refers to a token which will augment an original token and *Alteration* is a $\langle Term, Candidate \rangle$ pair that may be used to extend a query. Using the previous example, the term *automobile* can be expanded with the candidate *cars*, thus producing the alteration $\langle automobiles, cars \rangle$.

An important aspect of query expansion is thus to be able to generate good alterations for certain terms in a query. An alteration is considered good if it increases the NDCG value of the query. Generating good alterations for an arbitrary word in a query is not a trivial task. The current approach uses a range of techniques, from manually supervised lists of alterations to synonyms extracted from online repositories such as WordNet [Fellbaum (1998)].

In this chapter we explore a machine learning approach in which we aim to learn rules that identify common patterns for good alterations. Since the creation of new good alterations is a costly process, it is our goal to use the identified rules to generate good candidates for a given term.

From the query expansion component perspective, the aspect of being able to generate new candidates from the learned rules is more important than predictive accuracy. An ILP approach is thus particularly suitable for this problem as the model an ILP system learns, a set of Prolog rules, can also be easily used to construct new alterations.

4.2 Experiments

In this section we describe the whole experimentation procedure, starting from processing the raw data to learning an ILP model, and finally using the model to construct putative new good alterations.

4.2.1 *Materials*

We have gathered from internal resources five data files that were used for these experiments. The first is an English lexicon consisting of roughly 340,000 words. The other four files are query sets gathered from Bing search engine users in Great Britain, which were named *Head1*, *Tail1*, *Head2*, *Tail2*. The numerical suffix refers to the period from which the queries were sampled.

Head queries are randomly sampled from the top 100,000 queries performed by users, whilst Tail queries are randomly sampled from queries which have been issued fewer than 500 times during the time period 1 or 2.

Each of the four query sets is a tab separated file where each line has the format *Query<tab>Term<tab>Candidate*. Previous experimentation has determined that changing the word *Term* to *Candidate* in query *Query* increases the overall NDCG value and is, therefore, a good alteration.

In this investigation we are considering query-independent alterations only. Thus, we processed the four query sets to consider only the ⟨*Term*, *Candidate*⟩ pair. The alteration list was restricted to those in which both *Term* and *Candidate* occur in the English lexicon. We combined the query sets from the same period (Head1+Tail1 and Head2+Tail2) into two datasets *HT1* and *HT2*. The number of positive alterations in these datasets is 6,508 and 5,832, respectively.

Opposing the positive alterations, the negative ones will decrease or maintain the NDCG score of a query. Since our original sets do not contain negative alterations, we have randomly generated them from all the lexicon entries. Considering there are no more than 10 to 20 good alterations per *Term*, a randomly selected pair $\langle Term, Candidate \rangle$ is highly likely to be a bad alteration.

We used a ratio of 100 negatives to 1 positive to ensure the rules found would be specific. To generate the 100 negative examples per positive example, we fixed the *Term* to be the same as in the positive example and selected the 100 *Candidates* randomly from the full English lexicon.

Table 4.1 Background knowledge predicates.

Predicate type	Background Knowledge Predicates
unary word properties	word_length/2, num_vowels/2, num_glides/2, num_consonants/2, is_possessive/2
$\langle word, alteration \rangle$ properties	edit_distance/3, len_common_prefix/3, len_common_suffix/3, len_longest_common_substr/3, len_longest_common_subseq/3, is_substr/3, is_prefix/3, is_suffix/3
integer comparison	lteq/2, gteq/2

4.2.2 *Problem modeling*

To model this problem we used the features described in Table 4.1, whose names should be self explanatory.

The unary word properties features take a word as input and output an integer. An important $\langle word, alteration \rangle$ feature is the edit distance, also known as the Levenshtein distance [Levenshtein (1966)], the minimum number of edits needed to transform one string into the other.

On a previous experiment we focused on purely linguistic features, looking at grammatical and lexical (part-of-speech) categories. This, however, did not produce relevant results. Therefore we opted to focus on features that work at the pure string level, disregarding more language-specific or linguistic information. This also simplifies the process, limiting the input data to a valid word list of a given language and not being dependent on any type of linguistic annotation.

So instead of simply looking for general linguistic rules to define good alterations, such as "singular to plural", these features will attempt to look deeper at the way the alteration is being built. This approach allows the ILP system not to be dependent on linguistic restraints and to be free, for example, to identify specific plural morphemes as good alterations, while ignoring others.

4.2.3 *Rule learning*

We have implemented a program to generate the ILP background knowledge file containing ground facts for all the features of Table 4.1 applied to all the positive and negative alterations in our two datasets, *HT1* and *HT2*.

Note that all the predicates in Table 4.1 are determinate. That is, given the input, there is only one possible output. This determinism makes the hypothesis space relatively small and the coverage computation efficient, thus well suited to ILP systems like Aleph [Srinivasan (2007)] and FOIL [Quinlan and Cameron-Jones (1995)]. We employed both Aleph 5 and FOIL 6.4, with default settings, using *HT1* as training set and *HT2* as test set.

We selected the top two rules each system induced from the training set. Table 4.2 presents the rules and respective precision and recall on the training and test sets. Analyzing these results, we note that the precision and recall in the test set are identical to the ones in the training set, signaling that the rules generalize well. Also, Aleph rules tend to be more general and FOIL more specific.

A further analysis of the positive matches proved to be interesting in the sense that the rules grouped several linguistic processes. Thus, we were able to identify alterations that fall under specific linguistic rules. The most frequent cases are alterations that expand singular to plural ("ace to aces", "captain to captains") and add the possessive clitic *– 's* ("car to car's", "video to video's"). But we also note that these matches are not absolute,

Table 4.2 Rules found by ILP. The first two rules were found by Aleph, last two by FOIL.

Rule	An alteration from a term A to a candidate B is good if:	Training set Precision	Training set Recall	Test set Precision	Test set Recall
1	edit_distance(A,B,C), lteq(C, 3), is_substr(A,B,1)	98.9%	56.6%	98.4%	55.6%
2	edit_distance(A,B,C), lteq(C, 3), len_common_prefix(A,B,D), gteq(D,3), is_possessive(A,0)	98.5%	86.6%	98.2%	84.9%
3	edit_distance(A,B,C), C≤2, len_longest_common_subseq(A,B,D), D>2, is_possessive(A,0), num_consonants(B,E), E>1	97.7%	77.5%	97.4%	75.5%
4	num_vowels(B,C), edit_distance(A,B,D), len_common_prefix(A,B,E), D≤E, D≤2, C>D	99.4%	59.5%	99.5%	58.3%

meaning that they do not cover all that a singular to plural or a form possessive rule would.

We observe that we also encounter matches with denominal adjectives ("intelligence to intelligent", "gnosticism to gnostic", "apocalypse to apocalyptic", "angola to angolan"). Other interesting results extend the lemma of a verb to its present continuous ("access to accessing", "edit to editing") or to the regular past tense ("eye to eyed") or match contractions ("cannot to can't"). So each rule the system found is not specific to one phenomenon and covers different linguistic processes and that is what makes these rules relevant.

The relevance of these rules can therefore be justified by being independent of any linguistic background. We can, of course, always write this information in such a way that it would generate alterations based on the word formation rules of a given language, but by applying these rules, we identify specific occurrences of the patterns that were matched. Also relevant is the fact that the patterns that these rules match also allow the quick generation of alterations based on a simple list of words, instead of being dependent on annotated lexica. To find alterations with these rules, all that is required is a lexicon of valid words of a given language. This process will not only find alterations based on morphological rules, but others that would not necessarily be annotated within a list, such as orthographical variants ("ann to anne", "whisky to whiskey", "majorca to mallorca") or even, if it is the case, of misspelled words.

4.2.4 *From ILP rules to new alterations*

To test the rules found by ILP on the full lexica, we compiled a fresh list of 36 sample words and provided these as terms to the rules of Table 4.2 so that new candidates would be generated. The list of sample words compiled attempted to match lexical and grammatical categories: adjectives, nouns (loan words, singular, plural, possessive singular, possessive plural) and verbs (present participles, past tenses, infinitives). We have also selected test words by length, ranging from two to eight characters. While analyzing the results, and since we are only looking at query independent alterations, a generated alteration was considered to be relevant if the candidate maintained a semantic approximation to the term. Due to space restrictions, Table 4.3 shows only the coverage of one word category per rule. Not all the alterations are sensible but most are.

It was noted that rule behavior is not specific to lexical or grammatical categories. Word length, however, seems to be important when it comes

Table 4.3 Candidates generated from all lexicon for a sample list of words.

Rule	Word	Candidates
1	financer	financer's, financers, financers', refinancer, refinancers
2	acrylic	acrid, acrolect, acrolith, acromia, acronymic, acrostic, acryl, acrylate, acrylic's, acrylics, acrylics'
3	Moldavian	moldavia, moldavians
4	pianos'	pianism, pianist, piannas', piano, piano's, pianola, pianolas', pianos

to generating new candidates. Lengthier words (i.e. $\geq$ five characters) will return more relevant alterations than smaller words. This is explained by all rules computing the edit distance of the current term to a low value (two or three). The larger the word, the more likely it is that an arbitrary string at an edit distance of one to three will be an invalid word and thus not belong to the lexicon. It is interesting though, that neither Aleph nor FOIL captured the constraint on the word length. This is because the remaining constraints of the rule were enough to discriminate between the positive and negatives. However, if we were to further increase the ratio of negatives to positives, it would be more likely that the word length constraint would be learned by the ILP systems.

4.3 Conclusions and Future Work

In this chapter we have shown how ILP was used to learn a model which can generate relevant alterations. The learned model has both high predictive accuracy and recall and, more importantly, has been shown to be easily reversed in order to generate new good alterations. In future work we would attempt lifting the no-context restriction and consider the neighboring tokens of the query term, as well as determining the impact of these generated alterations on the overall NDCG. Improving the quality of both rules and generated alterations might pass from manipulating the lexicon so that it can contain more morphological variations or so that it can be stripped of specific lexical categories (such as articles, preposition or other groups of entries that could be considered stop words).

A more in-depth linguistic analysis would also be of relevance with the generated data, in which we would attempt to understand the relation between the rules and the linguistic coverage they support.

Currently, we are able to construct the candidates for a given term by running the rule against the background knowledge file. However, this process takes about one minute of central processing unit (CPU) time per term, for all the four rules, which limits scalability. We should look at the ILP rules as constraints over the good alterations and, using Constraint Logic Programming techniques and a constructive Prolog implementation of the predicates in Table 4.1, we would be able to generate the alterations in a more efficient way.

Acknowledgments

The authors would like to thank the Software Developer Engineers at the Microsoft Search Technology Center in Munich, especially Jonas Barklund, for the motivation to this problem.

Bibliography

C. Fellbaum (ed.). *WordNet: An Electronic Lexical Database.* The MIT Press, Cambridge, Massachusetts. 1998.

K. Järvelin and J. Kekäläinen. Cumulated gain-based evaluation of IR techniques. *ACM Trans. Inf. Syst.*, **20**, 4, 422–446. 2002.

Levenshtein. Binary codes capable of correcting deletions, insertions, and reversals. *Doklady Akademii Nauk SSSR*, **163(4)**, 845–848. 1965.

J. R. Quinlan and R. M. Cameron-Jones. Induction of Logic Programs: FOIL and Related Systems. *New Generat. Comput.*, **3&4(13)**, 287–312. 1995.

A. Srinivasan. *The Aleph Manual.* University of Oxford, Oxford.

Chapter 5

ILP for Cosmetic Product Selection

Hiroyuki Nishiyama and Fumio Mizoguchi

Faculty of Science and Technology, Tokyo University of Science, Japan

In this chapter, we design a real-world machine learning system using a smartphone. This system can acquire images taken with the camera of a smartphone using learners (ILP and SVM) and automatically diagnose the new image. To develop this system, we implement an image analysis function and a classifier function using learning rules (learned ILP) and learning data (learned SVM) in the smartphone. With this system, the user can collect image data with a smartphone camera and diagnose the new image data according to the learning rules and data in the smartphone. In this chapter, we apply this system to a cosmetics recommendation service and demonstrate its effectiveness by improving the user service.

5.1 Introduction

Recently, many multifunctional cellular phone terminals, such as smartphones (e.g., Android and iPhone), have been developed as a result of the evolution of the computer and of network infrastructure. Thus, the number of users is rapidly increasing. The smartphone is equipped with various sensors (e.g., an acceleration sensor, an infrared sensor, and a luminosity sensor), besides the camera function. Various researches and services can be performed with a smartphone using such features. Examples are the study of a service that recommends cosmetics appropriate for a skin condition by transmitting the skin image from the camera function to an analysis server [Hiraishi and Mizoguchi (2003); Nishiyama and Mizoguchi (2011)] and a navigation service using location information. With these services, information obtained from various sensors of the smartphone is transmitted to a server via the network; next, the server performs analysis and calculations; and finally, the result is displayed on the smartphone. Thus, the server should have sufficient computational performance and communication performance even if many requests are received at the same time [Hiraishi and Mizoguchi (2003)], as well as the ability to strengthen the server environment as the number of users increases. Moreover, the calculation ability of the smartphone and the portable terminal personal digital assistant (PDA) has advanced more rapidly than that of previous cellular phones such that these devices now have the same processing performance as a small notebook computer. Therefore, interest in research into data mining with a portable terminal has also increased [Stahl *et al.* (2010)].

Considering this background, we have designed a real-world machine learning system using a smartphone. This system can acquire images taken with a smartphone camera using learners (ILP and SVM) and automatically diagnose the new image. To develop this system, we implement an image analysis function and a classifier function using learning rules (learned ILP) and learning data (learned SVM) in the smartphone. With this system, the user can collect image data with a smartphone camera and diagnose the new image data according to the learning rules and data in the smartphone. To demonstrate its effectiveness, we apply this system to a user interface of a cosmetics recommendation service [Hiraishi and Mizoguchi (2003); Nishiyama and Mizoguchi (2011)]. With this service, users can photograph their own skin and transmit the skin picture to a diagnosis server by e-mail. The server analyzes the picture and judges the texture, tone, pores, and dryness of the skin, and recommends suitable cosmetics within one minute. The smartphone should be able to access the Internet to use this service [Hiraishi and Mizoguchi (2003)]. We also seek to enable the diagnosis of the skin image and the recommendation of cosmetics with a smartphone alone. To achieve this purpose, we have designed a system with the following three functions in a smartphone.

- Analyze skin images acquired by the user.
- Judge if a skin image can be diagnosed by using learning data obtained with an SVM [Vapnik (1995)].
- Diagnose skin by using learning rules obtained by ILP [Mizoguchi and Ohwada (1995)]. Finally, recommend cosmetics.

With these functions, a user can obtain recommended cosmetics appropriate for their skin even if the diagnosis server is not used through the Internet after user takes a picture of the skin.

In this chapter, we apply the learning data obtained with an SVM to judge whether the learning rules obtained with ILP for collected information can be applied. This method differs from Muggleton's research [Muggleton *et al.* (2005)] that combines SVM technology with ILP.

5.2 Previous Cosmetics Recommendation Service Using the Smartphone

Figure 5.1 depicts the process of a cosmetics recommendation service using a smartphone. First, the user takes a skin photo using a smartphone's camera (Fig. 5.1(1)). The picture will be displayed on the smartphone monitor, and the user chooses the domain of the skin photo to be diagnosed by tapping the rectangle on the monitor with a finger (Fig. 5.1(2)). The selected skin area is transmitted to the diagnosis and analysis server (refer to Fig. 5.2). In addition, the skin photograph is transmitted by e-mail. When the diagnosis is complete, the result is displayed on the monitor of the user's smartphone (refer to Fig. 5.1(3)). A radar chart indicates the

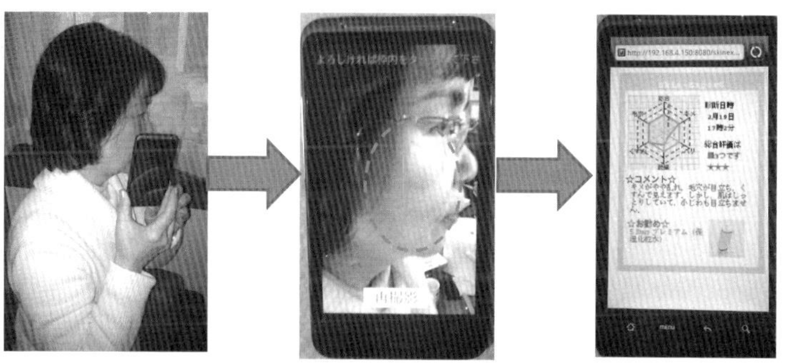

Fig. 5.1 Process of cosmetics recommendation service using a smartphone.

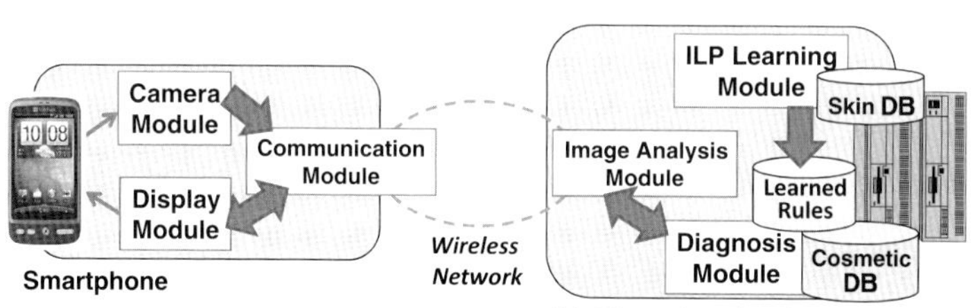

Fig. 5.2 Structure of a previous cosmetics recommendation service system.

texture, tone, pores, and dryness of the skin. This result involves comprehensive evaluation in five stages. After determining the condition of the skin, this service recommends suitable cosmetics. In addition, the result is displayed in the smartphone's browser. A homepage for the result of every diagnosis is created after diagnosis is completed by the diagnosis and analysis server [Hiraishi and Mizoguchi (2003)]. Thus, the user can check the diagnostic result at any time. (Each user's diagnostic result page is protected by a password.)

This cosmetics recommendation service system was to be executed skin diagnosis that applies learning rules created by ILP [Mizoguchi and Ohwada (1995)] in the diagnosis server as shown in Fig. 5.2. About 10,000 skin images evaluated by a skin specialist are used for ILP learning of the skin images. The following rule is an example rule for skin-grading:

```
1.        grade(A, every goodf):-  %rule(1)
2.        sex(A, efemalef),
3.        age(A, e40f),
4.        int_num(A, NI), 80<NI<90,
5.        int_depth(A, DI), 120<DI<130,
6.        line_thick(A, LT), 3.1<LT<5.1,
7.        line_depth(A, LD), 20<LD<130,
8.        line_strength(A, LS), 9.1<LS<12.5.
```

The grade in line 1 indicates that this rule (1) is for the grade "very good." This rule means that "If the sex is female (line 2), the age is in the 40s (line 3), the number of the intersections (NI) is between 80 and 90 (line 4), the image depth of the intersections (DI) is between 120 and 130 (line 5), the line thickness (LT) is between 3.1 and 5.1 (line 6), the image depth of the lines (LD) is between 20 and 130 (line 7), and the strength of the line direction (LS) is between 9.1 and 12.5 (line 8), then the skin is graded three stars." This system executes skin diagnosis based on the learning rules and recommends cosmetics appropriate for the state of the skin based on the diagnostic outcome [Hiraishi and Mizoguchi (2003)]. Actually, a total of 64 rules are created, and cosmetics have been selected for each rule by a cosmetics specialist.

Two problems of this system are that the learning rules may not be applied accurately depending on the state of the skin image acquired and the rules were created without using images of the smartphone. For instance, accurate diagnosis is impossible if the images are fake (images other than skin) or the image is out of focus. To resolve this problem, this system's Image Analysis Module judges whether a skin image can be diagnosed by extracting 45 parameters by image analysis. In addition, we need to create rules suitable for the camera function of the smartphone.

5.3 Design and Implementation of Diagnosis System by Smartphone

In this chapter, we diagnose a skin image in a smartphone with two learning tools (SVM and ILP). The structure of our system is illustrated in Fig. 5.3. In this system, the user takes a picture of the skin, and then the Image Analysis Module analyzes the skin image. Next, the SVM Prediction Module predicts whether the skin image can be diagnosed by using SVM learning data. This system requests the user to retake the photograph when the image is judged unfit for diagnosis. If this system judges that the image can be diagnosed, the Diagnosis Module applies the learning rule created by ILP to the parameters the Image Analysis Module extracted, diagnoses the parameters, and recommends cosmetics.

5.3.1 *Application of SVM learning data*

The Prediction Module uses learning data created by SVM learning. We used HTC Desire X06HT as the Android smartphone, and the Java version of LIBSVM[1] so that the SVM can be implemented on the Android.

Figure 5.4 presents data when collected parameters are learned by the SVM. The parameters of one line mean one image. The left-hand number

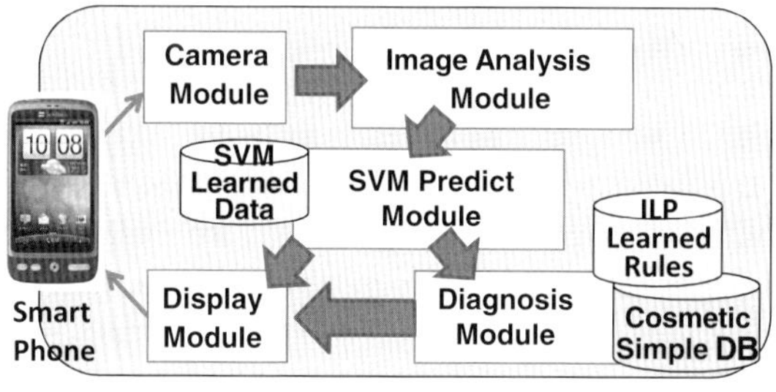

Fig. 5.3 System structure that implements the classification function by SVM and ILP.

[1]LIBSVM: A library for support vector machines. http://www/csie.ntu.edu.tw/~cjlin/libsvm/

Judge	NI	DI	LD	···	Blue
+1	17	126	134	···	113
−1	12	216	164	···	198
−1	84	136	149	···	145
−1	14	143	160	···	155
+1	18	176	157	···	101
⋮				⋮	

The number of images

← 13 parameters →

Fig. 5.4 Parameters used for SVM learning (before scaling).

(+1 or −1) indicates whether the skin image can be diagnosed (+1) or not (−1). The parameters are NI, DI, LD, LT, LS (refer to the foregoing paragraph), RGB parameter and etc. (13 parameters). After scaling, these parameters can be learned by the SVM, and learning data is created. We used the Gaussian kernel as the kernel function for SVM learning. The average time necessary for the Image Analysis Module to extract parameters by image analysis was 2.18 seconds. The average time necessary for the judgment using the learning data of the SVM of the extracted parameter was 0.46 seconds. Cross validation indicated that the learning accuracy of 156 images (78 images that can be diagnosed and 78 images that cannot be diagnosed) used for learning was 86.54%.

5.3.2 *Application of the ILP rules*

The Diagnosis Module uses ILP learning rules [Hiraishi and Mizoguchi (2003)] similar to those in Fig. 5.2 in the foregoing paragraph. However, the ILP rules were created without using smartphone images, so we modified the rules to make them suitable for the smartphone. We first corrected 8,083 skin images acquired by 1,482 users with cellular phones and smartphones. Next, we adjusted the parameters of the ILP rules with relative and statistical methods because we could not obtain a specialist's diagnostic result of the new images. In this method, we calculated the deviation of each parameter of the ILP rules from the old skin images (about 10,000 images) and the range of parameters of the new images (8,083 images). A suitable rule for a smartphone is thus generated from rule (1) in the foregoing paragraph as follows.

```
grade(A, every goodf):-  %rule(1')
sex(A, efemalef),
age(A, e40f),
```

```
4.        int_num(A, NI), 20<NI<31,
5.        int_depth(A, DI), 101<DI<120,
6.        line_thick(A, LT), 2.03<LT<3.10,
7.        line_depth(A, LD), 113<LD<125,
8.        line_strength(A, LS), 45.6<LS<75.5.
```

We adjusted all the ILP rules and realized skin diagnosis by the smartphone.

Our system uses the learning data created by the SVM to exclude skin images that cannot be diagnosed, and then diagnoses the remaining skin images using the learning rules created by ILP. We can take a picture, diagnose the skin image, and recommend cosmetics with a smartphone alone into the cosmetics recommendation service system illustrated in Fig. 5.3.

5.4 Conclusion

In this chapter, we designed a real-world machine learning system using a smartphone. This system can acquire images taken with a smartphone camera using learners (ILP and SVM) and automatically diagnose the new image. To develop this system, we implemented an image analysis function and a classifier function using ILP learning rules and SVM learning data in the smartphone. With this system, the user can collect image data with a smartphone camera and diagnose the new image data according to the learning rules and data in the smartphone. In this study, we applied this system to a user interface of a cosmetics recommendation service, diagnosed the skin image with the smartphone, and recommended cosmetics in an environment without Internet access, and demonstrated its effectiveness by improving the user service.

Bibliography

H. Hiraishi and F. Mizoguchi. A cellular telephone-based application for skin-grading to support cosmetic sales, *IAAI2003*, 19–24. 2003.

F. Mizoguchi and H. Ohwada. Constrained relative least general generalization for inducing constraint logic programs, *New Generation* Computing, **13**, 335–368. 1995.

S. H. Muggleton, H. Lodhi, A. Amini and M. J. E. Sternberg. Support vector inductive logic programming, *Discovery Science*, **2005**, 163–175. 2005.

H. Nishiyama and F. Mizoguchi. Cognitive support by smartphone — human judgment on cosmetic skin analysis support. *The 10th IEEE International Conference on Cognitive Informatics & Cognitive Computing*, pp. 175–180. 2011. ICCI&CC 2011: Banff, Alberta, 18–20 August 2011.

F. Stahl, M. M. Gaber, M. Bramer and P. S. Yu. Pocket Data Mining. Towards collaborative data mining in mobile computing environments, *The Proceedings of the 22nd International Conference on Tools with Artificial Intelligence*, pp. 323–330. 2010. ICTAI 2010: Arras, 27–29 October 2010.

V. Vapnik. *The Nature of Statistical Learning Theory*, Springer-Verlag, Berlin. 1995.

Chapter 6

Learning User Behaviours in Real Mobile Domains

Andreas Markitanis, Domenico Corapi, Alessandra Russo and Emil C. Lupu

Department of Computing, Imperial College London, UK

With the emergence of ubiquitous computing, innovations in mobile phones are increasingly changing the way users lead their lives. To make mobile devices adaptive and able to autonomously respond to changes in user behaviours, machine learning techniques can be deployed to learn behaviour from empirical data. Learning outcomes should be rule-based enforcement policies that can pervasively manage the devices, and at the same time facilitate user validation when and if required. In this chapter we demonstrate the feasibility of non-monotonic Inductive Logic Programming (ILP) in the automated task of extraction of user behaviour rules through data acquisition in the domain of mobile phones. This is a challenging task as real mobile datasets are highly noisy and unevenly distributed. We present two applications, one based on an existing dataset collected as part of the Reality Mining group, and the other generated by a mobile phone application called ULearn that we have developed to facilitate a realistic evaluation of the accuracy of the learning outcome.

6.1 Introduction

In the past few years, companies such as Apple and Samsung have really managed to develop cutting-edge mobile systems revolutionising the mobile phone industry. Often, the complexity of these systems prevent the user from utilising the device to its full potential. A more pervasive approach requires systems to be able to continuously adapt to the user's preferences and behaviour with near-to-zero intervention. Rules are an effective way of specifying how these systems should adapt in different contexts. Rule-based enforcement policies that govern system choices are increasingly becoming more popular in pervasive systems. Information about user behaviours can be collected through their phone usage and used together with past data and background knowledge about contextual information to compute new rule-based enforcement policies and/or make changes in existing ones. Such scenarios suggest the use of Inductive Logic Programming (ILP) [DeRaedt and Muggleton (1994)] as an appropriate learning mechanism. To our knowledge no existing ILP techniques have so far been applied to large and real data in the mobile phone domain.

In this context, to provide accurate solutions, the ILP technique has to make use of heuristics to guide the search in a (potentially large) search space to minimise computation time, cater for noise in the data and for uneven distribution of data. This chapter demonstrates that the non-monotonic inductive programming tool, TAL (Top-directed Abductive Learning) [Corapi *et al.* (2010)] can be appropriately customised to learn new mobile-user behaviours as well as revise existing rules with approximately 80% level of accuracy. TAL's main features suited this problem as it overcomes the completeness problems but also the expressiveness of learning in the context of learning logic programs. It is the first system that allows background theories and hypotheses to be normal logic programs. In particular, it handles negation during the learning process, has the ability to learn non-monotonic hypotheses and is complete, allowing to find a solution, if one exists. The key difference, which made it deal in this context, lies in its applicability to derive rules by handling large datasets and to perform a complete search over a large space and infinite domains.

A learning framework is presented where domain knowledge about contextual information and language bias are defined as normal logic programs, and applied to two real datasets. The former uses the mobile dataset collected as part of the Reality Mining group [Eagle *et al.* (2007)] whereas the latter has been collected through a proof-of-concept mobile phone application we have developed, called ULearn. The application collects contextual information about user mobility as well as user behaviour in terms of interactions with the device (e.g. accepting a call, rejecting a call, etc.). Additionally, it allows users to specify a language bias, and computes rule-based enforcement policies. These are presented to the user in the form of

English text for validation purposes and the user can refine the learning outcomes by selecting rules to revise and enforce constraints on the language. The evaluation of the learning outcomes in both applications shows that the learning accuracy changes according to the heuristics and considerably improves with the use of a standard cover loop.

The chapter is structured as follows. Section 6.2 summarises basic background notions used throughout the chapter. Section 6.3 presents our learning framework and introduces main parts of its background knowledge and language bias modelled in the specific domain of phone calls. Section 6.4 illustrates the application of the framework to two real mobile-domain datasets presenting some accuracy results of the learning outcomes. Finally, Section 6.5 concludes with final remarks and directions for future work.

6.2 Background

We assume the reader is familiar with basic notions and terminologies of Inductive Logic Programming. ILP is regarded as a machine learning technique that is used to enrich a knowledge base with rules that discriminate between positive and negative examples. Specifically, ILP is concerned with the computation of hypotheses H that together with a background knowledge B explain a given set of examples E, namely $B \cup H \models E$ under given semantics. In this chapter we consider the case when B and H are normal logic programs, E is a set of ground literals and $\models$ is the entailment relation under the stable model semantics.

The space of possible solutions is inherently large, particularly in real-domain applications with large datasets, so different levels of constraints can be imposed to restrict the search for hypotheses. A structure on the hypothesis can be employed to impose an instance-specific language bias S. Mode declarations are a common tool to specify a language bias [DeRaedt and Muggleton (1994)]. These define which predicates are to be used in the head and in each of the body conditions of the rules that form a hypothesis as well as how their arguments are unified or grounded. In the TAL system [Corapi *et al.* (2010)], the mode declarations are mapped into a top theory $\top$ that constrains the search by imposing a generality upper bound on the inductive solution. The system uses an abductive proof procedure instantiated on this top theory together with the background theory. The abductive derivation identifies the heads of the rules (of a hypothesis solution) and the conditions needed to cover positive examples and to exclude negative examples, ensuring consistency. The abductive solution is guaranteed to have a corresponding inductive hypothesis H that is a solution with respect to the examples. For further details on the ILP system, TAL, the reader is referred to [Corapi *et al.* (2010)].

6.3 Towards an Adaptive System Using ILP

In this section we briefly describe our learning framework for learning and revising mobile-user behaviour rules, with a brief overview of the concepts modelled in the background knowledge and language bias. As shown in Fig. 6.1, our learning framework includes a modelling step where background knowledge and examples are encoded as normal logic programs and a language bias is defined. The TAL learning system is then applied. Following that, rule refinement can be performed on the learned outcomes based on a subsequent collection of data. The framework also includes cross-validation mechanisms for assessing the accuracy of the rules learned.

In the application domain of mobile phones, as well as in many context-sensitive applications, the concept of time plays an important role in defining user behaviours. We answer phone calls at a particular point in time and we are at location Y at a time point X. These are often not instantaneous and have a certain time duration. Events are therefore modelled in our background knowledge using a notion of *timestamp span* defined in terms of a start-time and an end-time. A basic notion of time as $[Day, Month, Year]$ has been defined together with ordering relations over time (e.g. before and after). These have been used to define different notions of *duration*

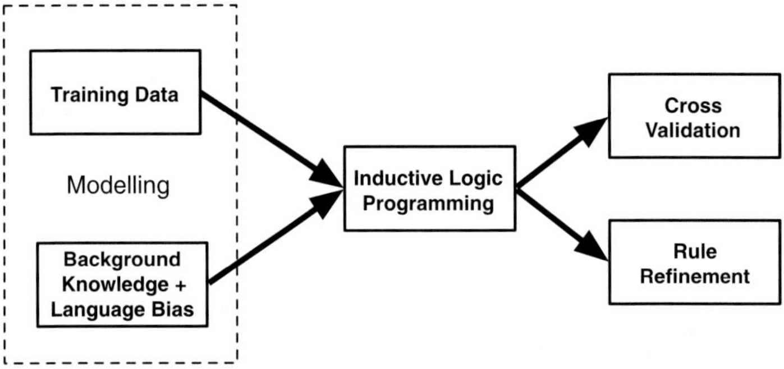

Fig. 6.1 The learning framework.

span which allow inference of specific knowledge from our collected data. Examples related to the domain of mobile phones include:

- **Activity span:** defines the period of a user's activity on the phone.
- **Application span:** denotes the period as well as the type of application a user is using. Application types are defined in the background knowledge.
- **Device span:** represents the period of time for which a device is present in the user's vicinity. Devices are also typed and defined in the background knowledge.
- **Cell span:** indicates the period in which the user is at a certain location. All locations traversed by the user are typed and included in the background knowledge.
- **On span:** Shows the period that the phone is switched on.

More abstract notions are defined in the background knowledge in terms of basic notions of time and duration span to allow the learning of user-behaviour rules that refer to more "high-level" concepts. These include concepts of time like weekend, morning, afternoon and evening, as well as the location of user, device proximity, user activity, application usage events, charge event, etc., each at a time point $[D, T]$. These are defined in terms of their respective span notions described above. For example, device proximity at time $[D, T]$ is defined in the background knowledge in terms of the existence of a device span such that $[D, T]$ is after $[D1, T1]$ but before $[D2, T2]$. As location also plays a crucial role in defining mobile-user behaviours, sufficient contextual information about a user's transition from one location to another can be collected through the device and is used to define a predicate that expresses the user being at a location X at time $[D, T]$.

Different language bias can be defined to specify the structure of the user-behaviour rules that we might be interested to learn. As proof of concept we have considered the task of learning when a user answers or rejects a phone call. The head declaration for such a task can be as rich as needed in order to compute rules that are dependent on few or many contextual aspects. An example of such head declaration is $modeh(accept(+date, +time, +contact))$ with a corresponding body bias declaration of the form $modeb(weekend(+date))$, $modeb(evening(+time))$, $modeb(= \ (+contact, \#contact), [\text{no ground constants}])$, and $modeb(\backslash + (= \ (+contact, \#contact)), [\text{no ground constants}])$, where the argument [no ground constants] defines the number of ground constants allowed in the search. For lack of space we omit the full definition of our language bias.

6.4 Real Mobile-Domain Applications

We have applied our framework to two different mobile-domain datasets. Each learning outcome has been cross validated using five folds[1] and we perform ROC[2] analysis on each fold in order to compute the total error estimate. We show, below, the solutions in English that have been produced automatically from the output of TAL by means of a translation mechanism that we have implemented.

The first dataset is the Reality Mining [Eagle *et al.* (2007)] dataset. This represents the largest mobile phone experiment attempted in the academic word. It consists of a large amount of data on human behaviour and group interactions collected using 100 Nokia 6600 smartphones with pre-installed software developed at the University of Helsinki. The information collected includes call and message logs, Bluetooth devices in proximity, cell tower IDs, application usage and phone status. The dataset has been anonymised and made available online to the general public.[3] We have selected a wide range of users, but ultimately focussed on studying the most problematic cases in terms of user's actions. Due to space constraints we only give an example of the most accurate user-behaviour rules that we have computed from this dataset. User #96 has a total number of 142 positive examples and 35 negative examples. The average error estimate turned out to be 19.2%. Listing 6.1 illustrates the best solutions while Table 6.1 shows some of the performance metrics of the ROC analysis.

Listing 6.1

```
solution(-106,[(accept(_,_,C):-$\+C=200)$])
solution(-104,[(accept(A,B,_):-not_nearDevice(A,B,413)),(accept(_,_,H):-$\+H
    =200)$])
solution(-104,[(accept(_,_,C):-C= -1),(accept(_,_,G):-$\+G=200)$])

Accept calls: not from contact 200
Accept calls: when you're not near device 413, OR not from contact 200
Accept calls: when the contact is not in your address book, OR not from
    contact 200
```

[1] We used five folds, as opposed to ten, due to the incredible amount of runtime taken to process each fold over large datasets.
[2] ROC: Receiver Operating Characteristic
[3] The Reality Mining Dataset: `http://reality.media.mit.edu/dataset.php`

Table 6.1 Performance measure results for user #96.

Fold	Accuracy	Error	Precision(PPV)
Fold 1	0.8571	0.1429	0.8529
Fold 2	0.9429	0.0571	0.9429
Fold 3	0.7143	0.2857	0.7143
Fold 4	0.6857	0.3143	0.6857
Fold 5	0.8378	0.1622	0.8378

Accuracy is the proportion of true results (both true positives and true negatives), and the accuracy of the above rule lies between 70% and 95%, a measure which is very promising. Precision is defined as the proportion of the true positives against all positive results (both true positives and false positives). In many cases, precision is equal to accuracy meaning that our results are both accurate and close to each other, showing that in each fold, the user's behaviour does not change much. Overall, the majority of the rules learned have one or two literals in the body and the best solutions always include the negation of a contact as the condition for accepting a call. This illustrates that the users' decision of accepting/rejecting calls is based on who the caller is, a result which is largely intuitive.

For the second dataset, we have developed a comprehensive client-server application called ULearn where data acquisition and user interaction takes place on an Android phone whilst the processing of data and execution of the learning algorithm happens on the server side. The rules, as a result of the training examples, background knowledge and language bias, are displayed to the user for validation. One of the main benefits of ULearn is the user's involvement in the learning process. The user can select any number of integrity constraints to impose restriction on the search space, or select already-learned rules for theory revision. We make use of the algorithm presented in [Corapi *et al.* (2008)] so that the existing rules are able to reflect and account for newly seen instances of examples and background knowledge. We have collected data from two users over a period of approximately two months. Here we present the best solutions for both users and also show how the results immediately improve when the cover loop approach is used. The score for each solution represents the accuracy of each rule.

User #2

```
/% Without cover loop %/
solution(-0.7065, [
 (accept(P,Q,R,_,_,_,_,_,_,_,Y,_):-\+user_is_active(P,Q),\+R=7517429133,\+Y=1280)
 ,
 (accept(A,B,C,_,_,_,_,_,_,_,_,_):-\+user_is_active(A,B),\+C=7517429133,
      timex_after_h(B,10))])

Accept calls: When you're not active, not from contact 7517429133, not when
      your phone's light level is 1280, OR when you're not active, not from
      contact 7517429133, after 10:00 o'clock

/% With cover loop %/
solution(-0.7717, [
 (accept(A,B,_,_,_,_,_,_,_,_,J,_):-not_at(A,B,1071.8253461),J=225),
 (accept(_,_,Q,_,_,_,_,_,_,_,_,_):-Q=1200490800),
 (accept(_,_,C1,_,_,_,_,_,_,_,_,_):-C1=447515692890),
 (accept(_,_,_,_,_,_,_,_,U1,_,_,_):-U1=0),
 (accept(Y1,Z1,A2,_,_,_,_,_,_,_,H2,_):-\+user_is_active(Y1,Z1),\+A2=7517429133,\+
      H2=1280)])

Accept calls: anywhere unless you're at 1071.8253461, when your light level is
      225, OR from contact 1200490800, OR from contact 447515692890, OR when
      your screen is off, OR when you're not active, not from contact
      7517429133, not when your light level is 1280
```

6.5 Conclusion

The work presented in this chapter demonstrates the applicability of the TAL system to real mobile domains for supporting the learning of mobile-user behaviours. With appropriate definition of a relevant domain of discourse, language bias and background knowledge, our evaluation results indicate that the system performs well when dealing both with large domains and large amounts of data. In particular, it has proven to be a powerful non-monotonic ILP system that tolerates noise and scales well with large domains and data because of its use of finite domain constraints that are not available in other systems. Further work includes enriching the background knowledge and language bias further. For example, using light-level information we can enrich the inference of context information, whether the user's mobile phone is inside their pocket or handbag. We can further use information about location to predict the user's next location. Last, but not least, we can explore the use of bagging, boosting together with bootstrapping datasets, in order to compute potentially richer rules with even higher accuracy.

Bibliography

D. Corapi, O. Ray, A. Russo, A. Bandara and E. C. Lupu. Learning rules from user behaviour, *2nd International Workshop on the Induction of Process Models*, September. 2008.

D. Corapi, A. Russo, and E. C. Lupu. Inductive logic programming as abductive search, *Technical Communications of the 26th International Conference on Logic Programming*, pp. 54–63. 2010. ICLP 2010: Edinburgh, 16–19 July 2010.

L. DeRaedt and S. H. Muggleton. Inductive logic programming: theory and methods, *J. Logic Program.*, **19/20**, 629–680. 1994.

N. Eagle, A. Pentland and D. Lazer. Inferring social network structure using mobile phone data, *PNAS*, **106(36)**, 15274–15278. 2007.

Chapter 7

Discovering Ligands for TRP Ion Channels Using Formal Concept Analysis

Mahito Sugiyama, Kentaro Imajo, Keisuke Otaki
and Akihiro Yamamoto

Graduate School of Informatics, Kyoto University, Japan

In this chapter, we propose an inductive approach to find candidates of ligands for *transient receptor potential (TRP) ion channels* from databases, which play crucial roles for sensory transduction of living things and are actively studied in biology and biochemistry. To study properties of TRP channels biologically, *ligands* are key tools. Ligands are chemical substances and activate or inhibit TRP channels by docking to them. However, finding a new ligand is difficult; choosing candidates of ligands relies on expert knowledge of biologists, and test experiments *in vitro* and *in vivo* cost high in terms of time and money. Thus an *in silico* approach to find candidates of ligands helps biologists. Here we achieve this task by treating as *semi-supervised learning* from ligand databases and using SELF (SEmi-supervised Learning via FCA) (recently proposed by two of the authors). SELF finds classification rules from mixed-type data including both discrete and continuous variables using FCA (Formal Concept Analysis). We show that SELF works well compared to other learning methods, and find candidates of ligands for TRP channels from more than a thousand ligands stored in a database.

7.1 Introduction

Transient receptor potential (*TRP*) *ion channels* form a class of ion channels, which are usually located on the plasma membrane. They play a crucial role for sensory transduction. In particular, *ThermoTRPs*, a subset of TRP channels, are activated by changes in temperature [Dhaka *et al.* (2006)]. Each channel has its own thermal thresholds and is considered

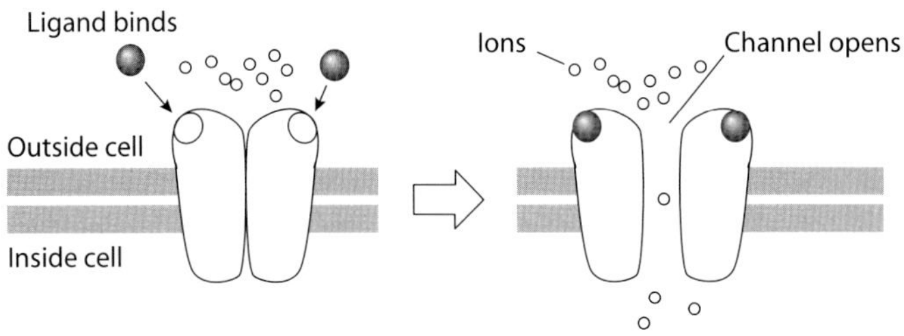

Fig. 7.1 Ligand-gated ion channels.

as a "gate" of temperature sensation, such as cold or hot [Bautista *et al.* (2007)]. To experimentally analyze TRPs (in biological sense), biologists use ligands, which are chemical substances and activate (called agonist or activator) or inhibit (called antagonist or inhibitor) TRPs' response (Fig. 7.1). Interestingly, each ligand has *selectivity*; i.e., binding cites of ion channels to which it can dock is limited and this is why they are convenient for experiments. However, finding ligands is difficult. Choosing candidates of ligands relies on expert knowledge of biologists, and experiments for testing ligands *in vitro* and *in vivo* are costly in terms of time and money. Thus an *in silico* approach to find candidates of ligands will help biologists.

In this chapter, we adopt an inductive data mining approach to find ligand candidates for TRPs from databases, and we use the framework of *semi-supervised learning* [Chapelle *et al.* (2006); Zhu and Goldberg (2009)] mainly studied in the machine-learning community. Semi-supervised learning is a special form of classification, where a learning algorithm uses both labeled and unlabeled data to obtain a classification rule (a label is an identifier of a class). Commonly, only few labeled data are available since labeling data costs high in a real situation. Currently, only few ligands for TRPs are discovered, and lots of ligands for other receptors are available. Thus if we use ligands for TRPs and the other ligands as labeled and unlabeled data, respectively, semi-supervised learning fits our goal.

Information about TRPs (and other ion channels) and ligands is donated to various databases, such as KEGG[1], and in this paper we use the IUPHAR database[2] [Sharman *et al.* (2011)]. In the database we can know which receptor each ligand binds to. Moreover, every ligand is characterized by seven attributes: hydrogen bond acceptors, hydrogen bond donors,

[1] `http://www.genome.jp/kegg/`
[2] `http://www.iuphar-db.org/index.jsp`

rotatable bonds, topological polar surface area, molecular weight, XLogP, and number of Lipinski's rules broken. Here, the forth, fifth, and sixth attributes are *real-valued* features, and the others are *nominal* features. Thus to learn classification rules for ligands from this database using the above seven attributes, a learning algorithm is required to handle mixed-type data including both discrete and continuous variables.

Various semi-supervised learning methods are available, but most of them are for learning from data with real-valued features. Moreover, to the best of our knowledge, only the semi-supervised learning method SELF [Sugiyama and Yamamoto (2011)], proposed by two of the authors, can directly handle mixed-type data. We therefore use SELF in this chapter to obtain classification rules and discover ligand candidates from ligand databases.

To date, no study treats mining of classification rules for ligands from databases. Some studies focus on predicting *affinity* of ligands, the strength of docking. Recently, the literature [Ballester and Mitchell (2010)] proposed a machine learning approach to predict affinity, but we cannot know whether or not a ligand binds to a receptor. Another approach was performed by King *et al.* [King *et al.* (1996)] for modeling structure-activity relationships (SAR), which can be applied to ligand finding. However, their goal is to understand the chemical model by describing relations using inductive logic programming (ILP), thus their approach is different from ours. Most studies have tried to construct a predictive model using domain-specific knowledge, such as the potential energy of a complex, the two-dimensional coordinates, and the free energy of binding [Moitessier *et al.* (2008)]. However, to use such a method, some special background knowledge is required and results depend on them. Our approach relies on only databases, hence the user do not need any background knowledge and can easily understand results.

This chapter is organized as follows: Section 7.2 gives methods: an overview of FCA and SELF, and experimental settings. Section 7.3 describes results and discussion of experiments.

7.2 Methods

SELF algorithm. SELF [Sugiyama and Yamamoto (2011)] learns classification rules from ligand data using FCA. SELF allows missing values and labels in databases; this is why it can be viewed as a semi-supervised learning method.

FCA [Davey and Priestley (2002); Ganter and Wille (1998)] is a mathematical and algebraic method used to derive a lattice structure, called a *concept lattice*, from a binary relation between objects and their attributes, called a *context* and given as a cross-table. In this study, each object corresponds to a ligand, and SELF translates features of ligands into attributes of the context in the data preprocessing phase. Each concept obtained by FCA is a pair of objects and attributes with the *closed* property; i.e., objects in a concept share a common subset of attributes and all attributes shared by the objects are in the concept. Many studies used FCA and the closed property for machine learning and knowledge discovery, such as classification [Ganter and Kuznetsov (2003)] and association rule mining [Pasquier *et al.* (1999)].

First, SELF makes a context from a given mixed-type database using both labeled and unlabeled data, where we use level-wise discretization for continuous variables. Next, it constructs the concept lattice from the context with FCA. Then SELF finds *maximal concepts* that are consistent with given class labels. Intuitively, their attributes correspond to the most general classification rules that explain a given labeled training data. We show a flowchart of SELF in Fig. 7.2.

To efficiently find all concepts, we use the algorithm proposed by Makino and Uno [Makino and Uno (2004)], which is known to be one of the fastest algorithms. Their algorithm enumerates all maximal bipartite cliques in a bipartite graph that coincide with the concept. Its time complexity is $O(\Delta^3)$, where Δ denotes the maximum degree of a given bipartite graph. For empirical experiments, we use the program LCM[3] [Uno *et al.* (2005)] to enumerate all concepts. As a result, time complexity of SELF is $O(nd) + O(\Delta^3) + O(\Lambda)$, where n is the number of objects, d the number of attributes, and Λ the number of concepts at discretization level 1, since data preprocessing takes $O(nd)$, making concepts takes $O(\Delta^3)$, and judging consistency of concepts takes less than $O(\Lambda)$.

Environment. All experiments were performed in R version 2.12.2 [R Development Core Team (2011)] since SELF was implemented in R. Note that LCM was implemented in C. We used Mac OS X version 10.6.5 with two 2.26-GHz Quad-Core Intel Xeon CPUs and 12 GB of memory.

Databases. We collected the entire 1,782 ligand data in the IUPHAR database[4] [Sharman *et al.* (2011)]. In the database, there are 44 ligands

[3] `http://research.nii.ac.jp/~uno/codes-j.htm`
[4] `http://www.iuphar-db.org/index.jsp`

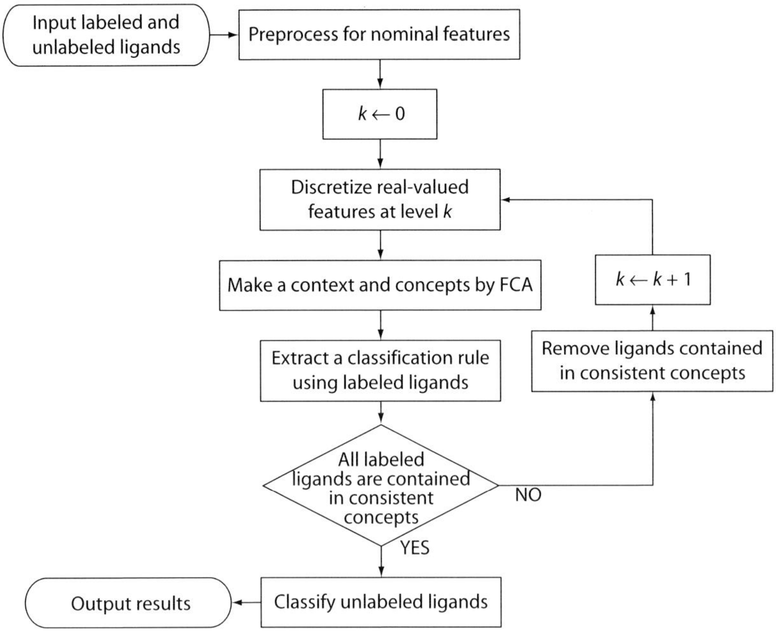

Fig. 7.2 A flowchart of classification by SELF. SELF learns classification rules from both labeled and unlabeled ligands (training data), and classifies unlabeled ligands. We say that a concept is consistent if all labels contained in the concept are the same.

that bind to TRPs, where seven TRPs exist: TRPA1, TRPC2, TRPM4, TRPM8, TRPV1, TRPV3, and TRPV4. From these ligands, we picked up nine ligands for labeled data, shown in Table 7.1, which are known as famous and convenient ligands of TRPs for biological experiments. Other ligands for TRPs are used as test data to evaluate performance of SELF. In the first experiment, we tested SELF in a *transductive setting* [Chapelle *et al.* (2006)], that is, we used both labeled and unlabeled data to obtain classification rules by SELF and predicted labels of unlabeled data. To measure the effectiveness of unlabeled ligand data, we performed three cases: using all ligands as unlabeled data, using the subset of ligands that bind to TRPs as unlabeled data, and using no unlabeled data. Moreover, to find new candidates of ligands for TRPs, we used all 44 ligands that bind to TRPs as labeled data in the second experiment.

Control Methods. As a control method for evaluation of SELF, we adopted the decision tree-based method implemented in R [Ripley (1996)]

Table 7.1 A subset of ligand database used for labeled data. Each ligand has seven attributes; hydrogen bond acceptors (HBA), hydrogen bond donors (HBD), rotatable bonds (RB), topological polar surface area (TPS), molecular weight (MW), XLogP, and number of Lipinski's rules broken (NLR), and has a receptor to which it binds as a class label.

	HBA	HBD	RB	TPS	MW	XLogP	NLR	Receptor
allicin	1	0	5	61.58	162.02	0.24	0	TRPA1
allyl isothiocyanate	1	0	2	44.45	99.01	1.72	0	TRPA1
DOG	5	1	18	72.83	344.26	5.80	2	TRPC2
phosphatidylinositol	19	8	44	332.00	1022.49	9.87	4	TRPM4
menthol	1	1	1	20.23	156.15	3.21	0	TRPM8
eucalyptol	1	0	0	9.23	154.14	2.60	0	TRPM8
capsaicin	2	2	10	58.56	305.20	4.23	0	TRPV1
camphor	1	0	0	17.07	152.12	2.13	0	TRPV3
epoxyeicosatrienoic acid	3	1	14	49.83	320.24	6.58	2	TRPV4

Table 7.2 Results of accuracy (%). We used all ligands as unlabeled data (SELF (ALL)), the subset of ligands which binds to TRPs (SELF (TRP)), or no unlabeled data (SELF). We used the decision tree-based method (Tree), SVM, and kNN ($k = 1, 5$).

SELF (ALL)	SELF (TRP)	SELF	Tree	SVM (RBF)	SVM (Pory)	1NN	5NN
0.52	0.48	0.37	0.18	0.39	0.43	0.50	0.34

since it can apply to mixed-type data. Note that this is a supervised learning method that cannot use unlabeled data in the learning phase. Moreover, we applied SVM with the RBF and the polynomial kernels and k nearest neighbor method ($k = 1$ and 5) for reference by using only real-valued features.

7.3 Results and Discussion

Results are summarized in Table 7.2. These results show that unlabeled ligand data can be used effectively in the learning of classification rules. Moreover, if we use the all ligands for learning, SELF shows the best result compared to other learning methods, and the accuracy is more than 50%, despite there being seven classes. Notice that even though the nearest neighbor also records good results, we cannot obtain any classification rules. Our results are therefore valuable for finding new ligands by biological experiments.

In the second experiment, 79 classification rules were obtained by using all ligands that bind to TRPs as labeled data and, by applying the rules, 762 candidates of ligands for TRPs were discovered from 1,782 ligands. These candidates are a novel result and can contribute to biological studies of TRP ion channels. Checking these candidates by actual biological experiments is a future work. Furthermore, this approach can be applied to any receptors, thereby discovering ligands for other receptors is an another interesting future work.

Acknowledgments

This work is inspired by the insightful ideas of Professor Shigeo Kobayashi. This work was partly supported by Grant-in-Aid for Scientific Research (A) 22240010 and for JSPS Fellows 22·5714.

Bibliography

P. J. Ballester and J. B. O. Mitchell. A machine learning approach to predicting protein–ligand binding affinity with applications to molecular docking. *Bioinformatics*, **26(9)**, 1169–1175. 2010.

D. M. Bautista, J. Siemens, J. M. Glazer, P. R. Tsuruda, A. I. Basbaum, C. L. Stucky, S. E. Jordt, and D. Julius. The menthol receptor TRPM8 is the principal detector of environmental cold. *Nature*, **448(7150)**, 204–208. 2007.

O. Chapelle, B. Schölkopf and A. Zien (eds). *Semi-Supervised Learning*. MIT Press, Cambridge, Massachusetts. 2006.

B. A. Davey and H. A. Priestley. *Introduction to Lattices and Order, 2nd edition*. Cambridge University Press, Cambridge. 2002.

A. Dhaka, V. Viswanath, and A. Patapoutian. TRP ion channels and temperature sensation. *Annu. Rev. Neurosci.*, **29**, 135–161. 2006.

B. Ganter and S. Kuznetsov. Hypotheses and version spaces. In A. de Moor, W. Lex, and B. Ganter (eds). *Conceptual Structures for Knowledge Creation and Communication*. LNCS, vol. 2746. Springer, Berlin, pp. 83–95. 2003.

B. Ganter and R. Wille. *Formal Concept Analysis: Mathematical Foundations*. Springer, Berlin. 1998.

R. D. King, S. H. Muggleton, A. Srinivasan and M. J. E. Sternberg. Structure activity relationships derived by machine learning: The use of atoms and their bond connectivities to predict mutagenicity by inductive logic programming. *P. Natl. Acad. Sci. USA*, **93(1)**, 438–442. 1996.

K. Makino and T. Uno. New algorithms for enumerating all maximal cliques. *Algorithm Theory-SWAT* **2004**, 260–272. 2004.

N. Moitessier, P. Englebienne, D. Lee, J. Lawandi and C. R. Corbeil. Towards the development of universal, fast and highly accurate docking/scoring methods: a long way to go. *Brit. J. Pharmacol.*, **153(S1)**, S7–S26. 2008.

N. Pasquier, Y. Bastide, R. Taouil and L. Lakhal. Efficient mining of association rules using closed itemset lattices. *Information Systems* **24(1)**, 25–46. 1999.

R Development Core Team. *R: A Language and Environment for Statistical Computing.* R Foundation for Statistical Computing. 2011.

B. D. Ripley. *Pattern Recognition and Neural Networks.* Cambridge University Press, Cambridge. 1996.

J. L. Sharman, C. P. Mpamhanga, M. Spedding, P. Germain, B. Staels, C. Dacquet, V. Laudet, and A. J. Harmar and NC-IUPHAR: IUPHAR-DB: New receptors and tools for easy searching and visualization of pharmacological data. *Nucleic Acids Res.*, **39(Database Issue)**, D534–D538. 2011.

M. Sugiyama and A. Yamamoto. Semi-supervised learning for mixed-type data via formal concept analysis. In S. Andrews, S. Polovina, R. Hill and B. Akhgar. (eds). *Conceptual Structures for Discovering Knowledge.* LNCS, vol. 6828. Springer, Berlin, pp. 284–297. 2011.

T. Uno, M. Kiyomi and H. Arimura. LCM 1 ver. 3: Collaboration of array, bitmap and prefix tree for frequent itemset mining. *Proceedings of the 1st International Workshop on Open Source Data Mining: Frequent Pattern Mining Implementations*, pp. 77–86. 2005. KDD 2005: Chicago, Ilinois, 21–24 August 2005.

X. Zhu and A. B. Goldberg. *Introduction to Semi-Supervised Learning.* Morgan and Claypool Publishers, San Rafael, California. 2009.

Chapter 8

Predictive Learning in Two-Way Datasets

Beau Piccart

Department of Computer Science,
Katholieke Universteit Leuven, Belgium

Hendrik Blockeel

Department of Computer Science,
Katholieke Universteit Leuven, Belgium
and Leiden Institute of Advanced Computer Science,
Universteit Leiden, The Netherlands

Andy Georges and Lieven Eeckhout

Electronic and Information Systems Department,
Universiteit Gent, Belgium

We introduce a new learning setting, called two-way predictive learning, as a special case of relational learning. We demonstrate that this learning setting has some properties that make an alternative learning approach, which we refer to as transposed learning, possible. We show how existing tasks fit this setting, discuss related work, and demonstrate experimentally that transposed learning can yield better results in multi-target learning.

8.1 Situating Two-Way Learning

Consider the following relational learning context: we have two types of objects $\mathcal{A}$ and $\mathcal{B}$, and a relation $\mathcal{R}$ between them. The objects of type $\mathcal{A}$ have attributes A_i, $i = 1, \ldots, n_A$; the objects of type $\mathcal{B}$ have attributes B_i, $i = 1, \ldots, n_B$; and the tuples in $\mathcal{R}$ have attributes R_i, $i = 1, \ldots, n_R$ as well as a special attribute T called the target attribute. We denote the set of

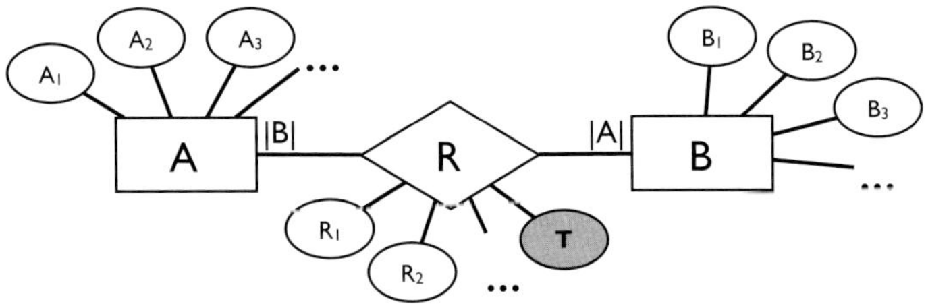

Fig. 8.1 ER diagram summarizing the data types available for learning. T is the target attribute.

attributes of $\mathcal{A}$, $\mathcal{B}$, $\mathcal{R}$ as $Attr(\mathcal{A})$, $Attr(\mathcal{B})$, $Attr(\mathcal{R})$, and their respective extensions as A, B, R. The relation R is complete: there is a relationship between each $\mathbf{a} \in A$ and each $\mathbf{b} \in B$. Figure 8.1 summarizes this in an entity-relationship (ER) diagram.

The task is to predict T from the other available information. This task is an instance of relational learning [De Raedt (2008)]: we predict an attribute of a relation from information about the participating objects. Propositionalization (representing the data using a single table) would cause redundancy (each object from A and B is described multiple times) and loss of information (the case where two rows refer to the same $\mathbf{a}$ can no longer be distinguished from that where two rows describe different objects with the same attribute values). Yet it is special, in the sense that the relation is complete (each $\mathbf{a}$ is linked to each $\mathbf{b}$), so there is no information in the structure of the relation itself.

This two-way learning setting is relevant for many applications; including molecular biology microarray data, recommender systems, multi-target prediction [Aho *et al.* (2009)], and the related problem of multi-task learning [Caruana (1997)]. Several toy examples in statistical relational learning, such as the student-course grade example [Getoor *et al.* (2001)], essentially describe a two-way prediction problem.

We can consider multiple specific settings, depending on what attributes are available. Table 8.1 provides an overview. The settings covered by the ER diagram can be called "relational learning with deterministic background" (since each instance of R is linked to exactly one A and B). Two-way learning, as defined here, covers the cases where $Attr(\mathcal{R}) = \{T\}$.

In the remainder of this chapter, we focus on *bare two-way learning*. Since, in this setting, R is complete, $Attr(\mathcal{A}) = Attr(\mathcal{B}) = \emptyset$, and $Attr(\mathcal{R}) = \{T\}$, the dataset D is simply a matrix. For each $\mathbf{a}_i$ and $\mathbf{b}_j$, we denote the corresponding T value as t_{ij}.

Table 8.1 Overview of two-way learning settings. In the table, * means "non-empty".

$Attr(\mathcal{A})$	$Attr(\mathcal{B})$	$Attr(\mathcal{R})\backslash\{T\}$	
$\emptyset$	$\emptyset$	$\emptyset$	bare two-way learning
**	$\emptyset$	$\emptyset$	single-decorated two-way learning
$\emptyset$	*	$\emptyset$	single-decorated two-way learning
**	*	$\emptyset$	double-decorated two-way learning
$\emptyset$/*	$\emptyset$/*	*	relational learning with deterministic background

This is the type of data we get in microarray data and in the context of recommender systems [Adomavicius and Tuzhilin (2005)].

It may seem strange that we want to predict t_{ij} from no information at all, since $Attr(\mathcal{A}) = Attr(\mathcal{B}) = \emptyset$, but the point is that the values of T themselves carry information. We can predict t_{ij} from the information in the $t_{ik}, k \neq j$, or from the $t_{kj}, k \neq i$, or even from the $t_{kl}, k \neq i, l \neq j$.

Bare two-way predictive learning can be addressed in different ways. Suppose we need to predict a single T_{ij} element. We distinguish the following main approaches:

Row-based: We learn a function f that predicts $T_{.j}$ from $T_{.k}, k \neq j$. That is, we reduce the task to a standard learning task, treating the rows as instances and the columns as attributes. The target attribute is $T_{.j}$, and the predictive attributes are $T_{.k}$ with $k \neq j$.

Column-based: This is the same as above, except that we treat the *columns* as instances and the *rows* as attributes; the target attribute is $T_{i.}$, and the predictive attributes are $T_{k.}$, $k \neq i$. We call this *transposed learning*, as it really corresponds to transposing the matrix that represents the dataset and then using a standard learning method.

These two alternatives also exist in single-decorated and double-decorated two-way learning, as shown on Fig. 8.2.

Matrix factorization [Lee and Seung (2000)]: In this approach, we try to find two matrix factors W and H such that $T \approx W \cdot H$. Each column $T_{.i}$ is then approximated by a linear combination of the columns of W, weighted by the components of $H_{.i}$. W forms a set of vectors optimized for the linear approximation of T, which will only give a good approximation if these basis vectors discover latent structure in the data. This method

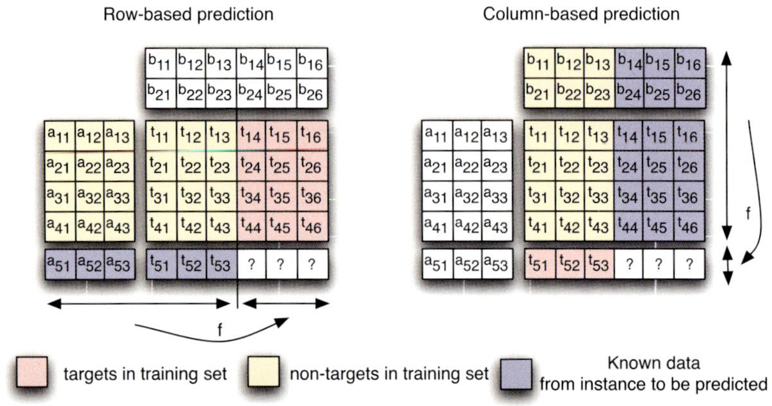

Fig. 8.2 We can learn a function f that generalizes over $\mathcal{A}$, predicting target values $t_{.i}$ from $a_{.j}$ and $t_{.k}$ or we can learn a function f that generalizes over $\mathcal{B}$, predicting target values $t_{i.}$ from $b_{j.}$ and $t_{k.}$. In the second case, the $t_{i.}$ targets will only become available when the new example becomes available.

predates the approaches proposed in this paper, and has been successfully applied in the field of recommender systems [Zhang *et al.* (2006)].

8.2 The Effects of Transposition

In the two-way learning setting, rows and columns are to some extent interchangeable. Consider again Fig. 8.2. Given a new object **a**, we need to predict the T_j values for it. First consider the user's point of view: rows are examples, columns are attributes. We get a new example and need to fill in some target values. If we have already learned a function f in the standard (row-based) way we can now apply it to predict those values.

Alternatively, we can consider a learner using the *transposed* view on the data. To this learner, **a** is a *new (target) attribute.* Since **a** is unknown during training, it is not possible to learn a function f till prediction time. At prediction time, f can be learned using the known components of **a** as known target values. In the column-based approach, our inductive learner is thus used lazily (or, transductively).

This transposition also turns a multi-target problem into a single-target problem and vice versa. This can be seen in the example in Fig. 8.2. The row-based approach results in a multi-target function f which predicts $(t_{.4}, t_{.5}, t_{.6})$ given $(a_{.1}, a_{.2}, a_{.3}, t_{.1}, t_{.2}, t_{.3})$ while the column-based approach results in a single-target function which predicts $t_{5.}$ given $(b_{1.}, b_{2.}, a_{1.}, t_{2.}, t_{3.}, t_{4.})$.

8.3 Applications

8.3.1 *Microprocessor-data*

For this application [Hoste *et al.* (2006)], the data consists of a set of performance numbers obtained by executing 26 benchmark programs[1] on a number of (different) machines. Based on these data, we wish to predict the performance of each of the machines for new programs. When a new program becomes available, the idea is to execute it on a limited number of machines ("predictive machines") and use this information together with the data about the benchmark programs to predict the performance of the remaining machines ("target machines"). Figure 8.3 illustrates the task. Since we use no descriptors of the machines or the programs, besides the performance numbers, this is a bare two-way learning problem.

We here compare row-based and column-based inductive learning. Our goal is to see whether the less natural column-based approach can offer an advantage over straightforward row-based learning.

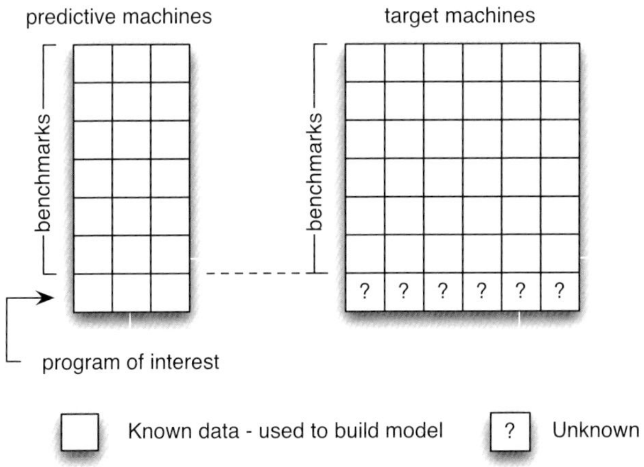

Fig. 8.3 Problem statement and terminology.

[1]From the SPEC CPU2006 suite, `http://spec.org/cpu2006`.

Table 8.2 Spearman's rank correlation for the predicted microprocessor data.

	Row-based	Column-based
Neural Network	0.82	**0.93**
SVM	0.77	**0.90**
Linear Regression	0.82	**0.91**
Matrix Factorization	0.85	0.85

We used three different machine learning algorithms from the Weka collection [Hall *et al.* (2009)]: a multi-layer perceptron (MLP), a Support Vector Machine using Sequential Minimal Optimization (SVM-SMO), and linear regression (Linear Regression). Each algorithm was run both row-based and column-based. The fourth algorithm to which we compare our results consist of a matrix factorization algorithm [Lee and Seung (2000)].

Default parameters were used for each algorithm and the performance is estimated using cross validation.

Table 8.2 shows that column-based prediction yields much better results than row-based prediction. One way to interpret this is that generalization over machines is easier than generalization over programs.

Of particular interest is the result of the Matrix Factorization (MF), which can only be applied to two-way datasets. As can be seen in Table 8.2, the MF algorithm outperforms all other algorithms for the row-based approach but the MF method is outperformed by the other algorithms in the column-based approach. The MF method does not benefit from a transposition.

8.3.2 *Ecological data*

Next, we consider an ecological application [Blockeel *et al.* (1999)]. Biologists take samples of river water to measure its quality, recording quantities of a number of micro-organisms, and physico-chemical parameters (such as oxygen concentration) in these samples. The goal is to learn to predict the physico-chemical parameters (PCP) from the micro-organism quantities. This problem corresponds to a standard multi-target problem on which we can perform both row-based and column-based learning.

We use the same four algorithms as for the micro-processor data. Results are shown in Table 8.3. Here, column-based prediction outperforms row-based prediction for the MLP and SVM, while row-based prediction works

Table 8.3 Mean Squared Error (MSE) for the ecological dataset.

	Row-based	Column-based
Neural Network	1.127	**0.9**
SVM-SMO	2.43	**1.46**
Linear Regression	**3.07**	4.04
Matrix Factorization	1.40	1.40

better for linear regression. This indicates that the optimal learning direction can depend on the learning algorithm.

8.4 Conclusions

We propose a new setting for machine learning that we call two-way predictive learning. The setting is characterized by the existence of two types of data elements, pairs of which are labeled with target values to be predicted. The two-way learning setting is encountered in many application domains. It covers multi-target learning as a special case, and is itself a special case of relational learning. It has some pecularities that motivate a separate study of this setting. In particular, it raises interesting questions about the interchangeability of examples and attributes, which itself sheds new light on the difference between inductive and transductive learning.

Experiments on two different application domains demonstrate the usefulness of this discussion: by running an inductive learner on the transposed data matrix, one can obtain better predictive results. While this approach is practically very simple, it is not straightforward to practitioners, partially because it requires a view of the data that is often unnatural (thinking of attributes as examples and vice versa), and partially because it requires one to use an inductive learner transductively (the learning process can only be started once a new test instance has arrived). Our experimental results show, however, that this alternative approach can yield important performance gains.

Acknowledgment

The work was funded by the Research Foundation: Flanders (FWO-Vlaanderen), project G.0255.08, "Efficient microprocessor design using machine learning".

Bibliography

G. Adomavicius and A. Tuzhilin. Toward the next generation of recommender systems: A survey of the state-of-the-art and possible extensions. *IEEE T. Knowl. Data En.*, **17(6)**, 734–749. 2005.

T. Aho, B. Zenko and S. Dzeroski. Rule Ensembles for Multi-target Regression. *The Ninth IEEE International Conference on Data Mining*, pp. 21–30. 2009. ICDM 2009: Miami, Florida, 6–9 December 2009.

H. Blockeel, S. Dzeroski and J. Grbovic. *Simultaneous Prediction of Multiple Chemical Parameters of River Water Quality with TILDE. Principles of Data Mining and Knowledge Discovery: Proceedings of the Third European Conference*, LNCS, vol. 1704. Springer-Verlag, Berlin, pp. 32–40. 1999. PKDD 1999: Prague, 15–18 September 1999.

R. Caruana. Multitask Learning. *Mach. Learn.*, **28**, 41–75. 1997.

L. De Raedt. *Logical and Relational Learning.* Springer, Berlin. 2008.

L. Getoor, N. Friedman, D. Koller and A. Pfeffer. Learning probabilistic relational models. In S. Džeroski and N. Lavrač, N. (eds). *Relational Data Mining.* Springer-Verlag, Berlin, 307–334. 2001.

M. Hall, E. Frank, G. Holmes, B. Pfahringer, P. Reutemann and I. H. Witten. The WEKA data mining software: An update. *SIGKDD Explorations*, **11(1)**, 10–18. 2009.

K. Hoste, A. Phansalkar, L. Eeckhout, A. Georges, L. K. John, and K. De Bosschere. Performance prediction based on inherent program similarity. *Proceedings of the 15th International Conference on Parallel Architectures and Compilation Techniques*, **9**, 114–122. 2006. PACT 2006: Seattle, Washington, 16–20 September 2006.

D. D. Lee and H. S. Seung. Algorithms for non-negative matrix factorization. *Adv. Neural Info. Proc. Syst.*, **13**, 556–562. 2001.

S. Zhang, W. Wang, J. Ford and F. Makedon. Learning from incomplete ratings using non-negative matrix factorization. *Proceedings of the 6th SIAM Conference on Data Mining*, pp. 549–553. SDM 2006: Bethesda, Maryland, 20–22 April 2006.

Chapter 9

Model of Double-Strand Break of DNA in Logic-Based Hypothesis Finding

Barthelemy Dworkin

National Institute of Informatics, Japan and University of Toulouse, France

Andrei Doncescu

National Institute of Informatics, Japan and Cancer Institute of Toulouse, France

Jean-Charles Faye

Cancer Institute of Toulouse, France

Katsumi Inoue

National Institute of Informatics, Japan

9.1 Introduction

Today the conception of artificial systems tries to imitate the natural systems by developing new concepts of reasoning able to handle a high level of heterogeneity and uncertainty. These complex systems have a dynamical evolution in terms of structure and organization. In order to model and control these systems there is a need to observe and reconstruct their behavior and make sense of large amounts of heterogeneous data gathered on various scales.

The science of complex systems (CSS) offers a theoretical framework for this holistic behavior by borrowing concepts from Statistical Physics, Dynamical System Theory, Theory of Computation and Machine Learning.

The main characteristic of a complex system is the emergent property which arises from the interactions of low-level entities and which cannot be deduced from or explained by the properties of low-level entities. Some of the most complex systems are the biological systems: if they cannot be reduced to the description of the properties of their elements, it is the manner of their evolution which modifies the characteristics of the constituting elements. Systems biology is expanding to cover almost all biological science, from protein interaction to whole organ and organism-level biomedical studies. Systems biology thus attempts to understand a life process as a whole system rather than as a collection of the parts considered separately. Understanding the interconnections among subsystems or elements involves a closed-loop thinking of causality, and also a great part of modeling. Modeling is the process of generating mathematical or computational theories that satisfy specifications or goals. Hence, a candidate model is a hypothesis for a theory of the system. The modeling and verification involve inference methods, hypothesis generation/update and hypothesis verification. Similarly, in biology and any scientific field, development of a scientific theory consists of a continuous cycle of observation explanation prediction experiment. Explanation of observed data is led by hypothesis generation, and experiments lead to data that could test inferred hypotheses. Over the course of this cycle, scientific models are frequently revised whenever discrepancies are encountered between observed and predicted results. In this chapter we propose an integrated framework for reasoning on a (partially observable) signaling pathway, possibly in the presence of global inconsistencies.

9.2 Double-Strand Break of DNA

A cell's response to a double-strand break of DNA (DSB) has been studied for some years, but the ATM-dependant signaling pathway has only been clarified since the discovery of γH2AX [Paull *et al.* (2000)], the phosphorylated form of histone H2AX. All the protein interactions of this pathway have been reported [Pommier *et al.* (2005)], including the signalization of the double-strand break (involving important proteins such as: γH2AX, MDC1, BRCA1 and the MRN complex), but also for the checkpoint mechanisms (involving p53, the Cdc25s and Chk2). In a general way, the cell can receive information by protein interactions that will transduce signals. First, the information is discovered by sensor proteins, which will recruit some other mediator proteins whose function will be to help all the interactions between the sensors and the transducers. These transducers are proteins that will amplify the signal by biochemical methods such as phosphorylation. In the end, the signal will be given to effectors that will engage an important cell process. In this pathway, the DSB is recognized by the MRN complex, which in turn will recruit ATM in its inactive dimer form, and then ATM will phosphorylate itself and dissociate to become an active monomer. This active form of ATM will phosphorylate many mediators such as γH2AX, MDC1, BRCA1 or 53BP1. Then, the signal is transduced by important proteins such as Chk2, p53 (a very important protein, which can cause cancer if mutated) or the Cdc25s. The effectors can be different with the context: some will induce the cycle arrest, whereas others will induce the cell apoptosis.

9.3 Ampliative Reasoning in Biological Systems

Understanding genetic and metabolic networks is of the utmost importance. These networks control essential cellular processes and the production of important metabolites in microorganisms, and modeling such networks from model organisms will drive applications to other less characterized organisms, which have a high biotechnological potential. The logical approach provides an intuitive method to provide explanations based on an expressive relational language. For example, logic can represent biological networks such as gene regulation, signaling transduction, and metabolic pathways. Unlike other approaches, this method allows a background theory, observations and hypotheses within a common declarative language, and provides the basis for the three main forms of inference, i.e., deduction (prediction), abduction (explanation) and induction (generalization). Deduction has traditionally been used for proving theorems of a given axiom set, but here we need to find new consequences (consequence finding), which is more general than theorem proving. Interestingly, the hypothesis-finding problem (abduction and induction) can be translated into consequence-finding problems, so that we can realize all three modes of inference using a deductive, consequence-finding procedure. We mention Inductive Inference as a type of reasoning that justifies some modification from one state of absolute belief to another, by adding new information to the initial assumes that is consistent with it but does not entail it.

9.3.1 *Hypothesis finding from first-order full clausal theories*

The importance of hypothesis generation has recently been recognized more and more for many innovative applications. SOLAR [Siegel] [Nabeshima *et al.* (2003)] is the state-of-the-art consequence-finding system in this field, whose performance is comparable with high-speed theorem provers when applied to theorem proving. It is the only system which is sound and complete for consequence finding in full clausal theories. SOLAR and CF-induction [Inoue (2004)] are the unique abductive and inductive reasoning systems, respectively, which are sound and complete for first-order full clausal theories. No other abductive or inductive system is comparable.

We will first present the case study and some behavioral rules. Next, we will present the limits of the classical logic and why we need the non-monotonic logic. We will explain the formalization of the behavioral rules with default logic. We use only normal defaults and Horn clauses in order to simplify the program, though we could extend this work to other case studies, with more complicated rules. Then, we explain the choice between the extensions thanks to preferences with simple probabilistic techniques.

9.4 Logical Model of a Double-Strand Break

Transfer reactions such as phosphorylation (and autophosphorylation), ubiquitination and methylation are specific cases of enzymatic stimulation. The mechanism is simple: an enzyme takes a substrate and makes a covalent bound with a marker.

$$Reaction(enzyme, substrate) \rightarrow product(marked - substrate) \quad (9.1)$$

Phosphorylation is a transfer of an inorganic phosphate and autophosphorylation is a special case where a protein can phosphorylate itself.

$$Phosphorylation(enzyme, substrate) \rightarrow product(P - substrate) \quad (9.2)$$

Ubiquitination is a transfer of a small peptide called ubiquitin and methylation is a transfer of a methyl component (CH3).

$$Ubiquitination(enzyme, substrate) \rightarrow product(Ub - substrate) \quad (9.3)$$

$$Methylation(enzyme, substrate) \rightarrow product(CH3 - substrate) \quad (9.4)$$

Unlike the other reactions, the transcription activation is not a transfer reaction, but still a very important one. It means that a protein will bind on a specific location of DNA and will induce the transcription of the target gene in RNA (along with a complex of other important proteins). After translation of the mRNA, a raw peptide will be produced and will eventually be modified by post-translational reactions such as phosphorylation, methylation or even glycosylation, which will give the protein related to this gene. We decided to model the transcription activation this way:

$$Activation(factor, promoter) \rightarrow product(translated - protein) \tag{9.5}$$

9.5 Results

This logical model contains two significant points for biological applications. On the first hand, nine different predicates are used to describe the biological interactions: enzymatic *stimulation* (general or not precise), *phosphorylation*, *autophosphorylation*, *ubiquitination*, *binding*, *transcriptionactivation*, *dissociation* and *product*. We precise that the "product" predicate describes the production of a protein following a reaction. It can be surprising but we did not choose to include a predicate for inhibition reactions, for in biology "inhibition" does not always describe the same mechanism. So we chose another way to say "if A exists, then B will not exist" (where A and B could be proteins or pathways). In order to still include inhibition without a specific predicate in our model, we decided to find another way: instead of the clause $product(A) \rightarrow inhibition(A, B)$ we use $product(A) \rightarrow \neg(product(B))$. This method has been revealed to have a good potential, and can be checked. Here is an example: normally in a cell, the protein $Cdc25A$ exists and prevents the cell cycle arrest. But if this protein is phosphorylated (by $Chk1$ for instance), it will be recognized by degradation effectors and will be dismantled. Without $Cdc25A$ the cell cycle stops. In the data, we modeled all the information this way:

(1) $stimulation(cdc25a, cell) \rightarrow \neg(product(cell\_cycle\_arrest))$
(2) $product(p\_chk1) \rightarrow phosphorylation(p\_chk1, cdc25a)$
(3) $phosphorylation(p\_chk1, cdc25a) \rightarrow product(p\_cdc25a)$
(4) $product(p\_cdc25a) \rightarrow$
$stimulation(p\_cdc25a, cdc25a\_degradation\_effectors)$
(5) $stimulation(p\_cdc25a, cdc25a\_degradation\_effectors) \rightarrow$
$product(cdc25a\_degradation)$
(6) $product(cdc25a\_degradation) \rightarrow \neg(stimulation(cdc25a, cell))$.

We used this top clause and production field for our inhibition test:

(1) $cnf(tp1, topclause, [-stimulation(cdc25a, X),$
$- product(cell\_cycle\_arrest), ans(X)]).$
(2) $pf([-stimulation(cdc25a, \_), -product(cell\_cycle\_arrest), ans(\_)]).$

It means we want to ask SOLAR to find all the *Cdc*25*A* substrates (by a simple stimulation) that will induce the cell cycle arrest. The only answer is:

(1) $conseq([+ans(\_0), -stimulation(cdc25a, \_0),$
$- product(cell\_cycle\_arrest)]).$

No other consequence was found, but that is normal as *Cdc*25*A* prevents the cell cycle arrest. We then asked SOLAR to find all the substrates of the phosphorylated Cdc25A on the same method:

(1) $cnf(tp1, top\_clause, [-stimulation(p\_cdc25a, X),$
$- product(cell\_cycle\_arrest), ans(X)]).$
(2) $pf([-stimulation(p\_cdc25a, \_), -product(cell\_cycle\_arrest), ans(\_)]).$

And here are the answers:

(1) $conseq([+ans(cdc25a\_degradation\_effectors),$
$- product(cell\_cycle\_arrest)]).$
(2) $conseq([+ans(\_0), -product(cell\_cycle\_arrest),$
$- stimulation(pcdc25a, \_0)]).$

We can see that the *Cdc*25*A* degradation effectors will induce cell cycle arrest, which is true because if *Cdc*25*A* is brought into degradation (after is phosphorylation), the cell cycle is stopped. In conclusion, our inhibition method by not creating a specific predicate is efficient.

We performed an experiment to see if our model could fix relations between proteins if we excluded a single protein. In a simple example of four proteins connected to each other by a series of simple implications $A \rightarrow B \rightarrow C \rightarrow D$, we wanted to prove that our model could find a relation from B to D if C was excluded. Here is the case of interactions with $RNF8$:

$$RNF8 \rightarrow RNF8\_bound \rightarrow RNF8/UBC13 \rightarrow Ub\_H2A$$

In biological words, $RNF8$ binds with the phosphorylated form of $MDC1$, thus allowing $UBC13$ to bind on $RNF8$. And finally, the complex $RNF8/UBC13$ can make an ubiquitination on the *H2A* histone, thus creating the ubiquitinated form *Ub_H2A*. We decided to delete the

$RNF8/UCB13$ complex to see if SOLAR could find a way to make a relationship between $RNF8\_bound$ and Ub_H2A: $RNF8 \rightarrow RNF8\_bound \rightarrow Ub\_H2A$. In our model, we structured the data biological data into SOLAR:

(1) $cnf(rnf\_02, axiom, [-binding(p\_mdc1, rnf8), product(rnf8\_bound)])$.
(2) $cnf(rnf\_03, axiom, [-product(rnf8\_bound),$ $binding(rnf8\_bound, ubc13)])$.
(3) $cnf(rnf\_04, axiom, [-binding(rnf8\_bound, ubc13),$ $product(rnf8\_ubc13)])$.
(4) $cnf(rnf\_05, axiom, [-product(rnf8\_ubc13),$ $ubiquitination(rnf8\_ubc13, h2a)])$.
(5) $cnf(rnf\_06, axiom, [-ubiquitination(rnf8\_ubc13, h2a),$ $product(ubc\_h2a)])$.

Then we deleted the predicate $product(rnf8\_ubc13)$ present in two clauses:

(1) $cnf(rnf\_02, axiom, [-binding(p\_mdc1, rnf8),$ $product(rnf8\_bound)])$.
(2) $cnf(rnf\_03, axiom, [-product(rnf8\_bound),$ $binding(rnf8\_bound, ubc13)])$.
(3) $cnf(rnf\_06, axiom, [-ubiquitination(rnf8\_ubc13, h2a),$ $product(ub\_h2a)])$.

The idea was to prove that $RNF8\_bound \rightarrow Ub\_H2A$ was true. We wanted to search all the products that would lead to the production of Ub_H2A in order to see if $RNF8\_bound$ was among these products. We used this top clause and this production field:

(1) $cnf(tp1, top\_clause, [-product(X), -product(ub\_h2a), ans(X)])$.
(2) $pf([-product(\_), -product(ub\_h2a), ans(\_)])$.

This experiment was tested on a computer under Windows 7, with an Intel Core i5 2.66GHz processor and 4096 of RAM. It lasted 163 seconds. As an answer, 527 new consequences have been found (with no time limit and no other parameters). Among these consequences, we found three of them that had the predicate product($rnf8\_bound$):

(1) $conseq([+ans(rnf8\_bound), -product(ub\_h2a),$ $-product(p\_mdc1)])$.
(2) $conseq([+ans(rnf8\_bound), -product(ub\_h2a),$ $-product(h2ax\_mdc1)])$.

(3) $conseq([+ans(rnf8\_bound), -product(ub\_h2a),$
$- product(gamma\_h2ax)])$.

These results show that, as we expected, $RNF8\_bound \rightarrow Ub\_H2A$ is true, and the production of the ubiquitinated histone is the consequence of the production of $\gamma H2AX$, of $MDC1$ bound to $H2AX$ and of the phosphorylated form of $MDC1(P\_MDC1)$.

9.6 Conclusion

We propose a complete logical model, respecting the protein interactions and biological veracity. Its first use is to act like a database: for instance, a biologist working on this pathway can ask all the proteins phosphorylated by Chk2, or all the proteins necessary for the ubiquitination of HA2 histone by RNF8 and UBC13. Depending on the SOLAR top clause, the question may be simple or complicated in biological terms. The other hypothetical use of our model is to give information of a new protein that would interact with proteins from this pathway. For instance, if a new protein is discovered and known to interact with a specific protein of the cell response to the DSB pathway, our model could find consequences of this interaction.

Bibliography

K. Inoue. Induction as consequence finding. *Machine Learning*, **55**, 109–135. 2004.

H. Nabeshima, K. Iwanuma, and K. Inoue. SOLAR: A consequence finding system for advanced reasoning. *Proceedings of the 11th International Conference*, LNAI, vol. 2796, pp. 257–263, Springer, Berlin. 2003. TABLEAUX 2003: Rome, 9–12 September 2003.

T. T. Paull, E. P. Rogakou, V. Yamazaki, C. U. Kirchgessner, M. Gellert, and W. M. Bonner. A critical role for histone H2AX in recruitment of repair factors to nuclear foci after DNA damage. *Curr. Biol.*, **10(15)**, 886–895. 2000.

Y Pommier, O. Sordet, V. A. Rao, H. Zhang and K. W. Kohn. Targeting chk2 kinase: molecular interaction maps and therapeutic rationale. Curr. Pharm. Design, **11(22)**, 2855–2872. 2005.

PART 2
Probabilistic Logical Learning

Chapter 10

The PITA System for Logical-Probabilistic Inference

Fabrizio Riguzzi
ENDIF, University of Ferrara, Italy

Terrance Swift
CENTRIA, Universidade Nova de Lisboa, Portugal

10.1 Introduction

Probabilistic Inductive Logic Programming (PILP) is gaining interest due to its ability to model domains with complex and uncertain relations among entities. Since PILP systems generally must solve a large number of inference problems in order to perform learning, they rely critically on the support of efficient inference systems.

PITA [Riguzzi and Swift (2010)] is a system for reasoning under uncertainty on logic programs. While PITA includes frameworks for reasoning with possibilistic logic programming, and for reasoning on probabilistic logic programs with special exclusion and independence assumptions, we focus here on PITA's framework for reasoning on general probabilistic logic programs following the distribution semantics, one of the most prominent approaches to combining logic programming and probability. Syntactically, PITA targets Logic Programs with Annotated Disjunctions (LPADs) [Vennekens *et al.* (2004)] but can be used for other languages that follow the distribution semantics, such as ProbLog [Kimmig *et al.* (2008)], PRISM [Sato (1995)] and ICL [Poole (2000)], as there are linear transformations from one language to the others [De Raedt *et al.* (2008)].

PITA is distributed as a package of XSB Prolog and uses tabling along with an XSB feature called *answer subsumption* that allows the combination of different explanations for the same atom in a fast and simple way. PITA works by transforming an LPAD into a normal program and then querying the program.

In this chapter we provide an overview of PITA and an experimental comparison of it with ProbLog, a state-of-the-art system for probabilistic logic programming. The experiments show that PITA has very good performances, often being faster than ProbLog.

10.2 Probabilistic Logic Programming

The distribution semantics [Sato (1995)] is one of the most widely used semantics for probabilistic logic programming. In the distribution semantics a probabilistic logic program defines a probability distribution over a set of normal logic programs (called *worlds*). The distribution is extended to a joint distribution over worlds and queries; the probability of a query is obtained from this distribution by marginalization.

The languages based on the distribution semantics differ in the way they define the distribution over logic programs. Each language allows probabilistic choices among atoms in clauses. As stated above, PITA uses LPADs because of their general syntax. LPADs are sets of disjunctive clauses in which each atom in the head is annotated with a probability.

Example 10.1. The following LPAD T_1 captures a Markov model with three states of which state 3 is an end state

s(0,1):1/3 ∨ *s(0,2):1/3* ∨ *s(0,3):1/3.*
s(T,1):1/3 ∨ *s(T,2):1/3* ∨ *s(T,3):1/3* ←
T1 is T-1, T1>=0, s(T1,F), \+ s(T1,3).

The predicate $s(T, S)$ models the fact that the system is in state S at time T. As state 3 is the end state, if $s(T, 3)$ is selected at time T, no state follows.

We now present the distribution semantics for the case in which a program does not contain function symbols so that its Herbrand base is finite.[1]

An *atomic choice* is a selection of the i-th atom for a grounding $C\theta$ of a probabilistic clause C and is represented by the triple (C, θ, i). A set of atomic choices κ is *consistent* if $(C, \theta, i) \in \kappa, (C, \theta, j) \in \kappa \Rightarrow i = j$.

[1]However, the distribution semantics for programs with function symbols has been defined as well [Sato (1995); Poole (2000); Riguzzi and Swift (2011)].

A *composite choice* κ is a consistent set of atomic choices. The probability of composite choice κ is $P(\kappa) = \prod_{(C,\theta,i)\in\kappa} P_0(C,i)$ where $P_0(C,i)$ is the probability annotation of head i of clause C. A *selection* σ is a total composite choice (one atomic choice for every grounding of each clause). A selection σ identifies a logic program w_σ called a *world*. The probability of w_σ is $P(w_\sigma) = P(\sigma) = \prod_{(C,\theta,i)\in\sigma} P_0(C,i)$. Since the program does not have function symbols the set of worlds is finite: $W_T = \{w_1,\ldots,w_m\}$ and $P(w)$ is a distribution over worlds: $\sum_{w\in W_T} P(w) = 1$.

We can define the conditional probability of a query Q given a world: $P(Q|w) = 1$ if Q is true in w and 0 otherwise. The probability of the query can then be obtained by marginalizing over the query $P(Q) = \sum_w P(Q,w) = \sum_w P(Q|w)P(w) = \sum_{w\models Q} P(w)$.

10.3 The PITA System

PITA computes the probability of a query from a probabilistic program in the form of an LPAD by first transforming the LPAD into a normal program containing calls for manipulating Binary Decision Diagrams (BDDs). The idea is to add an extra argument to each literal to store a BDD encoding the explanations for the answers of the subgoal. The extra arguments of these literals are combined using a set of general library functions:

- *init*, *end*: initialize and terminate the extra data structures necessary for manipulating BDDs;
- *zero(−D)*, *one(−D)*, *and(+D1,+D2,−DO)*, *or(+D1,+D2, −DO)*, *not (+D1,−DO)*: Boolean operations between BDDs;
- *get_var_n(+R,+S,+Probs,−Var)*: returns the multi-valued random variable associated to rule R with grounding substitution S and list of probabilities *Probs*;
- *equality(+Var,+Value,−D)*: D is the BDD representing *Var*=*Value*, i.e. that the random variable *Var* is assigned *Value* in D;
- *ret_prob(+D,−P)*: returns the probability of the BDD D.

The PITA transformation applies to atoms, literals and clauses. The transformation for a head atom H, $PITA_H(H)$, is H with the variable D added as the last argument. Similarly, the transformation for a body atom A_j, $PITA_B(A_j)$, is A_j with the variable D_j added as the last argument. The transformation for a negative body literal $L_j = \neg A_j$, $PITA_B(L_j)$, is the Prolog conditional $(PITA'_B(A_j) \rightarrow not(DN_j,D_j);one(D_j))$, where $PITA'_B(A_j)$ is A_j with the variable DN_j added as the last argument.

In other words, the input data structure, DN_j, is negated if it exists; otherwise the data structure for the constant function 1 is returned.

The disjunctive clause $C_r = H_1 : \alpha_1 \vee \ldots \vee H_n : \alpha_n \leftarrow L_1, \ldots, L_m$. where the parameters sum to 1, is transformed into the set of clauses $PITA(C_r)$:

$$\begin{aligned} PITA(C_r, i) = \; & PITA_H(H_i) \leftarrow one(DD_0), \\ & PITA_B(L_1), and(DD_0, D_1, DD_1), \ldots, \\ & PITA_B(L_m), and(DD_{m-1}, D_m, DD_m), \\ & get\_var\_n(r, VC, [\alpha_1, \ldots, \alpha_n], Var), \\ & equality(Var, i, DD), and(DD_m, DD, D). \end{aligned}$$

for $i = 1, \ldots, n$, where VC is a list containing each variable appearing in C_r. PITA uses tabling and a feature called *answer subsumption* available in XSB that, when a new answer for a tabled subgoal is found, combines old answers with the new one according to a partial order or (upper semi-) lattice. For example, if the lattice is on the second argument of a binary predicate p, answer subsumption may be specified by means of the declaration *table p(_,or/3-zero/1)* where *zero*/1 is the bottom element of the lattice and *or*/3 is the join operation of the lattice. Thus if a table has an answer $p(a, d_1)$ and a new answer $p(a, d_2)$ is derived, the answer $p(a, d_1)$ is replaced by $p(a, d_3)$, where d_3 is obtained by calling *or* (d_1, d_2, d_3).

In PITA various predicates of the transformed program should be declared as tabled. For a predicate p/n, the declaration is *table p(_1,...,_n,or/3-zero/1)*, which indicates that answer subsumption is used to form the disjunction of BDDs. At a minimum, the predicate of the goal and all the predicates appearing in negative literals should be tabled with answer subsumption. However, it is usually better to table every predicate whose answers have multiple explanations and are going to be reused often.

In Prolog systems that do not have answer subsumption, such as Yap, its behavior can be simulated on acyclic programs by using the transformation

$$\begin{aligned} PITA(C_r, i) = \; & PITA_H(H_i) \leftarrow bagof(DB, EV\hat{}(one(DD_0), \\ & PITA_B(L_1), and(DD_0, D_1, DD_1), \ldots, \\ & PITA_B(L_m), and(DD_{m-1}, D_m, DD_m), \\ & get\_var\_n(r, VC, [\alpha_1, \ldots, \alpha_n], Var), \\ & equality(Var, i, DD), and(DD_m, DD, DB)), L), \\ & or\_list(L, D). \end{aligned}$$

where EV is the list of variables appearing only in the body except DB and *or_list*/2 computes the *or*-join of all BDDs in the list passed as the first argument.

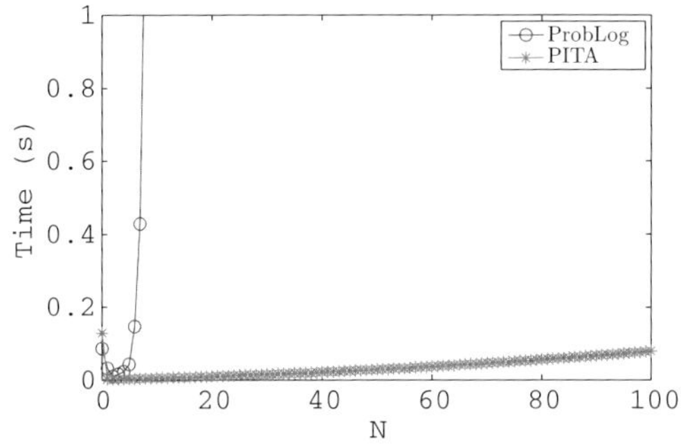

Fig. 10.1 Hidden Markov model.

10.4 Experiments

PITA was tested on six datasets: a Markov model from [Vennekens *et al.* (2004)], the biological networks from [De Raedt *et al.* (2007)] and the four testbeds of [Meert *et al.* (2009)]. PITA was compared with the exact version of ProbLog [Kimmig *et al.* (2008)] available in the git version of Yap as of 15 June 2011[2]. This version of ProbLog can exploit tabling, but as mentioned above, it cannot exploit answer subsumption which is not available in Yap.

The first problem is modeled by the program in Example 10.1. For this experiment, we query the probability of the model being in state 1 at time N for increasing values of N. For both PITA and ProbLog, we did not use reordering of BDDs variables[3] and we tabled the $s/2$ predicate. The graph of the execution times (Fig. 10.1) shows that PITA achieves a large speedup with respect to ProbLog.

The biological network programs compute the probability of a path in a large graph in which the nodes encode biological entities and the links represent conceptual relations among them. Each program in this dataset contains a non-probabilistic definition of path plus a number of links represented by probabilistic facts. The programs have been sampled from a very large graph and contain $200, 400, \ldots, 10{,}000$ edges. Sampling was repeated ten times, to obtain ten series of programs of increasing size. In each program we query the probability that the two genes HGNC_620 and HGNC_983 are related. For PITA, we used the definition of path from

[2]All experiments were performed on Linux machines with an Intel Core 2 Duo E6550 (2333 MHz) processor and 4 GB of RAM.
[3]For each experiment we used either group sift automatic reordering or no reordering of BDDs variables depending on which gave the best results.

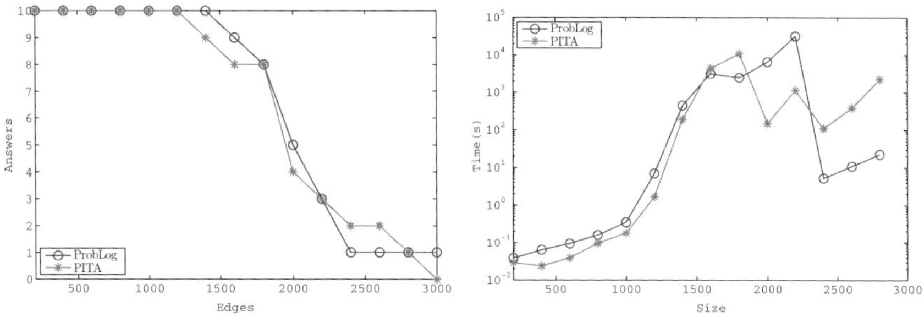

(a) Number of successes.

(b) Average execution times on the graphs on which both algorithms succeeded.

Fig. 10.2 Biological graph experiments.

[Kimmig *et al.* (2008)] that performs loop checking explicitly by keeping the list of visited nodes. For ProbLog, we used a definition of path in which tabling is exploited for performing loop checking. *path*/2, *edge*/2 and *arc*/2 are tabled in ProbLog, while only *path*/2 is tabled in PITA. We found these to be the best performing settings for the two systems. Figure 10.2(a) shows the number of subgraphs for which each algorithm was able to answer the query as a function of the size of the subgraphs, while Fig. 10.2(b) shows the execution time averaged over all and only the subgraphs for which both algorithm succeeded. Here there is no clear winner, with PITA faster for smaller graphs and ProbLog solving slightly more graphs and faster for larger graphs.

The four datasets of [Meert *et al.* (2009)] are: `bloodtype`, that encodes the genetic inheritance of blood type; `growingbody`, that contains programs with growing bodies; `growinghead`, that contains programs with growing heads; and `uwcse`, that encodes a university domain. The best results for ProbLog were obtained by using tabling in all experiments except `growinghead`. For PITA, all the predicates are tabled. The execution times of PITA and ProbLog are shown in Figs. 10.3(a), 10.3(b), 10.4(a) and 10.4(b).[4] In these experiments PITA is faster and more scalable than ProbLog.

[4]For the missing points at the beginning of the lines a time smaller than 10^{-6} was recorded. For the missing points at the end of the lines the algorithm exhausted the available memory.

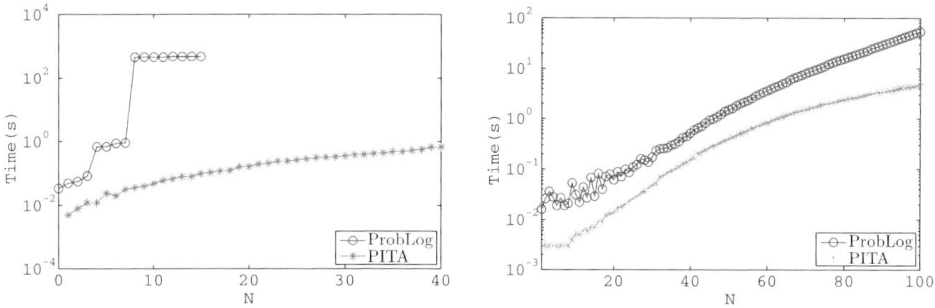

(a) bloodtype. (b) growingbody.

Fig. 10.3 Datasets from [Meert *et al.* (2009)].

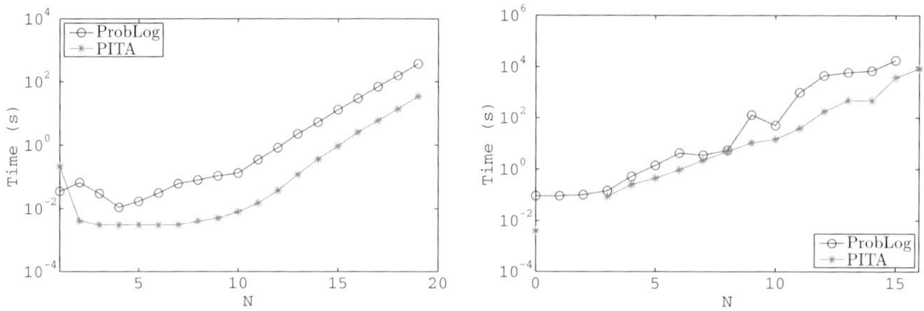

(a) growinghead. (b) uwcse.

Fig. 10.4 Datasets from [Meert *et al.* (2009)].

Bibliography

L. De Raedt, A. Kimmig and H. Toivonen. ProbLog: A probabilistic Prolog and its application in link discovery. *Proceedings of the 20th International Joint Conference on Artificial Intelligence,* pp. 2462–2467. 2007. IJCAI 2007: Hyderabad, 6–12 January 2007.

L. De Raedt, B. Demoen, D. Fierens, B. Gutmann, G. Janssens, A. Kimmig, N. Landwehr, T. Mantadelis, W. Meert, R. Rocha, V. Santos Costa, I. Thon and J. Vennekens. Towards digesting the alphabet-soup of statistical relational learning. *NIPS*2008 Workshop on Probabilistic Programming.* 2008. NIPS 2008: Whistler, 13 December 2008.

A. Kimmig, V. Santos Costa, R. Rocha, B. Demoen and L. De Raedt. On the efficient execution of ProbLog programs. *International Conference on Logic Programming,* LNCS vol. 5366, Springer, pp. 175–189. 2008.

W. Meert, J. Struyf and H. Blockeel. CP-Logic Theory inference with contextual variable elimination and comparison to BDD based inference methods.

International Conference on Inductive Logic Programming. LNCS vol. 5989, Springer, Berlin, pp. 96–109. 2009.

D. Poole. Abducing through negation as failure: stable models within the independent choice logic. *J. Log. Prog.*, **44(1–3)**, 5–35. 2000.

F. Riguzzi and T. Swift. Tabling and answer subsumption for reasoning on logic programs with annotated disjunctions. In *Technical Communications of the International Conference on Logic Programming, LIPIcs, vol. 7.* Schloss Dagstuhl–Leibniz-Zentrum fuer Informatik, pp. 162–171. 2010.

F. Riguzzi and T. Swift. Well-definedness and efficient inference for probabilistic logic programming under the distribution semantics. *Theor. Prac. Log. Prog.*, **13(2)**, 279–302. 2011.

T. Sato. A statistical learning method for logic programs with distribution semantics. In L. Sterling (ed.). *Proceedings of the 12th International Conference on Logic Programming.* MIT Press, Cambridge, Massachusetts, pp. 715–729. 1995.

J. Vennekens, S. Verbaeten and M. Bruynooghe. Logic programs with annotated disjunctions. *International Conference on Logic Programming.* LNCS vol. 3131, Springer, Berlin, pp. 195–209. 2004.

Chapter 11

Learning a Generative Failure-Free PRISM Clause

Waleed Alsanie and James Cussens

Department of Computer Science, University of York, UK

PRISM is a probabilistic logic programming formalism which allows learning parameters from examples through its graphical EM algorithm. PRISM is aimed at modelling generative processes in the compact first-order logic representation. It facilitates model selection by providing three scoring functions: *Bayesian Information Criterion (BIC)*, *Cheeseman–Stutz (CS)* and *variational free energy*. This chapter considers learning a failure-free single clause PRISM program by searching and scoring possible models built from observations and Background Knowledge (BK).

11.1 Introduction

PRISM is a probabilistic logic programming formalism in which a probability distribution is defined over possible worlds [Sato and Kameya (1997)]. Given a logic program $DB = F \cup R$ where F is a set of ground facts and R is a set of rules (definite clauses), a probability distribution P_F is defined over all possible assignments of truth values of the ground facts in F. Sampling from P_F will lead to a set $F' \subseteq F$ where the least Herbrand model of $F' \cup R$ represents a sample from all true ground atoms in DB. Thus P_F can be extended to P_{DB} which is known as *Distribution Semantics* [Sato and Kameya (1997, 2008)]. With this semantic, *generative models* can be represented in such a way that each sample of the ground atoms in DB explains a generation process of an observation. PRISM allows learning parameters from observations through its graphical EM algorithm. It also facilitates model (structure) scoring with three scoring functions: BIC, CS and variational free energy. However, general structure learning of PRISM has not been addressed much.

When learning generative models like *Probabilistic Logic Programs* (PLP), variables in the head are assumed to be an output of some predicates in the body, so each observation is fully explained by the program. This is different from learning *predictive models* where, typically, the aim is to learn the simplest (most general) model that is *complete* and *consistent* according to the positive E^+ and negative E^- examples, which is normally the setting in learning with *Inverse Entailment* (IE) [Muggleton and De Raedt (1994); Muggleton (1995)].

In subsequent sections we explain a technique to learn generative failure-free single clause PRISM programs. Such programs can represent static Bayesian networks. In Section 11.2, we briefly explain the variational free energy scoring function. Section 11.3 explains the formulation of the hypothesis space and the search strategies. Section 11.4 shows an experiment of learning the Asia network. Finally, we conclude with discussion and future directions.

11.2 Scoring with Variational Free Energy

In the *Variational Bayesian* (VB) approach, the marginal log-likelihood $L(M)$ is used in models scoring where $L(M) \stackrel{\text{def}}{=} \log p(D|M)$. As explanations Z of goals are hidden, the marginal log-likelihood can be written as:

$$L(M) = \log \sum_{Z} \int_{\theta} p(D, Z, \theta|M) d\theta \tag{11.1}$$

$$L(M) \geq F[q] \stackrel{\text{def}}{=} \sum_{Z} \int_{\theta} q(Z, \theta|D, M) \log \frac{p(D, Z, \theta|M)}{q(Z, \theta|D, M)} d\theta \tag{11.2}$$

$F[q]$ is the variational free energy and it is a lower bound of $L(M)$. The full derivation of approximating the distribution p by maximising the variational free energy is explained by Sato *et al.* [Sato *et al.* (2008)]. In VB learning, a further assumption is made that $q(Z, \theta|D, M) \approx q(Z|D, M)q(\theta|D, M)$. It can be noticed from this assumption and from the integral above that this score penalises complex models (ones that have a large parameter space). This trade-off between the complexity of the model and fitting the data is needed to avoid overfitting.

11.3 Building and Searching the Hypothesis Space

11.3.1 *Building the hypothesis space*

The search space is defined with respect to the observations and some BK. The BK considered so far is the PRISM switch definitions only. The outcomes of a switch are then added along with the switch separately as facts. For example, given the following BK:

```
values(smoking,[0,1]).
values(visitAsia,[0,1]).
```

BK will be transformed into facts as follows:

```
msw(smoking,0).
msw(smoking,1).
msw(visitAsia,0).
msw(visitAsia,1).
```

The transformed BK constitutes the base for building the search space. The search space is built by first approximating the *relative least general generalisation* (RLGG) of the first two observations relative to the BK. Then, after deleting all observations explained by the RLGG, an approximation of the *least general generalisation* (LGG)[1] of the resulting clauses (RLGG at first) and the clause formed by the first unexplained observation as a head and the BK as a body is built. The steps are repeated until all observations are explained. The LGG is approximated and not built exactly because some resulting predicates violate the PRISM condition that switches must be ground terms. For example, $lgg(msw(smoking, 1), msw(visitAsia, 1)) = msw(X, 1)$ which is not acceptable in PRISM. Some heuristics can also be used to approximate the LGG in order to reduce the resulting clause. Building the hypothesis space goes as follows:

(1) Build the LGG of the two clauses Obs_1*:-Conj(BK)* and Obs_2*:-Conj(BK)*, where Obs_1 is the first observation, Obs_2 is the second observation and *Conj(BK)* is a conjunction of the facts in BK. The result of the LGG is a clause *Head:-Body*.
(2) Delete all observations that are explained by the resulting clause (*Head:-Body*).
(3) Build the LGG of the resulting clause (*Head:-Body*) and the clause Obs_{n-m}*:-Conj(BK)*, where n is the number of observations, m is the number of observations explained by the previously resulting clause and Obs_{n-m} is the first unexplained observation.
(4) Repeat step 3 until all observations are explained.

[1]The idea of approximating the LGG was proposed by Idestam-Almquist [Idestam-Almquist (1997)] in solving ILP problems

Though the final clause explains all observations, it is extremely large and contains many predicates which would cause failures in most of the samples drawn from it. However, it defines a search space in which more salient clauses are contained which can be reached either by deleting literals or selecting some literals in a way that a generative process is achieved. This is the basic idea of the search algorithms which work on reducing the final clause resulting from the steps above until they reach a clause which gives the highest score amongst the visited clauses.

11.3.2 *Search*

The search algorithms aim at finding a clause with the highest score. As the aimed clause is assumed to be generative, two main conditions need to be met:

- All variables are range restricted.
- All switches are ground when they are invoked (this condition is imposed by PRISM).

11.3.2.1 *Greedy hill climbing*

The hill climbing search works by choosing the best candidate in the neighbourhood which is constituted by clauses with one literal deleted from the current clause. First it takes the massive clause generated by the steps described in Section 11.3.1, and then starts searching by selecting the best choice according to the variational free energy score. Given n literals in the body, hill climbing finds the best choice by deleting each one in turn, thus it runs VB learning n times and then $n-1$ times, and so on. So the cost of the search is $O(n^2)$ (this does not include the cost of the VB learning). Due to the large number of literals at the start of the search, this search strategy is considerably inefficient for big problems.

11.3.2.2 *Random generation search*

The random generation search takes the output of the steps in Section 11.3.1. It works by building generative clauses randomly. First, it considers the head of the resulting clause, and then it samples on body literal at a time until a generative clause is built. This clause is then scored and the process is repeated a pre-specified number of times. Finally, it produces the clause that has the best score. At each sampling stage, the set of body literals that are considered should not include any none ground switch. For example, the literal `msw(s(A),V)` must not be considered for sampling unless a literal that generates `A` has been sampled before in order for the switch `s(A)` to be ground. So the first sampling step works on literals with only ground switches (and other none `msw` predicates). Next, switches that are grounded by the sampled literal are added to the list that the algorithm will sample from, and the process is repeated until a generative clause is produced.

11.4 Experiment

In order to test the learning algorithms, we sampled 300 observations from the PRISM program shown in Table 11.2, representing the Asia network shown in Fig. 11.1(a). The observations were fed to the learning algorithm as training data along with the switch declaration part in Table 11.2 as

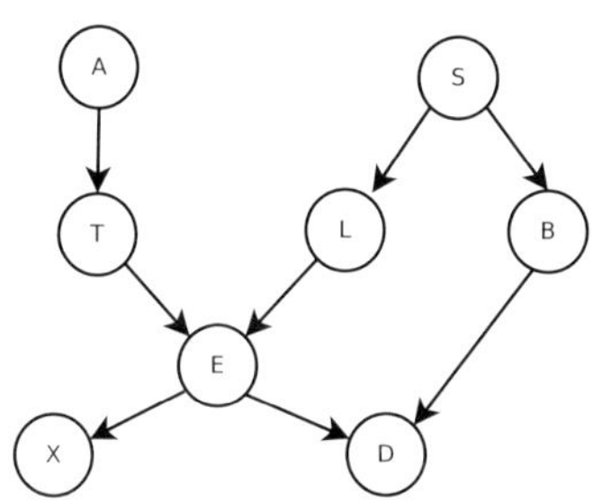

(a) The Asia Bayesian network from which 300 observations were sampled

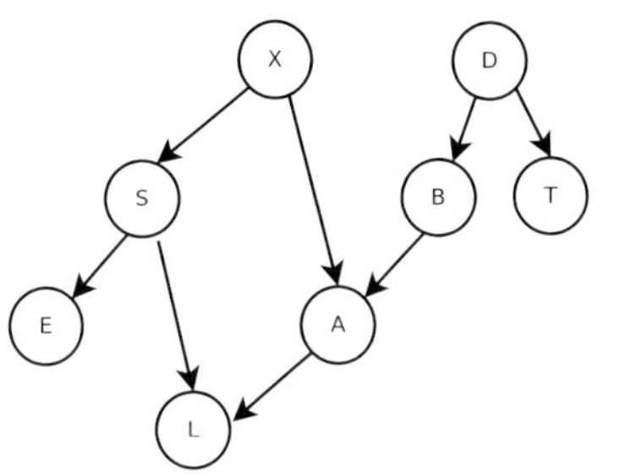

(b) The Bayesian network learned with greedy hill climbing

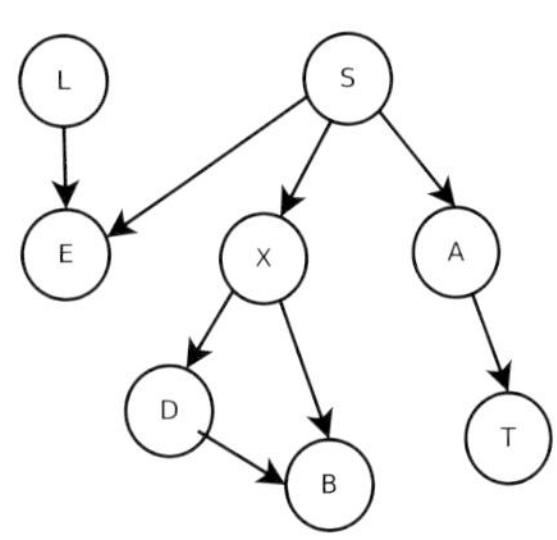

(c) The Bayesian network learned with random generation

Fig. 11.1 Learning Bayesian network encoded as a PRISM program.

Table 11.1 Result of learning a single-clause PRISM program encoding a Bayesian network with two search strategies.

	Variational free energy	Learning time
Original Net	−1459	N/A
Net learned by greedy hill climbing	−1464	>3 hours
Net learned by random generation	−1475	≈5 minutes

Table 11.2 A PRISM program encoding the Bayesian network where the training data was sampled from. The switch declaration part was used as a BK fed to the learning algorithm.

```
%Part of the switches declaration which also served as BK in learning
Bayesian network:
values(a,[0,1]).            values(s,[0,1]).            values(t_a(0),[0,1]).
values(t_a(1),[0,1]).       values(l_s(0),[0,1]).       values(l_s(1),[0,1]).
values(e_tl(0,0),[0,1]).    values(e_tl(0,1),[0,1]).
.
.
%Bayesian network modelling part:
asia(A,T,E,S,L,B,X,D):-
    msw(a,A),
    msw(s,S),
    msw(t_a(A),T),
    msw(l_s(S),L),
    msw(b_s(S),B),
    msw(e_tl(T,L),E),
    msw(d_eb(E,B),D),
    msw(x_e(E),X).
```

background knowledge. The learning algorithm is run twice with the two search strategies *greedy hill climbing* and *random generation*. The random generation search was set to generate 1,000 sample programs and return the program that with the highest score. The result is shown in Table 11.1. The greedy hill climbing search scored slightly higher than the random generation search. However, the time taken by the greedy hill climbing search is unsatisfactory. Taken into account that random generation search is completely random, this strategy could be improved with some guiding mechanisms.

11.5 Conclusion and Future Work

Probabilistic Inductive Logic Programming (PILP) is a challenging problem. PRISM is a well-developed formalism which generalises probabilistic models (e.g. Hidden Markov Model (HMM), Bayesian network, Stochastic Context-free Grammar (SCFG), etc) and Logic Programming (LP). This chapter presents a technique to learn single-clause failure-free PRISM programs and shows promising results. However, a challenging problem has yet to be solved. As the presented technique is based on constructing the LGG, though LGG is approximated and not constructed exactly, it could be problematic for big problems due to the combinatoric explosion of the number of literals. This problem needs further investigation.

There are different areas of improvement. One of which is learning recursive definitions as some models cannot be represented without recursive HMM with variable length. *Predicate Invention* (PI) can also be addressed as in some problems new predicates need to be invented to build the final theory.

Bibliography

P. Idestam-Almquist. Generalization of clauses relative to a theory. *Mach. Learn.*, **26(2–3)**, 213–226. 1997.

S. H. Muggleton and L. De Raedt. Inductive logic programming: Theory and methods. *J. Logic Program.*, **19**, 629–679. 1994.

S. H. Muggleton. Inverse entailment and Progol. *New Generat. Comput.*, Special issue on Inductive Logic Programming, **13**, 245–286. 1995.

T. Sato and Y. Kameya. PRISM: A language for symbolic-statistical modeling. *Proceedings of the 15th International Joint Conference on Artificial Intelligence*, pp. 1330–1339. 1997. IJCAI 1997: Nagoya, 23–29 August 1997.

T. Sato and Y. Kameya. New advances in logic-based probabilistic modeling by PRISM. In L. De Raedt, P. Frasconi, K. Kersting and S. H. Muggleton (eds). *Probabilistic Inductive Logic Programming*. Springer, Berlin, pp. 222–243. 2008.

T. Sato, Y. Kameya and K. Kurihara. Variational Bayes via propositionalized probability computation in PRISM. *Ann. Math. Artif. Intel.*, 54, 135–158. 2008.

Chapter 12

Statistical Relational Learning of Object Affordances for Robotic Manipulation

Bogdan Moldovan, Martijn van Otterlo and Luc De Raedt
Department of Computer Science,
Katholieke Universiteit Leuven, Belgium

Plinio Moreno and José Santos-Victor
Electrical & Computer Engineering, Instituto Superior Técnico, Portugal

We present initial results of an application of statistical relational learning using ProbLog to a robotic manipulation task modeled using affordances. Affordances encompass the action possibilities on an object, so previous works have presented models for just one object. However, in scenarios where there are multiple objects that interact, it is very useful to consider the advantages of the statistical relational learning (SRL).

12.1 Introduction

Robotics is a vast and active area seeking to develop mobile, *physical* agents capable of reasoning, learning and manipulating their environment. Early approaches such as those in Shakey used logical representations such as STRIPS, and many more approaches use various other kinds of symbolic knowledge representation [Hertzberg and Chatila (2008); Stulp and Beetz (2008)]. In addition to symbolic (or semantic) methodologies, the physical aspect of robots requires dealing with various kinds of *uncertainty* typically not handled by symbolic formalisms. These aspects include interpreting noisy sensors, processing image streams from cameras, controlling noisy physical actuators for manipulation and, in general, solving many *grounding* and *anchoring* problems. Therefore, much of current robotics research is concerned with *probabilistic reasoning and learning* techniques [Thrun *et al.* (2005)] instead of symbolic representations. Statistical relational learning (SRL) [De Raedt (2008); De Raedt and Kersting (2008)] combines logical representations, probabilistic reasoning and machine learning. Several recent works have explored the use of SRL and have shown how to effectively combine probabilistic and logical methods in robotics domains, e.g. see the kitchen scenario in [Jain *et al.* (2009)].

We outline initial results of using SRL, in particular ProbLog [De Raedt *et al.* (2007)], in a manipulation scenario with an iCub robot. We extend recent results in *imitation learning* in which (video) demonstrations of object manipulation (e.g. by a human) are used to learn *affordances* [Krunic *et al.* (2009); Lopes *et al.* (2007); Montesano *et al.* (2008)]. Affordances are a way to structure the robot's environment in terms of what it can do with specific objects. We extend this model by proposing an initial approach towards generalization, using probabilistic logical affordance models. This can be done by the use of SRL in a multiple-object scenario, which allows for the generalization over objects and actions by allowing the use of already-learned one- and two-object models together with known logical rules to be used for inference. This allows for a greater flexibility in modeling complex multi-object environments for robot manipulation than the previous approaches [Krunic *et al.* (2009); Lopes *et al.* (2007); Montesano *et al.* (2008)] of modeling the scene with a specific Bayesian network (BN). Next, we explain the one-object case and in Section 12.3 we discuss the learning of manipulation skills. Section 12.4 describes the relational extension and initial results after which we conclude with planned extensions, mostly carried out in the context of the EU project on *Flexible Skill Acquisition and Intuitive Robot Tasking for Mobile Manipulation in the Real World* (FIRST-MM)

12.2 Affordance-Based Models

We first discuss the affordance learning setting of [Krunic *et al.* (2009); Lopes *et al.* (2007); Montesano *et al.* (2008)]. Affordances capture *action opportunities* (e.g. what can one do with an object?) to structure the environment. The typical setup involves a robot (with an arm) and a table with physical objects (cubes, balls, etc.). Three main aspects of the approach are *actions* (A), *object properties* (O) and *effects* (E). These, and their relationships, are presented in Fig. 12.1. Actions are physical manipulation skills that can be applied to objects and include *grabbing* (and releasing),

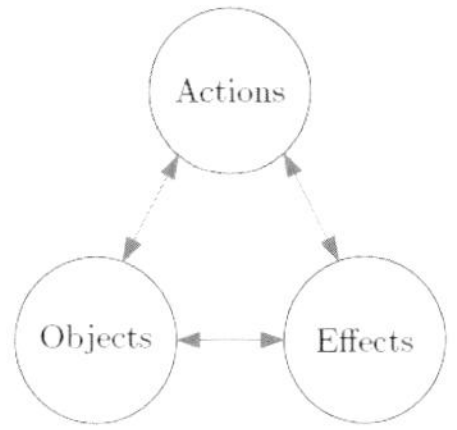

Inputs	Outputs	Function
(O, A)	E	Effect prediction
(O, E)	A	Action recognition/planning
(A, E)	O	Object recognition/selection

Fig. 12.1 Affordances model: relations between objects, actions, effects [Lopes *et al.* (2007); Montesano *et al.* (2008)].

pushing (in a plane away from the robot), and *tapping* (sideways). Object properties are aspects that can be measured from perceptual devices (such as vision) and involve color, shape and size. Effects are measurable features that change once an action is performed, e.g. the velocity of the hand, the velocity (or distance between) between the hand and the object, etc. Depending on which data is available to the robot and which aspects need to be predicted, the model can also be used for planning and other tasks, see the table in Fig. 12.1.

Learning to imitate manipulation actions is accomplished through several steps. First, data is collected from the robot performing several actions on different objects. All features for A, O and E are measured for each demonstration, and then processed, discretized and aggregated to acquire a dataset where all features have a relatively small (ordinal) set of values. A probabilistic model can then be learned that captures the dependencies between the three types of features. This can be used for various purposes; e.g. for imitation learning; the robot observes a human manipulating an object (with properties O), observes the effects of the demonstrated action (E) and computes the most likely action causing E and O, i.e. $\arg\max_A P(A|E, O)$. Note that the robot has now computed how to imitate a certain effect on an object in terms of his own action repertoire which is obviously different from that of the human.

12.3 Learning Relational Skills and Experiments

The setting we have just described focuses on learning to manipulate a single object. The data (E, A and O) is used to learn a (propositional)

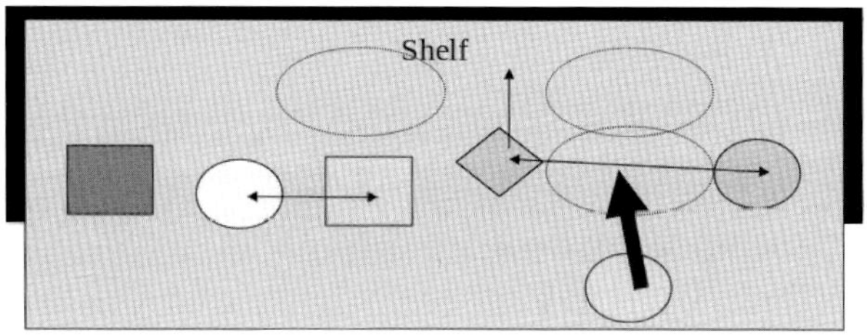

Fig. 12.2 Relational interactions on a shelf, with colored objects and possible goal locations.

BN and single actions for each object (e.g. large cubes should always be tapped to the left). We envision a more general setting in which manipulation skills involve (i) multiple objects, (ii) object interactions while manipulating, (iii) behaviors depending on spatial configurations of objects, and (iv) sequential actions.

A typical example in the First-MM project is the *shopping scenario*. Part of it is depicted in Fig. 12.2. The robot is given a shelf, where several objects are already present and their object properties (e.g. shape, location, orientation, etc.) are known. An additional object is present in front of the shelf, and the task of the robot is to place this object onto it, in a context of multiple other objects. We set up experiments where an iCub robot has to interact with one or two objects on the shelf. The *active* object is the one the robot acts upon, and the *passive* object may interact with the active one through the robot's actions. Once the setting is extended to more than one object, object interactions occur (e.g. pushing an object into another object), and the (spatial) relationships between objects have to be taken into account. We ran 87 experiments, 37 replicating the one object experiment in [Krunic *et al.* (2009); Lopes *et al.* (2007); Montesano *et al.* (2008)] and 50 involving two objects. Figure 12.3(l) illustrates the two objects setting. On the left is the robot's hand (white) and on the black table there is a yellow rectangular prism (active), and a blue rectangular prism (passive). The experiments were recorded using a top-view camera. The videos were processed in order to extract features (e.g. object shape, color, location, etc.), to compute the feature values for groups of frames, and then to cluster and discretise the values. From this data we first learn a BN using the K2 algorithm (using MATLAB), and then similar to [Lopes *et al.* (2007); Montesano *et al.* (2008)], we learn the parameters (i.e. the probabilities) of this BN. Figure 12.3(r) shows a subset of the BN, involving

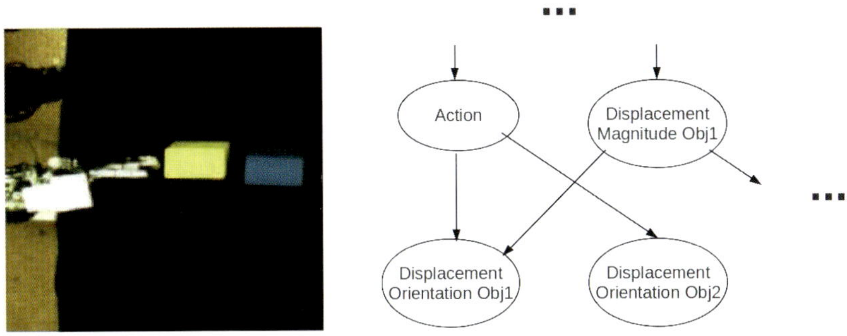

Fig. 12.3 **(l)** video still of the data showing the robot hand and two objects, **(r)** part of the Bayesian network obtained from structured learning.

the relations between the action, the magnitude of the displacement of the active object, and the displacement orientation of the two objects.

Learning an affordance model for these situations and the corresponding BN, the use of SRL allows us to achieve a generalization over multiple objects in this setting. Using SRL for affordances allows the robot to learn high-level skills, including motion planning, from low-level components such as the actions and their effects on objects with given properties. The ultimate goal of this research is the temporal aspect of the setting, in which a plan consists of a set of actions. To imitate the plan and learn necessary manipulation skills, the robot needs to recognize individual actions in the plan. The rest of the chapter will focus on recognizing individual actions.

12.4 ProbLog Modeling and Results

SRL [De Raedt and Kersting (2008)], a subfield of AI, studies the combination of logical representations, probabilistic reasoning mechanisms and machine learning. *Probabilistic programming languages* (PPL) are programming languages specially designed to describe and infer with probabilistic relational models. The PPL ProbLog is a probabilistic extension of the Prolog logic programming language, where facts are annotated with probabilities and for which several inference methods are available [De Raedt *et al.* (2007)]. Additionally, Prolog style logical rules can be used for defining (general) *background knowledge* to answer probabilistic queries.

We continue with the obtained experimental data described in Section 12.3, and add relational properties between objects (e.g. initial relative distance or orientation between two objects) in the two-object scenario as well as relational effects (e.g. final relative distance or orientation between two objects), and model it using ProbLog. The model supports inference for action recognition in this relational extension of [Krunic *et al.* (2009); Lopes *et al.* (2007); Montesano *et al.* (2008)]. Our approach has the advantage that data obtained from the one-object experiments can already be generalized to multiple objects through the use of variables that refrain from referring to specific, hardcoded objects. ProbLog rules generalize over the object displacement magnitude and orientation. Thus later this learning setting can be extended to more than the one and two objects that the experiments investigated, to the full-shelf scenario. Knowing that grabbing and moving an object does not involve a second object, the displacement of this main object can be generalized by using the data already obtained from the one-object experiment. ProbLog can be used for modeling the relations of the learned BN and parameters. As an example, in the subnet from Fig. 12.3(r), the following ProbLog statement using annotated disjunctions and the learned parameters models part of the relation between robot action and the magnitude of the displacement of the main object and the displacement orientation of that object:

$$
\begin{aligned}
0.8947 :: \texttt{dispOri}(\texttt{ObjMain}, 5); 0.1053 :: \texttt{dispOri}(\texttt{ObjMain}, 7) \\
\leftarrow \texttt{action}(\texttt{ObjMain}, \_, 3), \texttt{dispMag}(\texttt{ObjMain}, 1).
\end{aligned}
$$

This says that if the action type is tap ("3") *and* the displacement magnitude of the main object is small ("1"), then there is a probability of 0.8947 of the displacement orientation of the main object to be in a North (N) direction ("5"), while there is a probability of 0.1053 of it being in an East (E) direction ("7").

The full relation between the robot action and the displacement orientation of the secondary object is modeled as:

$$
\begin{aligned}
&0.0345 :: \texttt{dispOri}(\texttt{ObjSec}, 1); 0.9655 :: \texttt{dispOri}(\texttt{ObjSec}, 7) \\
&\qquad \leftarrow \texttt{action}(\_, \texttt{ObjSec}, 3). \\
&0.0476 :: \texttt{dispOri}(\texttt{ObjSec}, 1); 0.0952 :: \texttt{dispOri}(\texttt{ObjSec}, 3); \\
&\qquad 0.6190 :: \texttt{dispOri}(\texttt{ObjSec}, 5); 0.1429 :: \texttt{dispOri}(\texttt{ObjSec}, 6); \\
&\qquad 0.0952 :: \texttt{dispOri}(\texttt{ObjSec}, 7) \leftarrow \texttt{action}(\_, \texttt{ObjSec}, 4).
\end{aligned}
$$

Logical rules are used to specify general behavior. In the example, when an object is grabbed and moved, any other object in the scene remains unchanged (displacement magnitude and orientation are 0), which is modeled as:

$$\texttt{dispMag(ObjSec, 0)} \leftarrow \texttt{action(ObjMain, ObjSec, 1)}.$$
$$\texttt{dispOri(ObjSec, 0)} \leftarrow \texttt{action(ObjMain, ObjSec, 2)}.$$

General logical rules keep the relations as generic as possible. Similar to the examples presented above, the whole two-object model can be modeled using ProbLog. Because of limited data, not every relation is caught by structured learning. But using ProbLog is effective here too, as additional relations between objects, actions and effects, or constraints in the system can be modeled additionally with the use of logical rules.

After modeling the whole setting in ProbLog, we performed inference in order to do action recognition. It is assumed that the robot has knowledge of the object properties (O), and it can observe the effects (E), and it needs to infer which action (A) was performed. This resumes to querying for the condiditonal probabilities $P(A|O, E)$ in the ProbLog model for each of the four possible actions. As an example, an instance of action recognition that we ran had:

O: Object1=*Cube* Object2=*Cylinder*
Initial Relative Distance=*Big* Initial Relative Orientation=*NE*
E: Displacement Object1=*Medium* Displacement Object2=*Small*
Displacement Orientation Object1=*N*
Displacement Orientation Object2=*E* Contact Area=*Medium*
Predicted Action: Grasp, Release: 0% **Tap: 86.588%** Push: 13.412%

In this case, the action would be recognized by the robot as being a Tap.

One of the main advantages of using a probabilistic logic language is that it makes learning and inference so flexible by generalizing over the specific objects. Given that most object interactions in this setting involve two objects, the existing two-object model is a good approximation for the general shelf setting. Assuming no multi-way (> 2) interactions at the same time, extending this model to more than two-object on the shelf is easy, being enough to add all the new object property values to the model, and then do inference. Eventually, multi-way interactions can also be learned from experiments, just as the two-object interactions were, and this added to the model for it to become more exact. This can be used to find the best action the robot can do to place an object at the desired location given a configuration of objects around it.

12.5 Conclusion and Future Work

We described an initial approach towards generalization of robotic affordance model learning in a probabilistic relational setting. Moving to multi-object scenes requires expressive representation schemes to generalize over specific configurations of objects. Future work will involve the learning of full manipulation skills and generalization over more than two objects in a multiple-object scenario, and planning given partial knowledge about the environment. One direction in the multiple-object setting is that of *activity recognition* and *imitation learning*. Here, the robot detects the object properties and effects and tries to predict which action was performed. This involves recognizing the low-level "atomic actions" involving just one or two objects, by employing the learned models (for either one or two blocks). The whole demonstrated behavior consists of sequences of such actions, which would allow learning high-level manipulation strategies from demonstration by first distinguishing between their component low-level actions. A second interesting direction is to use the affordance models for *planning* of manipulation strategies. The long-term goal is to go towards a full-shelf/shopping scenario, in which the robot is instructed where and how to place objects by a human.

Acknowledgments

Bogdan Moldovan is supported by the IWT (agentschap voor Innovatie door Wetenschap en Technologie). This work is supported by the European Community's 7th Framework Programme, grant agreement First-MM-248258.

Bibliography

L. De Raedt. *Logical and Relational Learning*. Springer, Berlin, 2008.

L. De Raedt and K. Kersting. Probabilistic inductive logic programming. In L. De Raedt, P. Frasconi, K. Kersting, S. H. Muggleton (eds). *Probabilistic Inductive Logic Programming*. Springer, Berlin, pp. 1–27. 2008.

L. De Raedt, A. Kimmig and H. Toivonen. Problog: a probabilistic prolog and its application in link discovery. *Proceedings of the 20th International Joint Conference on Artificial Intelligence*, pp. 2462–2467. IJCAI 2007: Hyderabad, 6–12 January 2007.

J. Hertzberg and R. Chatila. AI reasoning methods for robotics. In B. Siciliano and O. Khatib (eds). *Springer Handbook of Robotics*. Springer, Berlin. 2008.

D. Jain, L. Mösenlechner and M. Beetz. Equipping robot control programs with first-order probabilistic reasoning capabilities. *IEEE International*

Conference on Robotics and Automation, pp. 3626–3631. 2009. ICRA 2009: Kobe, 12–17 May 2009.

V. Krunic, G. Salvi, A. Bernardino, L. Montesano and J. Santos-Victor. Affordance based word-to-meaning association. *IEEE International Conference on Robotics and Automation*, pp. 4138–4143. 2009. ICRA 2009: Kobe, 12–17 May 2009. In ICRA, 2009.

M. Lopes, F. S. Melo and L. Montesano. Affordance-based imitation learning in robots. *IEEE/RSJ International Conference on Intelligent Robots and Systems*, pp. 1015–1021. 2007. IROS 2007: San Diego, California, 29 October–2 November 2007.

L. Montesano, M. Lopes, A. Bernardino and J. Santos-Victor. Learning object affordances: From sensory-motor coordination to imitation. *IEEE T. Robot.*, **24**, 15–26. 2008.

F. Stulp and M. Beetz. Combining declarative, procedural, and predictive knowledge to generate, execute, optimize robot plans. *Robot. Auton. Syst.*, **56**, 967–979. 2008.

S. Thrun, W. Burgard and D. Fox. *Probabilistic Robotics*. MIT Press, Cambridge, Massachusetts. 2005.

Chapter 13

Learning from Linked Data by Markov Logic

Man Zhu and Zhiqiang Gao

School of Computer Science & Engineering, Southeast University, P.R. China

Semantic Web, with the vision of "Web of Linked Data", is becoming the data-holder for Description Logics learning algorithms. However, noise arises as an unavoidable issue to the effectiveness of these algorithms. To cope with this problem, we make use of the advantages of the Markov logic in handling uncertainties and modeling rich relations, and propose an $\mathcal{ALC}$ inclusion axioms learning algorithm. In this chapter, we describe the approach in detail and report the evaluations using a small illustrative data set, and four larger data sets. Experimental results show that the approach performs well on noisy data.

13.1 Introduction

As the "Web of Linked Data" vision of the Semantic Web is coming true, the size of Linked Data has kept growing over the last few years.[1] Although the Linked Data can provide plenty of examples for learning algorithms, as argued by Auer and Lehmann [Auer and Lehmann (2010)], many data sets on the Linked Data lack rich knowledge representation and contain noise.[2] Recent years have seen an increasing interest on this problem

[1] According to the 2009 report, there have been over 6 billion RDF triples, and over 148 million links in Linked Data [Bizer (2009)].

[2] We are particularly interested in handling two types of noise — *partiality* and *error* [Zhu (2011)] — in complement with the noise analyzed in [Hogan *et al.* (2010)]. Partiality means that concept assertions or the relationships between named individuals are actually true but missed, and error means that the RDF triples are not correct.

[Auer and Lehmann (2010); d'Amato *et al.* (2010)]. Learning from Linked Data is both worth investigating and challenging.

An important body of previous work has enlightened this chapter. In [Niepert *et al.* (2011)], Niepert proposed log-linear description logics, integrating description logics with log-linear models, to learn coherent Description Logic $\mathcal{EL}^{++}$ concept inclusions. Lehmann *et al.* have written a series of works on learning description logics, which have been implemented in the Description Logics learning tool DL-Learner. DL-Learner includes four class description learning algorithms, namely CELOE, a random guesser learning algorithm, and ISLE, a brute force learning algorithm. These algorithms select class expressions according to various heuristics [Lehmann *et al.* (2011)]. Völker and Niepert proposed a statistical approach, to be specific, an association rule mining, to learn OWL 2 $\mathcal{EL}$ from Linked Data in [Völker and Niepert (2011)].

We propose to learn $\mathcal{ALC}$ inclusion axioms inductively from Linked Data based on Markov logic [Richardson and Domingos (2006)]. As a combination of first-order logic and Markov network, Markov logic is able to handle Description Logic $\mathcal{ALC}$ (subsumed by first-order logic) in terms of expressivity. Using Markov logic, two challenges of learning from Linked Data can be easily handled: (1) Linked Data are highly structured due to the relations between entities and the underlying ontology; (2) Linked Data contains noises, here; we refer particularly to partiality and error. We make contributions in the following aspects: firstly, we tried to handle the noise issue in Linked Data, and explored the use of Markov logic to provide representation for Linked Data, and learn $\mathcal{ALC}$ inclusion axioms in a probabilistic way. Secondly, we adopted $\mathcal{ALC}$ downward refinement operator [Lehmann and Hitzler (2008)] to organize the hypotheses space during inclusion axioms learning with Markov logic.

13.2 Description Logic $\mathcal{ALC}$

Interpretation $\mathcal{I}$ (c.f. Table 13.1) consists of a non-empty set $\Delta^{\mathcal{I}}$ and an interpretation function.[3] In this chapter, the inclusions we learn are of the form $A \sqsubseteq C$, where A is an atomic concept, and C is a complex concept description (built from atomic concepts and atomic roles with $\mathcal{ALC}$

[3]Interpretation function assigns to every atomic concept A a set $A^{\mathcal{I}} \subseteq \Delta^{\mathcal{I}}$ and to every atomic role R a binary relation $R^{\mathcal{I}} \subseteq \Delta^{\mathcal{I}} \times \Delta^{\mathcal{I}}$.

Table 13.1 Syntax and semantics of Description Logic $\mathcal{ALC}$ [Baader and Nutt (2003)].

	Construct	Syntax	Semantics
	atomic concept	A	$A^{\mathcal{I}} \subseteq \Delta^{\mathcal{I}}$
	atomic role	r	$r^{\mathcal{I}} \subseteq \Delta^{\mathcal{I}} \times \Delta^{\mathcal{I}}$
	top concept	$\top$	$\Delta^{\mathcal{I}}$
	bottom concept	$\bot$	$\emptyset$
	conjunction	$C \sqcap D$	$(C \sqcap D)^{\mathcal{I}} = C^{\mathcal{I}} \cap D^{\mathcal{I}}$
	universal restriction	$\forall r.C$	$(\forall r.C)^{\mathcal{I}} = \{a \mid \forall b.(a,b) \in r^{\mathcal{I}}$ implies $b \in C^{\mathcal{I}}\}$
$\mathcal{U}$	*disjunction*	$C \sqcup D$	$(C \sqcup D)^{\mathcal{I}} = C^{\mathcal{I}} \cup D^{\mathcal{I}}$
$\mathcal{C}$	*negation*	$\neg C$	$(\neg C)^{\mathcal{I}} = \Delta^{\mathcal{I}} \setminus C^{\mathcal{I}}$
$\mathcal{E}$	*existential restriction*	$\exists r.C$	$(\exists r.C)^{\mathcal{I}} = \{a \mid \exists b.(a,b) \in r^{\mathcal{I}}$ and $b \in C^{\mathcal{I}}\}$

constructors). An interpretation $\mathcal{I}$ satisfies $A \sqsubseteq C$, if $A^{\mathcal{I}} \subseteq C^{\mathcal{I}}$. Equivalence $A \equiv C$ holds, if both $A \sqsubseteq C$ and $C \sqsubseteq A$ holds.

13.3 Learning from Linked Data

Given concept A, the algorithm will ideally learn an inclusion axiom of the form $\mathcal{A} \sqsubseteq \mathcal{C}$. Similar to the SEQUENTIAL-COVERING algorithm, the $\mathcal{ALC}$ learning algorithm we proposed contains a loop. Inside the loop, two operations are conducted. Firstly, the algorithm generates candidate concepts with $\mathcal{ALC}$ constructors for the current concept $C_{current}$ (c.f. Section 13.3.1) using $\mathcal{ALC}$ downward refinement opeartor [Lehmann and Hitzler (2008)]. Secondly, according to a performance evaluating function which selects the "best" one from the candidates according to the performance measure (c.f. Section 13.3.2). The loop breaks when the performance of the new candidate stops increasing.

13.3.1 *Generating candidate specializations*

We use the $\mathcal{ALC}$ downward refinement operator proposed by Lehmann [Lehmann and Hitzler (2008)] to generate candidate specializations. The refinement operator is a mapping $S \mapsto 2^S$ on a quasi-ordered space S. Subsumption is a quasi-ordering (reflexive and transitive) relation. An $\mathcal{ALC}$ downward refinement operator maps an $\mathcal{ALC}$ concept C to the $\mathcal{ALC}$ concept specializations of C. The learning algorithm conducts a general-to-specific search over the hypotheses space. According to our observations, the

Algorithm 1: Learning algorithm

input : target concept A, KB
output: concept C satisfying $A \sqsubseteq C$

current $\leftarrow \top$;
do
    oldconcept $\leftarrow$ current;
    candidates $\leftarrow$ `GenerateCandidates(`T, oldconcept`)`;
    current $\leftarrow$ `BestWeightConcept(`T, KB,candidates`)`;
while `performance(`oldconcept`)`$<$`performance(`current`)` ;
return $A \sqsubseteq$current;

Fig. 13.1 Learning algorithm.

refinement operator is particularly suitable for generating candidate specializations because it is well founded, and its good properties (for example, completeness) ensure the learning process will return the result if it exists.

The candidates are generated by an iterative process, which starts from a base set $\mathcal{B}$. $\mathcal{B}$ includes most general atomic concepts, negates most specific atomic concepts $\{\exists r.\top | r$ is an atomic role$\}$, and $\{\forall r.C | r$ is an atomic role, and $C \in \mathcal{B}\}$. We denote the set of atomic concepts as C_A, and for $A \in C_A$, the direct atomic subconcept of A can be defined as $dc_{\downarrow}(A) = \{A' | A' \in C_A$, there is no $A'' \in C_A$ with $A' \sqsubset A'' \sqsubset A\}$, the set of direct atomic superconcepts $dp_{\uparrow}(A)$ can be defined vice versa. The details of the $\mathcal{ALC}$ downward refinement operator $\rho_{\downarrow}(C)$ can be found from Table 13.2.

13.3.2 *Guiding the search*

At each step, candidate inclusions of the form $A \sqsubseteq C_i$ are assumed to be uncertain, that is, each inclusion is associated with a weight ($\prec A \sqsubseteq C_i, w_i \succ$). They construct a Markov logic network (MLN). Given the RDF triples in Linked Data, the MLN can be instantiated to be a Markov network $M_{L,C}$, in which each binary value node is a grounding of a predicate and each feature $f_{i,j}$ is a grounding of one of the concept descriptions. $M_{L,C}$ therefore encodes the joint probability distribution $P(X = x) = \frac{1}{Z}\exp(\sum_i w_i n_i)$, where $n_i = \sum_j \mathbf{1}\{f_{i,j}$ is true$\}$. In order to make both inferencing and learning tractable, this joint probability distribution is always approximated by pseudo-log-likelihood:

$$\log P^*_w(X = x) = \sum_{l=1}^{n} \log P_w(X_l = x_l | MB_x(X_l)) \qquad (13.1)$$

Table 13.2 $\mathcal{ALC}$ downward refinement operator $\rho_\downarrow(C)$ [Lehmann and Hitzler (2008)].

if C is	$\rho_\downarrow(C)$
$\bot$	$\emptyset$
$\top$	$\{C_1 \sqcup \ldots \sqcup C_n \mid C_i \in \mathcal{B}(1 \leq i \leq n)\}$
$A(A \in A_C)$	$\{A' \mid A' \in dc_\downarrow(A)\} \cup \{A \sqcap D \mid D \in \rho'_\downarrow(\top)\}$
$\neg A(A \in A_C)$	$\{\neg A' \mid A' \in dp_\uparrow(A)\} \cup \{\neg A \sqcap D \mid D \in \rho'_\downarrow(\top)\}$
$\exists r.D$	$\{\exists r.E \mid E \in \rho'_\downarrow(D)\} \cup \{\exists r.D \sqcap E \mid E \in \rho'_\downarrow(\top)\}$
$\forall r.D$	$\{\forall r.E \mid E \in \rho'_\downarrow(D)\} \cup \{\forall r.D \sqcap E \mid E \in \rho'_\downarrow(\top)\}$ $\cup\{\forall r.\bot D = A \in A_C \text{ and } dc_\downarrow(A) = \emptyset\}$
$C_1 \sqcap \ldots \sqcap C_n$ $(n \geq 2)$	$\{C_1 \sqcap \ldots \sqcap C_{i-1} \sqcap D \sqcap C_{i+1} \sqcap \ldots \sqcap C_n \mid$ $D \in \rho'_\downarrow(C_i), 1 \leq i \leq n\}$
$C_1 \sqcup \ldots \sqcup C_n$ $(n \geq 2)$	$\{C_1 \sqcup \ldots \sqcup C_{i-1} \sqcup D \sqcup C_{i+1} \sqcup \ldots \sqcup C_n \mid$ $D \in \rho'_\downarrow(C_i), 1 \leq i \leq n\}$ $\cup\{(C_1 \sqcup \ldots \sqcup C_n) \sqcap D \mid D \in \rho'_\downarrow(\top)\}$

After taking the derivative of (13.1), we get

$$\frac{\partial}{\partial w_i} \log P^*_w(X = x) = \sum_{l=1}^{n} [n_i(x) - P_w(X_l = 0 \mid MB_x(X_l)) n_i(x_{[X_l=0]}) - P_w(X_l = 1 \mid MB_x(X_l)) n_i(x_{[X_l=1]})] \tag{13.2}$$

In MLN, the weight represents the relative strength or importance of the class description (rule) [Richardson and Domingos (2006)]. The higher the weight, the greater the difference in log probability between a world that satisfies the concept description and the one that does not [Richardson and Domingos (2006)]. At each step, the concept description with the highest weight is selected. To select the most promising candidate from the candidates generated at each step, the weight vector is learned by L-BFGS algorithm [Liu and Nocedal (1989)], a quasi-Newton method suitable for large-scale optimization. Inasmuch as the joint probability distribution is a good indicator of the performance of the selected concept description, the iteration stops when the pseudo-log-likelihood stops increasing when a more specific description is selected.

13.4 Experiments

We adopt the measures frequently used in the information retrieval domain for the evaluations, namely precision, recall and F1-score. The experiments are conducted on two types of data sets. With the illustrative data sets, we focus on analyzing the capability of the approach on handling noises. As an illustrative example, we choose a small data set from the examples of DL-Learner,[4] and perform small modifications on it to show the noisy cases, which are difficult to illustrate on large data sets. As for the real-world ontology, we use four ontologies, namely, the Semantic Bible ontology, Adhesome ontology, financial ontology (obtained from DL-Learner), and SC ontology.

Learning Concept Definitions. To show the performance on noisy cases, we modify the ontology and add two positive examples, father(anna) and father(heinz), separately to correspond to error and incompleteness cases, and build two ontologies named family_error and family_incomplete.[5] Using DL-Learner GUI (version 2010-08-07) with CELOE algorithm under default settings for the class learning problem, the concept description for father can be correctly learned from family.owl to be $male \sqcap \exists hasChild.Thing$, but from family_error.owl and family_incomplete.owl the concept description cannot be learned correctly. However, our learner is able to learn the correct concept definition for concept father from all of these ontologies.

Learning Concept Inclusions. The evaluation results are shown in Table 13.3. We use positive examples for the target concept to learn inclusions. On Adhesome, the recall is only 0.1852, which can be explained from two views: on the one hand, Adhesome ontology contains more concepts with zero instances, thus data are not sufficient for the learner to go. On the other hand, the Adhesome ontology is expressive and contains number restrictions, which cannot be expressed by $\mathcal{ALC}$. Since SC ontology contains a large amount of instances compared with the amount of concepts, our learner tends to select restrictions prior to atomic concepts, which have led to a very low precision.

13.5 Conclusion and Remarks

To handle the noises that generally exist in Linked Data, we propose a naive but simple approach for learning Description Logic $\mathcal{ALC}$ inclusion axioms inductively by Markov logic. We use $\mathcal{ALC}$ downward refinement operator

[4] `http://aksw.org/Projects/DLLearner`
[5] `http://research.aturstudio.com/family\_noisy/`

Table 13.3 Learning results.

Data sets	Precision	Recall	F1-score
Adhesome	0.8333	0.1852	0.3030
Semantic Bible	0.8958	0.9302	0.9127
SC	0.2121	0.7000	0.3256
financial	0.7895	0.5455	0.6452

[Lehmann and Hitzler (2008)] to conduct a general-to-specific search. During the candidate selection process, we transform the problem by finding the candidate with the highest weight, which can be viewed as an indicator of the degree of consistency between the candidates and the facts in the Linked Data. Compared to other works of learning description logic, our approach is more insensitive to noise.

We note two issues here. (1) At first sight, we learn the "most" specific concept C to form $A \sqsubseteq C$. We know from Table 13.2 that other axioms $A \sqsubseteq C'$ with the fact $C' \sqsubseteq C$ (that are obtained by reasoners) can be easily reached. (2) Semantic Web languages generally make an open world assumption (OWA). We maintain OWA, and only take into account the facts that are known to be true.

Acknowledgment

We gratefully acknowledge funding from the National Science Foundation of China under grants 60873153, 60803061 and 61170165.

Bibliography

S. Auer and J. Lehmann. Making the web a data washing machine — creating knowledge out of interlinked data. *Semantic Web Journal*, **1(1)**, 97–104. 2010.

F. Baader and W. Nutt. Basic description logics. In F. Baader, D. Calvanese, D. McGuiness, D. Nardi and P. Patel-Schneider (eds). *The Description Logic Handbook*. Cambridge University Press, Cambridge, pp. 43–95. 2003.

C. Bizer. The emerging web of linked data. *IEEE Intell. Syst.*, **24(5)**, 87–92. 2009.

C. d'Amato, N. Fanizzi and F. Esposito. Inductive learning for the semantic web: What does it buy? *Semantic Web Journal*, **1(1–2)**, 53–59. 2010.

A. Hogan, A. Harth, A. Passant, S. Decker and A. Polleres. Weaving the pedantic web. In C. Bizer, T. Heath, T. Berners-Lee and M. Hausenblas (eds.).

Proceedings of the WWW2010 Workshop on Linked Data on the Web. 2010. Available online: `http://ceur-ws.org/Vol-628/`. Accessed 12 August 2014.

J. Lehmann and P. Hitzler. A refinement operator based learning algorithm for the alc description logic. In H. Blockeel, J. W. Shavlik and P. Tadepalli (eds). *Proceedings of the 17th International Conference on Inductive Logic Programming (ILP)*, LNCS, vol. 4894. Springer, Berlin, pp. 147–160. 2008.

J. Lehmann, S. Auer, Lorenz Bühmann and Sebastian Tramp. Class expression learning for ontology engineering. *Web Semantics: Science, Services and Agents on the World Wide Web*, **9(1)**, 71–81, 2011.

D. C. Liu and J. Nocedal. On the limited memory bfgs method for large scale optimization. *Math. Program.*, **45(1)**, 503–528. 1989.

M. Niepert, J. Noessner and H. Stuckenschmidt. Log-linear description logics. *22nd International Joint Conference on Artificial Intelligence*, pp. 2153–2158. IJCAI 2011: Barcelona 16–22 July 2011.

M. Richardson and P. Domingos. Markov logic networks. *Mach. Learn.*, **62(1)**, 107–136. 2006.

J. Völker and M. Niepert. Statistical schema induction. In L. Aroyo, P. Traverso, F. Ciravegna, P. Cimiano, T. Heath, E. Hyvönen, R. Mizoguchi, E. Oren, M. Sabou and E. Simperl (eds). *The Semantic Web: Research and Applications (Proceedings of the 6th European Semantic Web Conference)*, Springer, Berlin, pp. 124–138. 2011.

M. Zhu. Dc proposal: Ontology learning from noisy linked data. In *Proceedings of the 10th International Semantic Web Conference Part II*, LNCS, vol. 7032. Springer, Berlin, pp. 373–380. 2011

Chapter 14

Satisfiability Machines

Filip Železný
Department of Cybernetics, Czech Technical University in Prague, Czech Republic

We propose a probabilistic model for formulas, in which a formula's probability decreases with the number of pre-defined constraints it contradicts. Probability of ground conjunctions can be computed by a series of subsumption checks. The probability is equivalent (up to a multiplicative constant) to that computed by a Markov logic network (MLN) for conjunctions that fully describe a possible world. An experiment indicates that the two quantities correlate also for other conjunctions, with less variance for larger conjunctions. The proposed framework suggests a simple classification principle.

14.1 Introduction

In MLNs [Richardson and Domingos (2007)], the probability of an interpretation (possible world) decreases with the number of pre-defined constraints it violates. The probability of a formula is then the sum of probabilities of the worlds in which it holds. This quantity is intractable to calculate and sampling is usually adopted to approximate it. Here we explore an alternative probabilistic model enabling fast computation of a formula's probability. We embrace the key concept of MLNs but formalize it without regards to possible worlds: the probability of a formula decreases with the number of pre-defined constraints it contradicts. Instead of general formulas, we focus here specifically on ground conjunctions. Having a parametric probability model for ground conjunctions can be useful since they often represent learning examples (they correspond to partial interpretations

[De Raedt (1997)]). In the sequel we explore how such probabilities can be computed, how they relate to probabilities in the MLN framework, and how our framework can be used for classification.

14.2 Probabilistic Model

We consider a first-order logic language with Herbrand base (set of all ground atoms in the language) $\mathcal{H}$. As in most treatments of MLNs, we do not allow functions in the language so that $\mathcal{H}$ is finite. Extensions to the infinite case (e.g. along the lines of [Singla and Domingos (2007)]) are possible but not dealt with here. Given a finite set of formulas $F_1, F_2, \ldots F_n$ with real weights $w_1, w_2, \ldots w_n$, the probability of an interpretation $x \subseteq \mathcal{H}$ in the MLN framework is

$$P_M(x) = \frac{1}{Z_M} \exp \sum_{i=1}^{n} w_i n_i(x) \tag{14.1}$$

where n_i is the number of groundings of F_i that are true in x, i.e. denoting the set of all its grounding substitutions possible in the language as $\mathsf{GS}(F_i)$,

$$n_i(x) = |\{\theta \in \mathsf{GS}(F_i) \mid x \models F_i\theta\}| \tag{14.2}$$

Z_M is a normalizer ensuring that the above probability sums to 1 over all $2^{|\mathcal{H}|}$ interpretations x. As in most MLN studies, we shall assume that the F_is are clauses.

The probability of a formula φ in the MLN framework is the sum of probabilities of φ's models

$$P_M(\varphi) = \sum_{x \models \varphi} P_M(x) = \frac{1}{Z_M} \sum_{x \models \varphi} \exp \sum_{i=1}^{n} w_i n_i(x) \tag{14.3}$$

Computing this probability is not tractable except for minimalistic languages, and in practice it is estimated through sampling. Particular attention has been devoted to approximative methods for the case when $\varphi = c$ is a ground conjunction [Richardson and Domingos (2007)]. Here we instead aim at a conceptual simplification. Specifically, we maintain the F_is and w_is but we propose that

$$P_S(\varphi) = \frac{1}{Z_S} \exp \sum_{i=1}^{n} w_i m_i(\varphi) \tag{14.4}$$

where

$$m_i(\varphi) = |\{\theta \in \mathsf{GS}(F_i) \mid \varphi \wedge F_i\theta \nvdash \bot\}| \tag{14.5}$$

So the probability of a formula decreases with the number of constraints (groundings of the F_is) it contradicts. Calculating the normalizing constant Z_S is less obvious than calculating Z_M in the MLN case, however, it becomes straightforward if we again constrain ourselves to $\varphi = c$ being ground conjunctions (we will maintain the assumption throughout the paper). Then Z_S is such that $P_S(c)$ sums to 1 over all $3^{|\mathcal{H}|}$ possible ground conjunctions c (each atom from $\mathcal{H}$ can either be positive, negative, or absent in c).

Note that $c \wedge F_i\theta \vdash \bot$ is equivalent to $F_i\theta \vdash \neg c$. Since c is a ground conjunction, $\neg c$ is a ground clause and thus, unless F_i is self-resolving, $F_i\theta \vdash \neg c$ can be reduced to the subsumption check $\mathsf{lits}(F_i\theta) \subseteq \mathsf{lits}(\neg c)$. Equation 14.5 can now be expressed as

$$m_i(c) = |\{\theta \in \mathsf{GS}(F_i) \mid \mathsf{lits}(F_i\theta) \not\subseteq \mathsf{lits}(\neg c)\}| \tag{14.6}$$

Equivalently, $m_i(c) = |\mathsf{GS}(F_i)| - |\{\theta \in \mathsf{GS}(F_i) \mid \mathsf{lits}(F_i\theta) \subseteq \mathsf{lits}(\neg c)\}|$. The first summand is not significant since it does not depend on c and can simply be removed and reflected in the weight w_i. Thus, what remains to compute towards obtaining $m_i(c)$ is just the set of solutions to a subsumption check. This is particularly appealing due to extremely fast subsumption testers under energetic research that now achieve order-of-magnitude speed-ups by employing CSP algorithms [Maloberti and Sebag (2004)] or other heuristic approaches [Santos and Muggleton (2010)], language-biases [Kuzelka and Zelezny (2011)] or randomized search [Kuzelka and Zelezny (2008a,b)]. The approach [Kuzelka and Zelezny (2008a)] seems particularly relevant in the present context since it uses randomization to estimate the *number* of subsumption solutions, i.e. the $m_i(c)$ numbers directly.

14.3 Comparing $P_M(c)$ and $P_S(c)$

The relationship between $P_M(c)$ and $P_S(c)$ is clear for *model conjunctions* (conjunctions that have a single model). The model conjunction for an interpretation x is $c_x = \bigwedge_{a \in x} a \bigwedge_{b \in \mathcal{H} \setminus x} \neg b$. We have that

$$Z_S P_S(c_x) = Z_M P_M(c_x) \tag{14.7}$$

for any model conjunction c_x. Comparing Eqs (14.4) and (14.3), we see that the above is true if

$$\exp \sum_{i=1}^{n} w_i m_i(c_x) = \sum_{y \models c_x} \exp \sum_{i=1}^{n} w_i n_i(y)$$

However, since the only model of c_x is x, the first summation on the right-hand side vanishes and we only need to check that for each i,

$m_i(c_x) = n_i(x)$. As follows from Eqs (14.5) and (14.2), this is the case if the relation $c_x \wedge F_i\theta \nvdash \bot$, i.e. $\mathsf{lits}(F_i\theta) \nsubseteq \mathsf{lits}(\neg c_x)$ is equivalent to the relation $x \models F_i\theta$. Since $\neg c_x = \bigvee_{a\in x} \neg a \bigvee_{b\in \mathcal{H}\setminus x} b$, the former relation means that either for some negative literal $\neg a$ of $F_i\theta$, a is not in x, or some positive literal of $F_i\theta$ is not in $\mathcal{H} \setminus x$, i.e. (since $x \subseteq \mathcal{H}$), is in x. That, however, is precisely the definition of the latter relation and we have thus proven the equivalence of both relations. Thus Eq. (14.7) indeed holds.

For ground conjunctions c other than model conjunctions, the relationship between $P_S(c)$ and $P_M(c)$ is less clear. For this general case, we have not yet been able to relate the quantities analytically as in Eq. (14.7) and so we approached the question empirically. To this end, we implemented in YAP Prolog both MLNs inference, and the herewith proposed subsumption-based inference, both exact and sampling-based.[1]

For this particular experiment, we considered the following four clauses from a toy university domain, each with weight $w_i = 1$

$$F_1 = \text{false} \leftarrow \text{studies}(P, C) \wedge \text{teaches}(P, C) \tag{14.8}$$

$$F_2 = \text{false} \leftarrow \text{teaches}(\mathsf{john}, C) \wedge \text{teaches}(\mathsf{jack}, C) \tag{14.9}$$

$$F_3 = \text{teaches}(\mathsf{john}, C) \vee \text{teaches}(\mathsf{jack}, C) \leftarrow \text{studies}(P, C) \tag{14.10}$$

$$F_4 = \text{studies}(\mathsf{john}, C) \vee \text{studies}(\mathsf{jack}, C) \leftarrow \text{teaches}(P, C) \tag{14.11}$$

We used a *typed* Herbrand base $\mathcal{H}$, which consists of atoms made of one of teaches/2 and studies/2 predicate symbols with the first argument being either jack or john and the second argument being one of $\{\mathsf{math}, \mathsf{cs}, \mathsf{ai}\}$. $\mathcal{H}$ contained exactly 12 atoms. We randomly generated 500 ground conjunctions. Each one was sampled independently from the others, by going over all atoms in $\mathcal{H}$. Each atom in $\mathcal{H}$ had 1/2 probability of being included in the conjunction; if it was included, it produced a positive (negative) literal with 1/2 probability. For each such conjunction c we computed both $Z_M P_M(c)$ and $Z_S P_S(c)$. The 500 value pairs are shown diagrammatically in Fig. 14.1. The main insight provided by the experiment is that the two quantities are clearly correlated and the satisfiability framework is characterized by a rougher probability scale. As expected, the conditional variance $\mathrm{var}(P_M(c)|P_S(c))$ is smaller for large conjunctions c (red marks in the figure) than for arbitrary conjunctions; this is because large conjunctions are

[1] The implementation (sporadically commented) is available at `http://labe.felk.cvut.cz/~zelezny/sm.yap`

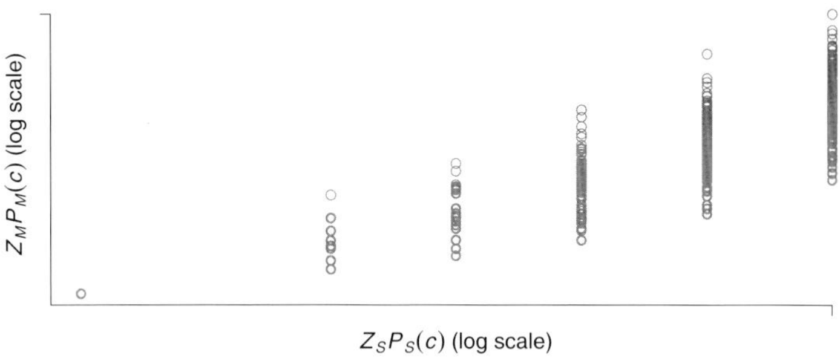

Fig. 14.1 MLN-probabilities vs. SM-probabilities of random ground conjunctions. The mean length of a conjunction is six literals, conjunctions of this or greater length are shown in red.

closer to model conjunctions for which we have already established the deterministic relationship (Eq. (14.7)).

While $P_S(c)$ has its own intuitive meaning (as worded in introducing the quantity), the experiment shows that it can be also viewed as an estimator of $P_M(c)$. Note that unlike $P_M(c)$, $P_S(c)$ is reasonable for modeling only those domains where the constraints F_i are independent of each other; otherwise it may fail intuition. For example, given $F_1 = p \leftarrow q$, $F_2 = q \leftarrow r$, and $c = r \wedge \neg p$, then $P_S(c)$ is a mode of the P_S distribution since c does not violate any of the two constraints. The fact that it contradicts their conjunction is not reflected by $P_S(c)$. We think, however, that the said independence assumption is not problematic for modeling real-world domains, as essentially the same assumption is made by the generally successful propositionalization systems.

The natural question is what benefits $P_S(c)$ brings us in comparison to $P_M(c)$. The key advantage lies in the fact that the exact computation of $Z_M P_M(c)$ takes time exponential in the size of $\mathcal{H}$ and this size in turn grows combinatorially with the number of constants in the language. To appreciate this complexity, we calculated $Z_M P_M(c)$ for the (randomly drawn) conjunction $c = \neg\text{teaches}(\mathsf{john}, \mathsf{math}) \wedge \text{teaches}(\mathsf{john}, \mathsf{ai}) \wedge \neg\text{teaches}(\mathsf{jack}, \mathsf{ai}) \wedge \neg\text{studies}(\mathsf{john}, \mathsf{math}) \wedge \neg\text{studies}(\mathsf{jack}, \mathsf{math}) \wedge \neg\text{studies}(\mathsf{jack}, \mathsf{ai})$ for the previously shown F_is and for different numbers of constants in $\mathcal{H}$, obtaining the following runtimes:

number of course-constants in $\mathcal{H}$	2	3	4	5
time to compute $Z_M P_M(c)$ [s]	0.02	0.47	10.25	242.67

In contrast, the time to exactly calculate $Z_S P_S(c)$ is zero (below measurability) in all these cases. This is understandable since the runtime here does not depend on the size of $\mathcal{H}$. Indeed, the computation is just a series of subsumption checks between the F_i's and $\neg c$, wherein the complexity is only given by the sizes of these clauses.

Of course, exact probability inference is replaced by faster sampling-based approximative methods in the MLN framework. On the other hand, the unification-based algorithm for subsumption checking that we used above can also be replaced by much faster subsumption testers as we have already commented. An experimental comparison including such features is left for an extended version of the chapter.

Lastly, the comparison above regarded the computation of the unnormalized quantities $Z_M P_M(c)$ and $Z_S P_S(c)$. Exact computation of $P_S(c)$ would obviously be intractable since it would involve a loop over $3^{|\mathcal{H}|}$ conjunctions. This could be remedied by Monte-Carlo sampling (independent of any randomization possibly adopted in the subsumption-checking step) as in the MLN framework, except that each atom would be in one of three (positive, negative, absent) rather than two states. Nevertheless, we will now exemplify a situation where we can simply rely on the unnormalized quantity.

14.4 Discriminative Learning

In the MLN context, discriminative learning usually refers to the situation where the probabilistic model is used to predict the truth value of some atoms given the truth value of other atoms. Here we adopt a view more usual in supervised machine learning, where examples (here, ground conjunctions) are partitioned into classes (here we assume exactly two classes) and the model is used to predict the classes of given examples. A straightforward way to classification, based on likelihood odds, is to predict class one if $P_S^1(c)/P_S^2(c) > \tau$, where P_S^1 and P_S^2 are two class-specific distributions in the form (14.4) and τ is a real threshold. The inequality can be rewritten as

$$\frac{Z_S^1 P_S^1(c)}{Z_S^2 P_S^2(c)} > \tau \frac{Z_S^1}{Z_S^2} \equiv \tau' \tag{14.12}$$

From the training set, we would estimate the structure (F_is) and parameters (w_is) for both distributions as well as the parameter τ' with the objective of maximizing training-set accuracy (modulo overfitting counter-measures). As follows from the expression above, we only need the unnormalized quantities $Z_S^1 P_S^1(c)$ and $Z_S^2 P_S^2(c)$ along with the learned parameter τ' to classify c.

Perhaps a more pragmatic way to classification learning, however, is to drop the exponential form while maintaining the proposed $m_i(c)$ concept. We would classify c into class 1 iff $\sum_{i=1}^{n} w_i m_i(c) > \tau$. This form gives a simple clue for structure learning, in particular, we would search for clauses F_i that contradict as many (few) as possible training examples of class 1 (2). Then, parameters w_i and τ would be tuned. This approach in fact corresponds to a sort of propositionalization with subsequent learning of a linear classifier. The kind of propositionalization entailed by the present framework differs from current propositionalization approaches mainly in that (1) full (function-free) clausal logic is used to express features F_i (in current propositionalization systems, features are usually queries or Horn clauses), and (2) rather than a Boolean value, a feature is assigned an integer for a given example, capturing the number of the feature's groundings that contradict the example.

14.5 Conclusion

We have proposed satisfiability machines, a conceptual simplification of MLNs. A full discussion of its relationships to propositionalization as well as classification experiments on gene expression data under gene-ontology background knowledge is left for an extended version of this paper.

Acknowledgment

This work was supported by the Czech Science Foundation project P103/10/1875 "Learning from Theories".

Bibliography

L. De Raedt. Logical settings for concept-learning. *Artif. Intell.* **95(1)**, 187–201. 1997.

O. Kuzelka and F. Zelezny. Fast estimation of first-order clause coverage through randomization and maximum likelihood. In A. McCallum and S. Rowies. *Proceedings of the Twenty-Fifth International Conference on Machine Learning*, pp. 504–511. 2008a. ICML 2008: Helsinki, 5–9 July 2008. Available online: `http://icml2008.cs.helsinki.fi/papers/503.pdf`. Accessed 12 August 14.

O. Kuzelka and F. Zelezny. A restarted strategy for efficient subsumption testing. *Fund. Inform.*, **89(1)**, 95–109. 2008b.

O. Kuzelka and F. Zelezny. Block-wise construction of tree-like relational features with monotone reducibility and redundancy. *Mach. Learn.*, **83(2)**, 163–192. 2011.

J. Maloberti and M. Sebag. Fast theta-subsumption with constraint satisfaction algorithms. *Mach. Learn.*, **55(2)**, 137–174. 2004.

M. Richardson and P. Domingos. Markov logic networks. *Mach. Learn.*, **62(1–2)**, 107–136. 2007.

J. Santos and S. H. Muggleton. Subsumer: A Prolog theta-subsumption engine. In M. Hermenegildo and T. Schaub (eds). *Technical Communications of the 26th International Conference on Logic Programming*, Schloss Dagstuhl–Leibniz-Zentrum fuer Informatik, Dagstuhl, pp. 172–181. 2010.

P. Singla and P. Domingos. Markov logic in infinite domains. *23rd Conference on Uncertainty in Artificial Intelligence*, pp. 368–375. 2007. UAI 2007: Vancouver, 19–22 July 2007.

PART 3

Implementations

Chapter 15

Customisable Multi-Processor Acceleration of Inductive Logic Programming

Andreas K. Fidjeland, Wayne Luk, and Stephen H. Muggleton
Imperial College London, UK

Parallel approaches to Inductive Logic Programming (ILP) are adopted to address the computational complexity in the learning process. Existing parallel ILP implementations build on conventional general-purpose processors. This chapter describes a different approach, by exploiting user-customisable parallelism available in advanced reconfigurable devices such as Field-Programmable Gate Arrays (FPGAs). Our customisable parallel architecture for ILP has three elements: a customisable logic programming processor, a multi-processor for parallel hypothesis evaluation, and an architecture generation framework for creating such multi-processors. Our approach offers a means of achieving high performance by producing parallel architectures adapted both to the problem domain and to specific problem instances. The coverage test in Progol 4.4 is performed up to 56 times faster using our multi-processor.

15.1 Introduction

Inductive Logic Programming (ILP) is a powerful paradigm for symbolic machine learning, since it can incorporate existing theories and produce human-readable output. ILP systems have been successfully applied in a number of areas. For example, in molecular biology they have been used for learning rules for prediction of protein fold signatures [Turcotte *et al.* (2001)], mutagenesis [Srinivasan *et al.* (1994)], toxicity [Lodhi *et al.* (2010)], and structure activity relationships for pharmacaphores [Sternberg and Muggleton (2003)]. However, ILP systems are computationally demanding. Several approaches to speeding up ILP have been developed with parallelisation being exploited at different levels [Dehaspe and De Raedt

(1995); Fidjeland and Luk (2003); Fonseca *et al.* (2005, 2009); Ohwada *et al.* (2000); Skillicorn and Wang (2001); Wielemaker (2003)]. Common to these approaches is the reliance on conventional general-purpose processors, with parallel processing units either being nodes in a distributed computer or cores in a multi-core processor.

This chapter describes a different approach, based on advanced reconfigurable hardware such as FPGAs, to provide multi-processors with a customisable architecture. Similar approaches have been used in speeding up various demanding applications, such as those in financial modelling [Jin *et al.* (2009)] and in medical imaging [Tsoi *et al.* (2009)]. Our approach is developed for speeding up the ILP system Progol [Muggleton (1995)], using customised instruction processors and multi-processors. Its unique features include:

(1) Arvand, an instruction processor for logic programming, which can be customised to particular classes of data sets for learning (Section 15.3);
(2) a Progol multi-processor, which exploits data parallelism in hypothesis evaluation (Section 15.4);
(3) a multi-processor architecture generation framework for logic programming, which is used to create customised multi-processors (Section 15.5).

Reconfigurable hardware has been used in emulating Intel architectures [Schelle *et al.* (2010)]. Such emulation, however, does not exploit the reconfigurability of FPGAs to provide a customisable architecture. Moreover, our research demonstrates how fine-grained parallelism on an FPGA can significantly enhance ILP performance.

15.2 Background: Sequential and Parallel ILP

Inductive logic programming [Muggleton and De Raedt (1994)] is a learning paradigm based on first-order logic. Such systems learn predicate hypotheses from background information and examples. This approach has the advantages that both the specified background knowledge and the generated hypotheses are in a human-readable format, and that the system can build on partial theories by incorporating existing background knowledge.

ILP systems come in several variations, but in general they take as input a set of positive (E_+) and negative (E_-) examples, some background knowledge (B), and a language bias defining the hypothesis space. From this it produces a theory (H) explaining the examples. ILP algorithms employ different strategies for constructing and searching through the hypothesis space and in assessing the quality of each hypothesis.

The ILP system Progol [Muggleton (1995)] is based on the method *mode-directed inverse entailment*. For each positive example it constructs a lattice bounded by the most and least general hypothesis. This hypothesis space is explored using an A*-like algorithm, where the quality of a hypothesis is determined by a combination of the number of positive and negative examples as well as the clause length.

To illustrate ILP, Fig. 15.1 shows a hypothesis, part of the background knowledge, and some examples taken from a data set for learning mutagenic activity for nitro-aromatic compounds [Srinivasan *et al.* (1994)]. The

(a) Hypothesis

```
active(A) :-
   atm(A,B,c,27,C),
   bond(A,D,E,1),
   bond(A,D,B,7).
```

(b) Examples

```
active(d48).
active(d60).
...
```

(c) Background

```
atm(d1,d1_1,c,22,-0.117).
atm(d1,d1_2,c,22,-0.117).
...
bond(d1,d1_1,d1_2,7).
bond(d1,d1_2,d1_3,7).
...
```

`c-alt` 3 j_0 j_1 j_3	← beginning of clause with frame size →	`c-alt` 0 $j1$ $j2$ $j3$
`h-fstvar` r_0	and address offsets for indexing	`h-const d1`
`c-goal atm/5`		`h-const d1_1`
`g-nxtvar` r_0	constant →	`h-const c`
`g-fstvar` r_1	integer literal →	`h-int` 22
`g-const c`		`h-fix` −0.117
`g-int` 27	end of unit clause →	`c-nogoal`
`g-void`	← void variable	
`c-call`		`c-alt` 0 j_1 j_2 j_3
`c-goal bond/4`	← beginning of goal	`h-const d1`
`g-nxtvar` r_0		`h-const d1_2`
`g-fstvar` r_2	← first instance of variable with	`h-const c`
`g-void`	binding in register 2	`h-int` 22
`g-int` 1		`h-fix` −0.117
`c-call`	← end of goal	`c-nogoal`
`c-goal bond/4`		
`g-nxtvar` r_0	← subsequent instance of variable	...
`g-nxtvar` r_2	with binding in register 0	
`g-nxtvar` r_1		
`g-int` 1		
`c-lastcall`	← end of clause	

Fig. 15.1 A small part of the mutagenesis data set [Srinivasan *et al.* (1994)] showing the Prolog form (top) and VAM/Arvand code (bottom, hypothesis and two clauses of background only).

Table 15.1 Parallelisation strategies for ILP.

Strategy	Unit of work	Granularity	Examples
Search	whole or part of search tree	coarse	[Dehaspe and De Raedt (1995); Ohwada *et al.* (2000); Wielemaker (2003)]
Data	search tree based on part of example set	coarse	[Fonseca *et al.* (2005); Skillicorn and Wang (2001)]
Evaluation	hypothesis test	fine	[Fidjeland and Luk (2003); Skillicorn and Wang (2001)], this work

background contains a number of facts (12,000+) regarding atoms and bonds in chemical compounds of interest. The examples specify the compounds which are known to be mutagenically active. There may be hundreds of such examples. The hypothesis in Figure 15.1(a) is a rule that specifies that an atom A is mutagenically active provided it contains atoms and bonds with certain properties and relationships. The number of hypotheses depends on how the hypothesis space is defined, but may be numbered in the tens of thousands. The computationally demanding nature of ILP is a result of the size of this hypothesis space.

The parallelisation strategies in the literature come in different levels. Fonseca *et al.* [Fonseca *et al.* (2009)] identify three levels, summarised in Table 15.1. First, *search parallelism* can be exploited by running sequential versions of independent learning tasks in parallel, performing the cross-fold validation in parallel, learning independent concepts in parallel, or, at a finer level, by searching the hypothesis space in parallel [Dehaspe and De Raedt (1995); Ohwada *et al.* (2000); Wielemaker (2003)]. Second, *data parallelism* can be exploited by partitioning the data set and learning in parallel based on subsets [Fonseca *et al.* (2005); Skillicorn and Wang (2001)]. Third, in *evaluation parallelism* the coverage tests, i.e. the scoring of hypotheses, are performed in parallel [Fidjeland and Luk (2003); Skillicorn and Wang (2001)]. We take the third of these approaches in this chapter. Previous approaches to evaluation parallelism have shown limited speedups compared with other parallelisation strategies [Fonseca *et al.* (2009)]. However, we make use of a much larger number of processors which have a low overhead in task creation.

15.3 The Arvand Processor

Our approach to accelerating ILP is built around a customisable processor, Arvand. The processor is specialised for performing coverage tests in Progol. A coverage test involves evaluating candidate hypotheses by determining how well each hypothesis explains the example set. Background knowledge in the form of domain-specific rules and facts provides a program, and each example test provides a program call whose return status (success or failure of the test) is used in the scoring of the hypothesis. The execution of each example test involves heavy use of *unification* and *backtracking*, the support for which is reflected in the instruction set and microarchitecture of Arvand. The processor is distinguished by a small high-level data-centric instruction set, a two-stream architecture, and hardware support for special stack operations. The processor microarchitecture can be customised to particular types of background knowledge, with the aim of reducing the resource usage which can be a limiting factor when the core is used in a chip multi-processor.

15.3.1 *Instruction set*

The Arvand processor is based on the Vienna Abstract Machine (VAM) [Krall and Neumerkel (1990)], an execution model for Prolog. The basic instructions and the two-stream model are taken from the VAM, but with adaptations for use in a hardware implementation, aiming to simplify instruction decoding and reducing the number of branches. The VAM model was chosen over the more common Warren Abstract Machine [Warren (1983)] for two reasons. First, the two-stream model naturally lends itself to a dual-issue processor implementation, which can easily be exploited in a hardware implementation. Second, the model affords more opportunities for simplifying microarchitecture customisations, in that less data require heap storage. This is because when both the goal and head streams are ground structures, the one-stream model creates data on the heap, whereas the two-stream model does not. A direct implementation of an abstract machine has advantages over compilation to a 'traditional' instruction set (which could be used in optimized off-the-shelf soft processor cores) in that programs are much smaller. This means that more data can be cached in the limited embedded memories available on the target devices and that fewer (albeit potentially more complex) instructions are required to execute a given program.

Instructions can broadly be divided into control and data instructions. Prolog clauses are encoded in this instruction set by having control instructions delineating the structure of the clause (see `c-goal`, `c-nogoal`, `c-call`, and `c-lastcall` in Fig. 15.1), while data instructions encode the constant and variables terms in the clause (see `g-const`, `g-fstvar`, and `g-nxtvar` in the same figure).

Two instruction streams are active at the same time (for the head and goal), so the true instruction set of the processor is the set of all valid basic instruction pairs. Combinations of data instructions are unified, resulting in either failure or success with possible variable bindings. Combinations of control instructions result in a procedure call or return with a possible follow-up procedure call. The necessary stack operations are implicit in these combined control instructions.

Data instructions are divided into variable and non-variable data. Variable data instructions refer to a slot in the current activation record, possibly residing in a register, whose contents are either read from or written to, depending on the type of variable instruction. Variables fall into one of several classes depending on its position within a data structure and the number of times it is referenced. The variable opcode dictates, along with the opcode from the *other* instruction stream, whether the variable requires a write operation, a read operation, or can be ignored, and furthermore whether it requires any stack space. Non-variable data instructions use an immediate operand. Data can be simple (a symbolic constant, integer, or fixed-point number), or compound structures. Compound structures are expressed as flattened trees in prefix order.

Execution can be non-deterministic, in that a computation can have several valid execution paths. Alternative execution paths are dealt with by prefixing the code for each clause with offsets to the code for alternative clauses to try on backtracking (see `c-alt` instructions in Fig. 15.1). There are three such offsets to deal with different situations. In highly non-deterministic programs the number of potential execution paths can be very large. As an optimisation, clauses are grouped according to the first data instruction (the indexing argument). Execution paths which can be guaranteed to fail can thus simply be skipped. Run-time first-argument indexing is handled via a special index goal instruction which dispatches to a table of possible procedures, and switches the processor to a special execution mode to find the correct table entry.

15.3.2 *Microarchitecture*

The Arvand processor executes the above instruction set on a two-stream pipelined architecture. Figure 15.2 shows the data flow in the Arvand processor in its most basic form. There are four stages: two for fetch (combined in the figure), one for decode/read, and one for write. For the fetch and decode stages the head and goal instruction streams are treated separately, with the head stream shown in the top half of Fig. 15.2, and goal stream shown in the bottom half.

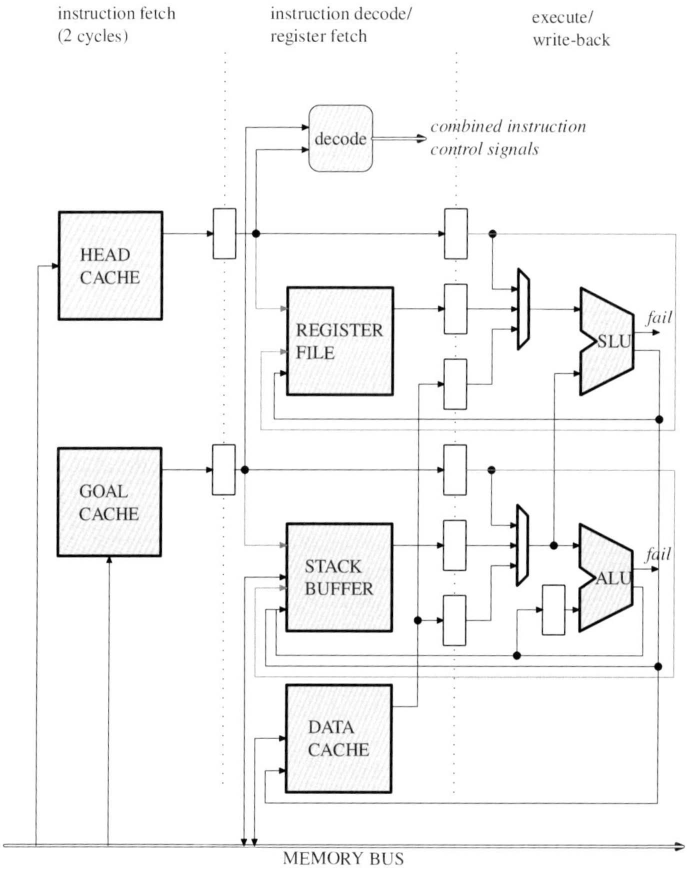

Fig. 15.2 Arvand processor in a typical configuration.

The two instruction streams are cached independently in direct-mapped caches. On a cache miss, data are fetched from an off-chip memory unit which is typically shared with other processors. The instruction streams alternate between data instructions and control instructions.

The register file holds the activation record (local variables and continuation) for the current head, as well as the topmost choice point. The stack buffer holds the top part of the stack, which includes the current activation record for the goal. The stack buffer holds a window of the full stack containing the goal frame pointer. Both the register file and stack buffer are dual-ported, so both a head and a goal variable can be read (in the decode stage) in a single cycle, while also potentially updating another head and goal variable (in the execute stage). Executing (combinations of) control instructions move activation records between the register file and the stack buffer.

Variables referred to in data instructions are read from the register file or stack buffer during the decode stage. Such references to data in either the head or the goal frame, and may or may not be bound at run-time. Bound head frame variables reside in the register file. Bound goal frame variables reside in the stack buffer which contains the top of the stack. Both head and goal variables may contain a reference to data on the heap, possibly through a chain of references. If a variable instruction contains such a reference and the value is required (which depends on the exact instruction combination), the instruction pipeline stalls while the reference is resolved. Such reference chains are typically short and the processor can perform one dereference operation per cycle, so the execution time overhead of this is usually small.

Unification is done on two terms, i.e. on two instruction sequences. On a per-instruction basis the unification unit determines whether unification is a success or a failure and may, depending on the instruction combination, do a combination of: writing to a data register, writing to an entry in the goal activation record in the stack buffer, or creating a new entry on the heap. These operations are performed in a single cycle for non-compound data. The processor contains forwarding and hazard detection logic to deal with read-after-write (RAW) hazards.

In order to handle backtracking, the stack contains non-determinate activation records (choice points), in addition to the regular activation records (environments). There are therefore two interleaved stacks. A non-determinate activation record contains the information necessary to restart computation from a previous state, which is done if unification fails. The topmost choice point is stored in a special register file in order to speed up backtracking. Four registers point into the local stack to, respectively, the next available slot, the most recent choice point, the head environment, and the goal environment.

15.3.3 *Customisation*

The Arvand processor can be customised for a particular program type, or to exploit different run-time characteristics of a program. The processor customisations affect the usage of both programmable fabric space (used for processor logic) and embedded memory (used for caches and buffers), and can additionally affect execution time, and the class of programs supported (Table 15.2). Customisations come in four different forms: microarchitecture, memory interface, memory size, and data width.

First, the microarchitecture of Arvand can be customised to cater for subsets of the full instruction set. The processor can thus be customised for particular (classes of) data sets. These are defined with respect to the minimal processor of interest, which can only support programs where all terms are ground, and all clauses except for the initial goal are unit. Instructions for non-ground terms and non-unit clauses allow execution of a larger set of programs. Dynamic indexing instructions can be added to avoid unneeded non-deterministic branches of execution. A general-purpose ALU is not required for programs which use symbolic data exclusively. Most data are stored on the stack, so a heap is not included by default. Heap support is required if the program contains certain combinations of variable instructions or structured data. Data instructions for structures are required if the program contains compound terms.

Second, memory interface customisations make some memory units (goal program code, stack, or heap) purely local units rather than being caches/buffers backed by off-processor data. This simplifies the processor

Table 15.2 Arvand processor customisation types.

	Effect on		
Type	Space	Memory	Execution
Microarchitecture	Major	None	limits *types* of supported programs
Memory interface	Minor	Major	possibility of overflow
Memory size	None	Major	cache performance
Data width	Minor	Minor	arithmetic, number of supported symbols

control logic. If the data set is small enough, the head and goal instruction caches can be replaced by local buffers, eliminating cache miss overheads and shortening the fetch stage. In particular, when the *unit clause* customisation is used, the only goal code is the initial goal. The goal cache can be used as a local memory buffer which is loaded during processor initialisation. For data sets where the execution depth is limited (e.g. no recursion allowed, depth limitation in the language bias), the local stack can be implemented as a buffer. Where the heap is enabled the data cache can either be global, caching a larger heap in main memory, or can be local only.

Third, memory size customisations modify the size of the different caches and buffers. Such customisations can be applied to all types of programs, but affect both the performance and the resource usage of the processor. While conceptually straightforward this type of customisation leads to interesting trade-offs between the total number of processors and the performance of each.

Fourth, data width customisations adapt the word width to the requirements of particular data sets. Where the programs contain arithmetic instructions, this raises issues of precision. Where only symbolic data are used, the data width can be set based on the number of distinct symbols in the program, and on the size of the program.

15.4 Multi-Processor Architecture for ILP

The Arvand processor requires only a fraction of the resources found on a modern reconfigurable device, even when using one of the more demanding processor configurations. It is therefore possible to place a large number of processors on a single chip, creating a customised multi-core processor for ILP. Our multi-processor (Fig. 15.3) acts as an accelerator for a host system which directs the search through the hypothesis space.

The multi-processor receives a stream of candidate hypotheses over the system bus via the IO unit. For each hypothesis, a number of queries for the positive and negative coverage tests are generated in the 'Job gen' unit, which stores the example set locally. These queries are distributed to the available processors using the 'Fork' unit, which writes the relevant query (a short program) to a designated per-processor input buffer in RAM, and signals for the next available processor (one of P_i in the figure) to process the query. The results (successes or failures) from all the queries related to a hypothesis are collected via the 'Join' unit, summed, and returned to the host system via the IO unit. The multi-processor fully completes

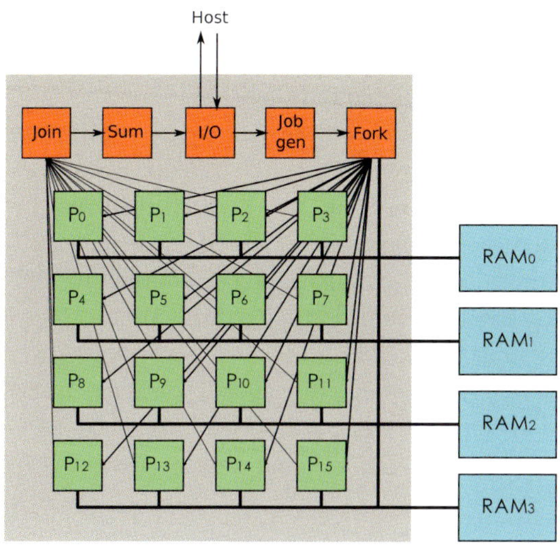

Fig. 15.3 Arvand multi-processor architecture for parallel evaluation of hypotheses. Each processor is a unit as described in Fig. 15.2.

the coverage test for a hypothesis before starting a new coverage test. The maximum parallelism is thus limited by the cardinality of the example set.

Parallelisation is done at the level of coverage testing, rather than at a higher level, for three reasons. First, this approach is conceptually simple, thus obviating the need for complex changes to the overall search algorithm. Second, the coverage test is a computationally demanding part common to ILP systems, so this approach to acceleration could be applied to other ILP systems, not just Progol. Third, the level of parallelism attainable in this way is a good match with the level of parallelism attainable on modern FPGAs. On a general-purpose processor the fine task granularity of the parallel coverage test could be an issue due to task creation overheads. This is not an issue in this multi-processor since we can design the communication architecture to match the problem at hand.

The single-processor customisations affect the configuration of the multi-processor. For a given device, there is a fixed amount of resources (both programmable fabric and memory). There is thus a general trade-off between the resource usage of a single processor and the number of constituent processors in a multi-processor. For a given data set, the processor architecture, memory interface, and data width can be fixed. The amount of local memory dedicated to caches and buffers can be varied, however. The trade-off is therefore in practice between the number of processors and the cache sizes of each processor. The single-processor performance will typically be better if caches are larger, but a multi-processor with more nodes may better exploit the available parallelism.

Figure 15.3 shows that there are dedicated connections to each processor from the Fork element, while the results from each processor are also sent by dedicated connections to the Join element. In practice, however, multiple dedicated connections can be implemented by a bus which enables processors along a row or along a column to share communication resources to the Fork and Join elements. While this method reduces the number of connections, additional bus controllers are required which complicates the implementation. The need to share connection resources depends on the specific FPGA used: many advanced FPGAs are rich in connection resources, so even a large number of dedicated connections may not be an issue.

15.5 Multi-Processor Architecture Generation

To facilitate generation of multi-processor systems based around Arvand, we have developed an architecture-description language, Archlog, which ties together software compilation, processor configuration and instantiation, and multi-processor configuration and generation [Fidjeland and Luk (2006)]. Archlog includes a domain-specific language in Prolog that covers multi-processor architectures using a number of primitives (including Arvand) and communication streams between them.

The Archlog system (Fig. 15.4) takes an architecture description and a Prolog program, and generates a hardware configuration tailored for this

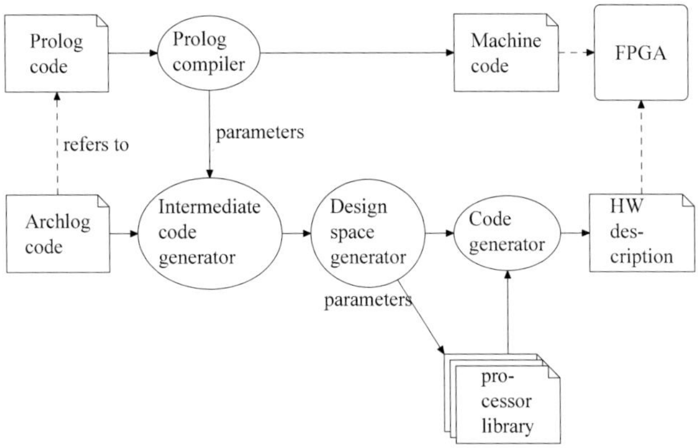

Fig. 15.4 The Archlog system for multi-processor architecture generation.

combination of architecture and software. Analysis of the input Prolog program(s) provides part of the processor configuration, by specifying the minimal processor configuration that can support the program. An architecture description may not fully specify all parameters of the design, for example the level of parallelism in a multi-processor design. The system explores the space of possible designs, and can return a number of pareto-optimal designs. The user can choose between these, although in an extended system run-time reconfiguration could be used to determine the optimal architecture dynamically.

15.6 Results

15.6.1 *Data sets*

We use two ILP data sets to evaluate the multi-processor performance: mutagenesis [Srinivasan *et al.* (1994)] and protein folding [Turcotte *et al.* (2001)]. The two data sets have different features (Table 15.3). The former uses a smaller processor than the latter due to simpler background knowledge and lack of arithmetic.

Mutagenesis is a well-known ILP application for learning mutagenic activity for nitro-aromatic compounds [Srinivasan *et al.* (1994)]. The background knowledge for this data set contains the structural descriptions of the chemical compounds of interest, a number of relevant properties of these compounds, as well as rules describing ring concepts. For benchmarking we use the structural descriptions only, which means that the background knowledge contains ground unit clauses only and no arithmetic. Consequently, a simple processor configuration can be used. A high degree of non-determinacy in this data set leads to an example test dominated by shallow backtracking. We extract a benchmark suite consisting of all the hypotheses explored when generalising from the first example. We use only the 188 "regression-friendly" examples.

The protein folding data set is based on a study by Turcotte *et al.* [Turcotte *et al.* (2001)] into discovering rules governing protein folds. We use the

Table 15.3 Data sets used for evaluation.

Name	$\lvert B\rvert$	$\lvert E_+\rvert$	$\lvert E_-\rvert$	$\lvert H\rvert$	Notes
Mutagenesis	12203	125	63	846	Ground unit clauses only, no arithmetic
Protein folding	2780	42	40	1498	No structures

part of the data set referring to immunoglobulin. The background knowledge is described using 2,780 clauses, describing structures and properties of proteins, as well as high-level rules. These benchmarks use the full range of control instructions, including dynamic indexing instructions. There are no structures and some use of arithmetic. Again we extract a benchmark suite consisting of all the hypotheses explored when generalising from the first example.

15.6.2 *Resource usage*

Resource usage for both programmable fabric and embedded memory can vary greatly with processor customisation. Figure 15.5(a) shows the usage of both these kinds of resources for processors in various configurations. We use all valid combinations in microarchitecture customisation for a total of 17 different processor architectures. For each of these we use the smallest stack and heap (both 1K words), and vary the two instruction cache sizes independently over the sizes 1K, 2K, and 4K words. The programmable fabric usage is measured in device-independent flip-flops as reported by the Handel-C compiler (v5.3.2). Both the programmable fabric usage and the memory usage vary by a factor of around three. The potential resource savings realised by customisation translate into increased parallelism, since more small processors can fit on a particular chip.

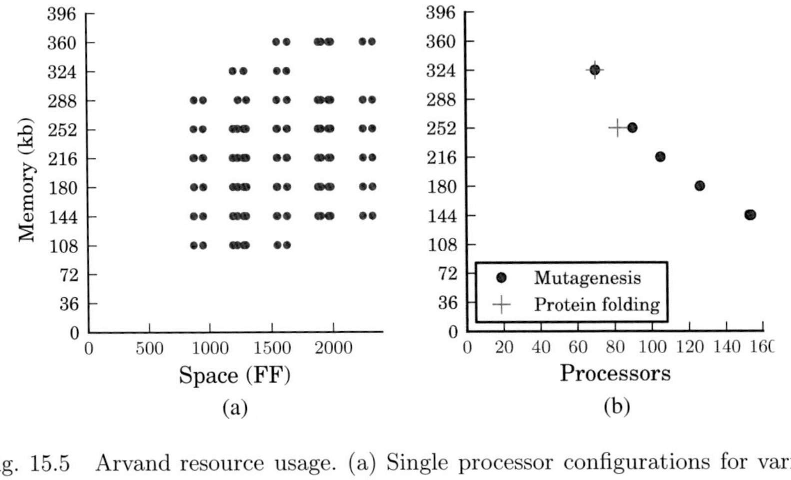

Fig. 15.5 Arvand resource usage. (a) Single processor configurations for variations in architecture, data width, and cache sizes. (b) Optimal multi-processor configurations for selected architectures.

Figure 15.5(b) shows the resource usage of multi-processor configurations which optimally exploit the available resources on a Xilinx Virtex 6 (LX550T) device.[1] The resource usage is shown for multi-processor configurations optimised for the two data sets described above. For the simple processor architecture up to 152 processors can fit on a chip, whereas for the more complex architecture up to 82 processors can fit. The designs can run at 100 MHz. Each configuration maximally exploits either the programmable fabric or the embedded memory. The resource usage results are acquired based on a simple resource model and place-and-route results from Xilinx ISE 13.2.

15.6.3 *Performance*

We measure the performance of several different multi-processor configurations on the two data sets described above using a detailed multi-processor simulator, and compare this with Progol 4.4 (Fig. 15.6). The performance is for the coverage test only, rather than the full application. Results are taken from multi-processor configurations which maximally exploit the resources, as well as several smaller configurations (single processor and multiples of 16 nodes). These smaller multi-processors require less area (and could therefore fit on a smaller chip) and consume lower power.

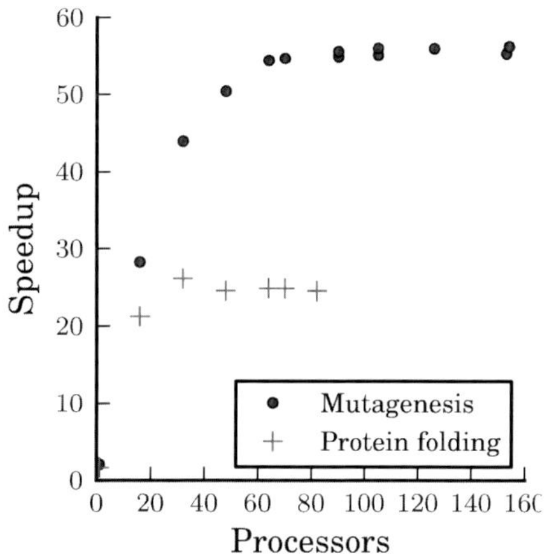

Fig. 15.6 Speedup w.r.t. Progol 4.4 for different multi-processor configurations for two different data sets.

[1] Virtex 6 Family Overview. Xilinx, Inc., San Jose, CA. 2011.

The performance results of the Arvand multi-processors are compared with run-time results from Progol 4.4. The time required for the coverage test in Progol is estimated based on total execution time and CPU utilization (as reported by system timing tools) and profiling results (using gprof) when running on an Intel i7-950 processor (3.07 GHz, 25.6 GB/s). A comparison could have been made with other systems with additional optimizations such as query transformations [Santa Costa *et al.* (2003)] and demand-driven indexing [Santa Costa *et al.* (2007)]. However, comparing with Progol 4.4 gives an indication of the kinds of speedup that can be attained by using custom hardware. Optimisations could be applied to software and custom hardware alike.

Even a single Arvand processor performs the coverage test faster than Progol, although it is clocked at a much lower frequency. This is to a large extent due to the specialised architecture of the processor, which needs to execute far fewer instructions. Progol performs the coverage test by running its built-in Prolog interpreter. Prolog implementations based on byte-code or native-code compilation outperform Progol's built-in interpreter, and can be slightly, but not significantly, faster than a single Arvand processor [Fidjeland (2007)].

Part of the speedup achieved by the Arvand multi-processor is due to software optimisations. In particular we employ a variation of the cut-transformation [Santa Costa *et al.* (2003)] which reduces non-determinacy at run-time by removing choice points to which backtracking would not alter the final result (due to not having any output variables). This is a valid optimization in the coverage test, although it is not applicable in general Prolog programs. This optimization could in principle be applied in Progol as well, but there it would incur an overhead to check if choice points can be removed. In the hardware implementation there is no overhead in execution time as the test is done in parallel with the rest of the decode stage, and only a small space overhead. With this optimisation the speedup for the mutagenesis is around 56 times, but even without this optimisation the speedup is around 8.3 times. The effect of this optimisation on the protein folding data set is not significant.

The overall speedup of the Arvand multi-processor with respect to Progol is around 56 times (mutagenesis) and 26 times (protein folding), both results showing the promise of this approach to accelerating ILP. Multiprocessors scale only up to a point, after which performance plateaus. This happens for two reasons. First, the sequential nature of the overall hypothesis search algorithm imposes a natural limit to parallelisation. Each hypothesis results in a batch of related jobs all of which are run to completion before a new batch is started, with the result that some processors end up having to wait for long-running jobs to complete. Relaxing the sequentiality constraint would reduce this problem. Second, congestion on the shared memory buses provides a second limit to parallelisation. The very large number of processors in question means that even fairly modest cache miss rates can result in congestion. This limit could be reduced by more refined job dispatch methods which improve temporal locality and by amending the existing instruction caches with scratchpad memory to hold commonly used parts of the background knowledge.

15.7 Concluding Remarks

Customisable architectures show good promise in speeding up demanding ILP applications. Our building blocks and architecture generation framework other than Progol can be adapted to enable ILP systems to exploit this technology, without the need for hardware design expertise. Moreover, to realise the full potential of our approach, we are integrating the multi-processor design tools seamlessly with Progol, targeting the latest high-performance FPGA systems.

Another theme of ongoing research involves studying how variations in run-time characteristics of inductive logic programming can be used in optimising performance and energy consumption. Such variations can be exploited by adapting the resources in a multi-processor system to match the run-time characteristics, making use of hardware reconfigurability. A key challenge is to automate such exploitation for realistic applications while minimising overheads in run-time reconfiguration, such that efficient designs can be produced cost-effectively.

Acknowledgments

The research leading to these results has received funding from EPSRC awards EP/F033516/1 and EP/I012036/1, and from the European Union Seventh Framework Programme under grant agreement no. 257906 and 287804.

Bibliography

V. Santa Costa, A. Srinivasan, R. Camacho, H. Blockeel, B. Demoen, G. Janssens, J. Struyf, H. Vandecasteele and W. Van Laer. Query transformations for improving the efficiency of ILP systems. *J. Mach. Learn. Res.*, **4**, 465–491. 2003.

V. Santa Costa, K. Sagonas and R. Lopes. Demand-driven indexing of Prolog clauses. In V. Dahl and I Nimelä. *Proceedings of the 23rd International Conference on Logic Programming*, LNCS, vol. 4670. Springer, Berlin, pp. 395–409. 2007.

L. Dehaspe and L. De Raedt. Parallel Inductive Logic Programming. In Y. Kodratoff, G. Nakhaeizadeh and G. Taylor (eds). *Proceedings of the MLnet Familiarization Workshop on Statistics, Machine Learning and Knowledge Discovery in Databases*, pp. 112–117. 1995.

A. Fidjeland. *Custom Architectures for Logic Programming.* PhD Thesis. 2007.

A. Fidjeland and W. Luk. Customising parallelism and caching for machine learning. *Proceedings of the IEEE International Conference on Field-Programmable Technology*, pp. 204–211. 2003. FPT 2003: Tokyo, 15–17 December 2003.

A. Fidjeland and W. Luk. Archlog: High-level Synthesis of Reconfigurable Multiprocessors for Logic Programming. *Proceedings of the IEEE International Conference on Field-Programmable Logic and Applications*, pp. 335–340. 2006. FPL 2006: Madrid, 28–30 Aug. 2006.

N. A. Fonseca, F. Silva and R. Camacho. Strategies to Parallelize ILP Systems. *Proceedings of the 15th International Conference on Inductive Logic Programming*, LNAI, vol. 3625. Springer-Verlag, Berlin, pp. 136–153. 2005.

N. A. Fonseca, A. Srinivasan, F. Silva and R. Camacho. Parallel ILP for distributed-memory architectures. *Mach. Learn.*, **74**, 257–279. 2009.

Q. Jin, D. Thomas, W. Luk and B. Cope. Exploring Reconfigurable Architectures for Tree-Based Option Pricing Models. *ACM T. Reconf. Tech. Syst.*, **4(2)**, 1–17. 2009.

A. Krall and U. Neumerkel. The Vienna abstract machine. *Proceedings of the International Workshop on Programming Language Implementation and Logic Programming*, LNCS, vol. 456, 121–135, Springer-Verlag, Berlin. 1990.

H. Lodhi, S. H. Muggleton and M. J. E. Sternberg. Multi-class mode of action classification of toxic compounds using logic based kernel methods. *Molecular Informatics.* 2010.

S. H. Muggleton. Inverse entailment and Progol. *New Generat. Comput.*, **13**, 245–286. 1995.

S. H. Muggleton and L. De Raedt. Inductive Logic Programming: Theory and Methods. *J. Logic Program.*, **19,20**, 629–679. 1994.

H. Ohwada, H. Nishiyamai and F. Mizoguchi. Concurrent execution of optimal hypothesis search for inverse entailment. *Proceedings of the 10th International Conference on Inductive Logic Programming*, LNAI, vol. 1866. Springer, Berlin, pp. 165–173. 2000.

G. Schelle, J. Collins, E. Schuchman, P. Wang, X. Zou, G. Chinya, R. Plate, T. Mattner, F. Olbrich, P. Hammarlund, R. Singhal, J. Brayton, S. Steibl, and H. Wang. Intel Nehalem processor core made FPGA synthesizable. *Proceedings of the 18th Annual ACM/SIGDA Internaional Symposium on Field Programmable Gate Arrays*, pp. 3–12. 2010. FPGA 2010: Monterey, California, 21–23 February 2010.

D. B. Skillicorn and Y. Wang. Parallel and Sequential algorithms for data mining using inductive logic. *Knowl. Inf. Syst.*, **3**, 405–421. 2001.

A. Srinivasan, S. H. Muggleton, R. King and M. Sternberg. Mutagenesis: ILP experiments in a non-determinate biological domain. *Proceedings of the 4th International Workshop on Inductive Logic Programming*, pp. 217–234, 1994.

M. J. E. Sternberg and S. H. Muggleton. Structure activity relationships (SAR) and pharmacophore discovery using inductive logic programming (ILP). *QSAR Comb. Sci.*, **22**, 527–532. 2003.

K. H. Tsoi, D. Rueckert, C. H. Ho, and W. Luk. Reconfigurable acceleration of 3D image registration. *Proceedings of the IEEE 5th Southern Programmable Logic Conference*, pp. 95–100. 2009. SPL 2009: Sao Paolo, 1–3 April 2009.

M. Turcotte, S. H. Muggleton and M. J. E. Sternberg. Automated discovery of structural signatures of protein fold and function. *J. Mol. Biol.*, **306**, 591–605. 2001.

D. Warren. *An Abstract Prolog Instruction Set.* Technical Report 309, SRI International. 1983.

J. Wielemaker. Native preemptive threads in SWI-Prolog. *Proceedings of the 19th International Conference on Inductive Logic Programming*, pp. 331–345. 2003. ICLP 2003: Mumbai, 9–13 December 2003.

Chapter 16

Multivalue Learning in ILP

Orlando Muoz Texzocotetla and Ren Mac Kinney Romero
Departamento de Ingeniería Eléctrica,
Universidad Autónoma Metropolitana, México

In this chapter we present an approach to make more expressive the hypotheses searched by ILP algorithms. This approach allows us to use more than one value in literals. We propose the construction of new clauses using information obtained analysing values in literals, which will allow multivalue learning. In order to discover such information, we draw from techniques used in inducing tree algorithms.

16.1 Introduction

Learning can be viewed as a search for a hypothesis H which satisfies some quality criteria [Mitchell (1997)]. In Inductive Logic Programming (ILP), the learning task can be described as follows: given a set of positive and negative examples (E^+ and E^-), and a background knowledge B, an ILP learner searches for an hypothesis H such that $B \wedge H \models E^+$.

The learner, in general, "can be described in terms of the structure of its search space, its search strategy and search heuristics" [Lavrac and Dzeroski (1994)]. Regarding search space, ILP is determined by the language of logic programs, which are formed with program clauses of the form $T \leftarrow Q$, where T is an atom $p(X_1, \ldots, X_n)$ and Q is a conjunction of literals $L_1, \ldots, L_m$. Also, the search space's clauses are syntactically restricted by a bias language. This bias determines which clauses are searched from the vocabulary of predicates, function symbols and constants that are in the background knowledge [Lavrac and Dzeroski (1994)]. When bias language is stronger (and therefore lacks expressiveness), the search space becomes smaller and more efficient, but it is likely that the final hypothesis cannot represent an appropriate solution for the target problem. For instance, if the language restricts the use of the target atom into the clause's body then no hypothesis will represent an appropriate solution to any recursive problem.

Each ILP algorithm defines a language in order to construct theories with the highest expressiveness degree. However, current algorithms test only a single value in constructing literals, thus forcing the hypothesis search space to be constructed with lots of rules. If the background knowledge is large then it is more likely that the final theory contains many rules, hence making it more difficult to interpret the solutions found.

In this chapter we present an approach to make the hypotheses constructed by ILP algorithms more expressive. It allows us to build literals that use sets of values instead of single ones. It constructs new clauses using information obtained discretizing values in literals, which are selected by the user. This discretizing is binary, thus obtaining two possible sets for values present in literals with multivalue learning.

To discover and extract that information, we implemented and adapted the algorithm of selection of split point used by two decision tree inducers: QUEST (Quick Unbiased Efficient Statistical Tree) [Loh and Shih (1997)] and CRUISE (Classification Rule with Unbiased Interaction Selection and Estimation) [Kim and Loh (2001)]. To choose the best attribute those algorithms use *analysis of variance* (ANOVA) or *Levene's test* for numeric attributes and *Pearson chi-square test* for categorical attributes.[1] In the case of CRUISE, this algorithm performs a *BOX-COX transformation* before *Quadratic Discriminant Analysis* (QDA). To find the split point, we use QDA.

These new clauses (we call them multivalue clauses) are added to the background knowledge, thus allowing new literals to be used by the ILP algorithm search. This, we believe, allows ILP algorithms to construct hypotheses with fewer rules.

This chapter is organised as follows: in Section 16.2 we describe, with an example, the problematic that we want to address; in Section 16.3, we present the approach to create new multivalue clauses and to make more

[1] A categorical attribute takes values unordered, and a numerical attribute takes values on the real line.

literals available; in Section 16.4 we show the experiments performed and the results obtained. Finally our conclusions and future work are presented in Section 16.5.

16.2 Univalue Clauses

To describe our main goal, we present a pattern recognition problem from [Bongard (1970)]. This problem consists of finding a theory which describes a pattern that relates the positive examples, all of which contain at least a triangle which points to some of the following directions: west (w), northwest (nw) and north (n). The target literal is: **bongard (Example)** $\leftarrow$. Hypotheses will be created from each value of following literals contained in the background knowledge:

- *triangle* (*Example, NumT*). *circle* (*Example, NumC*). *square* (*Example, NumS*)
- *direction* ($NumT$, *Direction*) where $Direction \in \{w, nw, n, ne, e, sw, s, se\}$

In this case Aleph [Srinivasan (2004)] (a program that implements Stephen Muggleton's Progol [Muggleton and De Raedt (1994)] algorithm) returns the following theory, consisting of three rules:

(1) $bongard(A) : -triangle(A, B), direction(B, w).$
(2) $bongard(A) : -triangle(A, B), direction(B, nw).$
(3) $bongard(A) : -triangle(A, B), direction(B, n).$

To create this theory, ILP algorithms use clauses whose literals declare a single value to each literal. For instance, the second argument of the literal *direction*, *Direction*, is a categorical attribute with eight possible values. Each time that *direction* appears in some of the clauses which are contained in the search space, *Direction* uses only one of its values. This type of clauses, we'll call them *univalue*. Namely, if all the arguments of each literal within a clause's body declare only one value, then this is a *univalue clause*. If at least one argument presents more than one value, then we will call it *multivalue clause*.

Thus if the number of values for attributes (categorical and/or numeric) increases significantly, then hypotheses may have lots of rules, therefore making these hypotheses more difficult to interpret. We can see that it would be very helpful to create multivalue clauses which would allow ILP algorithms to create smaller hypotheses. Therefore we can ask: is it possible that ILP algorithms can test more than one value (a set of values) at a time? How should each set of values be created? Will multivalue clauses help to create hypotheses with fewer rules? We believe that the approach we propose answers these questions. It is given in detail in the following section.

16.3 Multivalue Clauses

The proposed approach discovers information at the examples. This information is used to create new clauses. These clauses will be added to the background knowledge to allow the ILP algorithms to use them adding the necessary literals to the search space. We will use the most popular ILP algorithms FOIL [Quinlan (1990)] and [Muggleton and De Raedt (1994)] Progol. Our approach has the following steps:

(1) **Creation of subsets of values.** In this step we make a binary split on the set of all values for the given literal. For this we implemented the split point selection algorithm presented in Section 16.1. Thus for each categorical value with a set $C = \{v_1, \ldots, v_m\}$, we will obtain two disjoint subsets C_1 y C_2 such that $C_1 \cap C_2 = \phi$. We also use this when we have a small number of discrete numeric values. For each numeric value we will obtain a split point d, which will divide the full set of values in two subsets. The first one will contain values less than or equal to d ($C_1 = \{x \bullet x \leq d\}$), and the second one will contain values greater than d ($C_1 = \{x \bullet x > d\}$). $C_1 \cap C_2 = \phi$.
(2) **Creation of multivalue clauses.** The subsets of values will be used to create multivalue clauses. For categorical attributes, each subset of values will be declared in the appropriate literal rather than a single value. Thus we will create two multivalue clauses. For numeric attributes, we will also create two clauses. In the first one the split point will determine the values less than or equal to d. In the second one the split point will determine the values greater than d.
(3) **Background knowledge modification.** In this step we add the multivalue clauses to the background knowledge.
(4) **Learning.** The new information is used by the ILP algorithm. The literals for the new clauses are made available to the ILP search.

16.3.1 *Example*

In order to better explain our approach, we present a simple ILP example. We must find a theory on the number of sides that must have a figure that belongs to one of the following classes: quadrilateral or non_quadrilateral. The target literal is $\mathbf{class}\ (\mathbf{Fig}, \mathbf{Class}) \leftarrow$. The background knowledge declares the relation $\mathbf{side}\ (\mathbf{F}, \mathbf{S})$, which indicates the number of sides S of the figure F.

Aleph returns the following theory:

- $\mathbf{class}\ (A, quadrilateral) \leftarrow \mathbf{sides}\ (A, 4)$
- $\mathbf{class}\ (A, non\_quadrilateral) \leftarrow \mathbf{sides}\ (A, 3)$
- $\mathbf{class}\ (pentagon, non\_quadrilateral) \leftarrow \mathbf{sides}\ (A, 5)$
- $\mathbf{class}\ (hexagon, non\_quadrilateral) \leftarrow \mathbf{sides}\ (A, 6)$

Now let's compare the above theory to our approach. In the next steps we show how the proposed approach is used for this problem.

(1) **Creation of subsets of values.** This problem has a small number of discrete numeric values so we work on it as a categorical value which indicates the number of sides of each figure. We obtain two subsets of categories: $A = \{4\}$ and $B = \{3, 5, 6\}$.

(2) **Creation of multivalue clauses.** For each subset of categorical values our approach creates multivalue clauses, the corresponding pair is:

$$\mathbf{sidesA}\ (F) \leftarrow \mathbf{sides}\ (F, L), \mathbf{member}\ (L, [4])$$

$$\mathbf{sidesB}\ (F) \leftarrow \mathbf{sides}\ (F, L), \mathbf{member}\ (L, [3, 5, 6])$$

(3) **Background knowledge modification.** In this step the new clauses are added to the background knowledge.

(4) **Learning.** Finally, this new background knowledge is used by adding literals *sidesA* and *sidesB* to the possibilities of constructing hypotheses the ILP algorithms. In this example the final theory (with Aleph) is:

$$\mathbf{class}\ (A, quadrilateral) \leftarrow \mathbf{sides}\ (A, L), \mathbf{member}\ (A, [4]).$$

$$\mathbf{class}\ (A, non\_quadrilateral) \leftarrow \mathbf{sides}\ (A, L), \mathbf{member}\ (A, [3, 5, 6]).$$

16.4 Experiments

The databases analysed were obtained from the UCI Repository [Frank and Asuncion (2010)], and each one was divided tenfold to perform a cross validation analysis. In order to compare our approach with univalue learning, we analysed each problem with the following ILP systems:

- **Aleph.** This is the ILP system created by Ashwin Srinivasan [Srinivasan (2004)]. Aleph implements the Progol algorithm ([Muggleton (1995)]).
- **multivalue FOIL.** FOIL adapted [Quinlan (1990)] with our approach.
- **multivalue Aleph.** Aleph adapted with our approach.

For each problem, we compared the number of rules for each theory, percentage of the covered examples, and the running time. We also compared the results from Aleph and multivalue Aleph. All experiments were performed on a modern multicore PC machine. In the following subsections we present the experiments that were carried out.

16.4.1 *Student loan and Japanese credit*

For the *Student Loan Problem* the goal is to create a logic program which indicates if a student must repay a loan. The goal predicate is **no_payment_due** (**Student**) ←. The declared predicates in the background knowledge provide information about gender, longest absence from school, school, employment, etc. This problem has two numeric attributes and two categorical attributes.

The second database is *Japanese Credit Screening Dataset* and contains information about people who were granted bank credit. This database was generated from Japanese enterprises which granted bank credits. The goal relation is **creditscreen** (**Person**) ←. In order to grant a credit the following information is taken into account: employment, type of good purchased for credit, gender, marital status, age, problematic region, etc. This database has five numeric attributes and one categorical attribute.

Results. Table 16.1 shows the results for these databases. We can observe that the number of rules decreases with our approach. We can also see that by using multivalue clauses the percentage of covered examples increases. Although our experience has been very positive, a deeper analysis is necessary in order to confirm that our approach increases accuracy.

Table 16.1 Student loan and Japanese credit results.

Student Loan Number of rules	**Avg** ===	**Student Loan Percentage of covered examples**	**Avg** ===
Aleph without multivalue clauses	9 rules	Aleph without multivalue clauses	71%
Aleph with multivalue clauses	6.2 rules	Aleph with multivalue clauses	89%
FOIL with multivalue clauses	5 rules	FOIL with multivalue clauses	87%
Running time	===		
Aleph without multivalue clauses	1.658 sec.		
Aleph with multivalue clauses	2.8868 sec.		
Japanese Credit Number of rules	**Avg** ===	**Japanese Credit Percentage of covered examples**	**Avg** ===
Aleph without multivalue clauses	17.8 rules	Aleph without multivalue clauses	79.87%
Aleph with multivalue clauses	14.7 rules	Aleph with multivalue clauses	82.23%
FOIL with multivalue clauses	10.1 rules	FOIL with multivalue clauses	96.66%
Time of performance	===		
Aleph without multivalue clauses	1.39 sec.		
Aleph with multivalue clauses	1.97 sec.		

16.5 Conclusions and Future Work

With the creation of the subsets of values (categorical or numerical) the ILP algorithms identify significant information which is contained in the examples and background knowledge. This information is the split point d, which, as seen from the results, we can use to reduce the number of rules for the theories induced. In order to confirm that the accuracy is improved with our approach, we need to analyse more ILP databases with multivalue clauses.

It must be noted that not all values can be processed with our approach. Only those attributes on literals whose values are applicable for all the objects in the domain. For instance, an attribute like name or surname is not applicable for all persons, and therefore it can not be used by our approach. A value like age is applicable for all persons, making it appropriate to use with our approach. It is left to the user to choose the literals.

Regarding future work, there are many avenues to explore. We can perform some improvements in the implemented algorithm in order to improve the results obtained to create new clauses. We can go further, on one hand, by obtaining more than one split point, thus dividing the values into more than two subsets. Or, on the other hand, in addition to the multivalue clauses, we could also design a method which creates multivariate clauses. It might be productive to look into other decision tree inducer techniques that extract significant information.

Finally it would be interesting to implement all ILP algorithms in one system like Weka [Bouckaert and Frank (2008)] to make the comparison on them simpler.

Bibliography

M. M. Bongard. *Pattern Recognition.* Hayden Book Co./Spartan Books, Rochelle Park, New Jersey. 1970.

R. R. Bouckaert and E. Frank. WEKA Manual for Version 3-6-0. University of Waikato, Hamilton, New Zealand. 2008.

A. Frank and A. Asuncion. UCI Machine Learning Repository. University of California, School of Information and Computer Sciences, Irvine, California. 2010.

H. Kim and W. Y. Loh. Classification trees with unbiased multiway splits. *J. Am. Stat. Assoc.*, **96**, 589–604. 2001.

N. Lavrac and Saso Dzeroski. *Inductive Logic Programming: Techniques and Applications.* Ellis Horwood Harlow. 1994.

W. Y. Loh and Y. S. Shih. Split selection methods for classification trees. *Statistica Sinica*, **7(4)**, 815–840. 1997.

T. M. Mitchell. *Machine Learning.* McGraw-Hill, New York. 1997.

S. H. Muggleton and L. De Raedt. Inductive logic programming: Theory and methods. *J. Logic Program.*, **19**, 629–684. 1994.

S. H. Muggleton. Inverse Entailment and Progol. *New Generat. Comput.*, **13**, 245–286. 1995.

R. Quinlan. Learning Logical Definitions from Relations. *Mach. Learn.*, **5**, 239–266. 1990.

A. Srinivasan. *The Aleph Manual.* 2004. Available online: `http://www.cs.ox.ac.uk/activities/machinelearning/Aleph/`. Accessed 11 August 2014.

Chapter 17

Learning Dependent-Concepts in ILP: Application to Model-Driven Data Warehouses

Moez Essaidi, Aomar Osmani and Céline Rouveirol

LIPN – UMR CNRS 7030, Université Paris-Nord, France

This chapter studies a new machine learning application with a possible challenging benchmark for relational learning systems. We are interested in the automation of a *model-driven data warehouse* using machine learning techniques. The main goal is to automatically derive the transformation rules to be applied in the model-driven process. This aims to reduce the contribution of transformation designers, thereby reducing the time and cost of development. We propose to express the model transformation problem as an *Inductive Logic Programming* (ILP) one: existing project traces (or project experiences) are used to define the background knowledge and examples. The *Aleph* ILP engine is used to learn best transformation rules. In our application, we need to deal with several dependent-concepts. Taking into account the work in *Predicate Invention*, *Layered Learning*, *Cascade Learning* and *Context Learning*, we propose a new methodology that automatically updates the background knowledge of concepts to be learned. Experimental results support the conclusion that our approach is suitable to solve this kind of problem.

17.1 Overview

Model-driven engineering [Bézivin (2005, 2006)] is an approach that organizes the development of a system around the design of models (conform to metamodels) and the definition of transformations to generate required components. The *model-driven data warehouse* represents approaches [Zepeda *et al.* (2008); Mazón and Trujillo (2008); Essaidi and

Osmani (2010a)] that apply the MDA[1] standard for the development of the data warehouse systems [Wrembel and Koncilia (2007)]. The approach presented in [Zepeda *et al.* (2008)] describes derivation of *Online-Analytical-Processing* (OLAP) schemas from *Entity-Relationship* (ER) schemas. The source and target schemas respectively conform to ER and OLAP metamodels of the *Common-Warehouse-Metamodel* (CWM). Authors describe how an ER schema is mapped to an OLAP schema and provide, also, a set of *Query-View-Transformation* rules (e.g., *EntityToCube, AttributeToMeasure, RelationShipToDimension*) to ensure this. The approach presented in [Mazón and Trujillo (2008)] extends the *Unified-Modeling-Language* (UML) and the CWM to multidimensional modeling with MDA. Authors focus on the transformation of the multidimensional conceptual model (i.e., conceptual OLAP schema) to the multidimensional logical model (i.e., logical OLAP schema). They provide, using the *Query-View-Transformation* language, transformations (e.g., *Fact2Table, Dimension2Table*, etc.) to derive the logical schema from the conceptual one.

We provide in [Essaidi and Osmani (2010a)] a unified model-driven data warehouse approach including an integrated design framework and transformation process. We propose the UML CORE metamodel to design the operational source-model and the CWM OLAP metamodel to design the multidimensional target-model. However, model transformation definition requires serious skill within metamodel and transformation languages. In this context, the *model transformation by example* approach [Balogh and Varró (2009); Strommer and Wimmer (2008); Dolques *et al.* (2009); García-Magariño *et al.* (2009)] proposes to automatically create model transformation from pairs of source and target model examples. Then, in [Essaidi and Osmani (2010b)], we extend our proposal by a conceptual transformation-by-example framework for the model-driven data warehouse context. For example, the $ClassToCube$ relation represents a mapping of $Class$, *Property* and *RelationShip* elements of the UML CORE into $Cube$, $Measure$ and $CubeDimensionAssocition$ elements of the CWM OLAP. The input instances (i.e., a, p, rse) of $Class$, *Property* and *Relationship* define elements of a candidate source model; this input-pattern gives the context in the source model when a class is transformed into $Cube$. The output instances (i.e., c, m, cda) of $Cube$, $Measure$ and $CubeDimensionAssocition$ define the generated elements of

[1]The Object Management Group (`http://www.omg.org/mda`) proposes the Model-Driven Architecture (MDA) as standard implementation of the model-driven engineering.

a target-model; this output-pattern states the context in the target-model where a *Cube* is generated from a *Class*.

This work extends the proposed method (in previous works) by machine learning in order to reduce expert contribution in the transformation process. We propose to express the model transformation problem as an ILP [Lavrac and Dzeroski (1994); Muggleton and De Raedt (1994)] one and to use existing projects trace to find the best transformation rules. To the best of our knowledge, this work is the only one that has been developed for automating model-driven data warehouse with relational learning and it is the first effort that provides real experimental results in this context. In the model-driven data warehouse application, we find dependencies between transformations. We investigate a new machine learning methodology stemming from the application needs: learning dependent-concept. Following work about *Layered Learning* [Gustafson and Hsu (2001); Nguyen *et al.* (2004); Stone and Veloso (2000)], *Predicate Invention* [Muggleton and Road (1994); Stahl (1994, 1995)], *Context Learning* [Bieszczad and Bieszczad (2006); Turney (1993); Varró (2006)] and *Cascade Learning* [Gama and Brazdil (2000); Ting and Witten (1997); Xie (2006)], we propose a *Dependent-Concept Learning* (DCL) approach where the objective is to build a pre-order set of concepts on this dependency relationship: first learn non-dependent concepts, then at each step, the theories of learned concepts are added as background knowledge to the future concepts to be learned with the respect to this given pre-order, and so on. This DCL methodology is implemented and applied to our transformation learning problem using Aleph.[2] The experimental evaluation shows that the DCL system gives significantly better results.

The remainder of the chapter is structured as follows. Section 17.2 provides background definitions and presents the application domain. Section 17.3 details the machine learning algorithms used and introduces the DCL approach. Section 17.4 reports experimental results. Section 17.5 gives our conclusions and future work.

17.2 Background Definitions

Definition 1 (Model). A model $M = (G, MM, \mu)$ is a tuple where: $G = (N_G, E_G, \Gamma_G)$ is a directed multigraph,[3] MM is itself a model called the

[2]http://www.cs.ox.ac.uk/activities/machlearn/Aleph/

[3]A directed multigraph $G = (N_G, E_G, \Gamma_G)$ consists of a finite set of nodes N_G, a finite set of edges E_G, and a function $\Gamma_G : E_G \rightarrow N_G \times N_G$ mapping edges to their source and target nodes [Jouault and Bézivin (2006)].

reference model of M (i.e., its metamodel) associated to a graph $G_{MM} = (N_{MM}, E_{MM}, \Gamma_{MM})$, and $\mu : N_G \cup E_G \rightarrow N_{MM}$ is a function associating elements (nodes and edges) of G to nodes of G_{MM}.

The relation between a model and its reference model (metamodel) is called conformance and is noted *conformsTo*. Elements of MM are called meta-elements (or meta-concepts). μ is neither injective (several model elements may be associated to the same meta element) nor surjective (not all meta-elements need to be associated to a model element) [Jouault and Bézivin (2006)]. In the ILP framework (regarding the background knowledge and examples), a model M_i is characterized by its description MD_i, i.e., a set of predicates that correspond to the contained elements. The predicates used to represent M_i as logic programs are extracted from its metamodel ω_i. For example, consider a data model used to manage customers and invoices. The classes *Customer* and *Invoice* are defined respectively by $class(customer)$ and $class(invoice)$. The one-to-many association that relate *Customer* to *Invoice* is mainly defined by $association(customer - invoice, customer, invoice)$ (other predicates, presented next, are used to define multiplicities of the association). Then, the logical description of models from the project's traces constitutes the generated background knowledge program in ILP.

***Definition 2* (*Metamodel and Meta-Metamodel*).** A meta-metamodel is a model that is its own reference model (i.e., it conforms to itself). A metamodel is a model such that its reference model is a meta-metamodel [Jouault and Bézivin (2006)]. The metamodeling architecture (part of the MDA standard) is based on meta-levels: $M3$, $M2$, $M1$ and $M0$. $M3$ is the meta-metamodel level and it forms the foundation of the metamodeling hierarchy (the *Meta-Object-Facility* is an example of meta-metamodel). $M2$ consists of the metamodel level and the UML and the CWM are examples of metamodels. $M1$ regroups all user-defined models and $M0$ represents the runtime instances of models.

The basic idea is to specify the relations among source and target element types using constraints. However, declarative constraints can be given executable semantics, such as in logic programming. In fact, logic programming with its unification-based matching, search, and backtracking seems a natural choice to implement the relational approach, where predicates can be used to describe the relations [Czarnecki and Helsen (2006)]. For example, in [Gerber *et al.* (2002)] the authors explore the application of logic programming. In particular *Mercury*, a typed dialect of *Prolog*, and *F-logic*, an object-oriented logic paradigm, implement transformations. In [Rutle *et al.* (2008)] authors discuss a formalization of modeling and model transformation using a generic formalism, the *Diagrammatic Predicate Logic* (DPL). The DPL [Diskin and Wolter (2008); Rutle *et al.* (2009)] is a graph-based specification format that takes its main ideas from both categorical and first-order logic, and adapts them to software engineering needs.

Definition 3 **(*Model Transformation*).** A model transformation consists of a set of transformation rules which are defined by input and output patterns (denoted by $\mathbb{P}$) in $M2$ level. Formally, a model transformation is associated to a relation $R(MM, MN) \subseteq \mathbb{P}(MM) \times \mathbb{P}(MN)$ defined between two metamodels which allows obtainment of a target model N conforming to MN from a source model M that conforms to metamodel MM [Stevens (2010)].

Definition 4 **(*Transformation Example*).** A transformation example (or trace model) $R(M, N) = \{r_1, \ldots, r_k\} \subseteq \mathbb{P}(M) \times \mathbb{P}(N)$ specifies how the elements of M and N are consistently related by R. A base of examples is a set of transformation examples. The transformation examples represent the project's traces or they can be collected from different experts [Kessentini *et al.* (2010)].

For instance, we are interested in the transformation of the *Data-Source PIM* (denoted DSPIM) to the *Multidimensional PIM* (denoted MDPIM). The DSPIM represents a conceptual view of a data-source repository and its *conformsTo* the UML CORE metamodel (part of the *Unified-Modeling-Language*). The MDPIM represents a conceptual view of a target data warehouse repository and its $conformsTo$ the CWM OLAP metamodel (part of the CWM). The (i) definitions and examples of DSPIM/MDPIM, (ii) their respective metamodels (UML CORE and CWM OLAP) and (iii) details about the proposed transformation-by-example framework for *Model-Driven Data Warehouse* are provided in our recent work [Essaidi *et al.* (2011)]. The predicates extracted from the UML CORE metamodel to translate source models into the logic program are: *type(name)*, *multiplicity(bound)*, *class(name)*, *property(name, type, lower, upper)*, *association(name, source, target)*, *associationOwnedAttribute(class, property)*, and *associationMemberEnds(association, property)*. Then, according to the CWM OLAP metamodel, the predicates defined to describe target models are: *cube(Name)*, *measure(Name, Type, Cube)*, *dimension(Name, isTime, isMeasure)*, *cubeDimensionAssociation(Cube, Dimension)*, *level*

(Name), *levelBasedHierarchy(Name, Dimension)*, and *hierarchyLevelAssociation(LevelBasedHierarchy, Level)*.

By analyzing the source and target models, we observe that structural relationships (like aggregation relation, composition relation, semantic dependency, etc.) define a restrictive context for some transformations. For INSTANCE, let us consider the concept *PropertyToMeasure*. We know there is a composition relation between *Class* and *Property* and there is also a composition relation between *Cube* and *Measure* in the metamodels. This implies that the concept *PropertyToMeasure* must be considered only when the concept *ClassToCube* is learned. Therefore, the *ClassToCube* concept must be added as background knowledge in order to learn the *PropertyToMeasure* concept. This domain specificity induces a pre-order on the concept to be learned and defines a dependent-concept learning problem. Therefore, in our approach, concepts are organized in order to defined a structure called *dependency graph*. In [Esposito *et al.* (2000)], Esposito *et al.* use the notion of dependency graph to deal with hierarchical theories. Authors define the dependency graph as a directed acyclic graph of concepts, in which parent nodes are assumed to be dependent on their offspring.

***Definition 5* (*Dependency Graph*).** A dependency graph is a directed acyclic graph of predicate letters, where an edge (p, q) indicates that atoms with predicate letter q are allowed to occur in the hypotheses defining the concept denoted by p [Esposito *et al.* (2000)].

17.3 Relational Learning of Dependent-Concept

The data warehouse is a database used for reporting; therefore a candidate language used to describe data is a relational database language. This language is close to *datalog* language used in relational learning (or ILP). In addition, the conceptual models are defined in term of relations between elements of different types (properties, classes and associations). Therefore, it is natural to use supervised learning techniques handling concept languages with the same expressive level as manipulated data in order to exploit all information provided by the relationships between data. Even if there are quite a number of efficient machine learning algorithms that deal with attribute-value representations, relational languages allow encoding structural information fundamental for the transformation process. This is why ILP algorithms [Lavrac and Dzeroski (1994); Muggleton and De Raedt (1994)] have been selected to deal with this learning problem. As ILP suffers from a scaling-up problem, the proposed architecture [Essaidi and Osmani (2010a,b)] is designed in order to take into account this limitation. Thus, it is organized as a set of elementary transformations such that each one concerns a few number of predicates only, to reduce the search space. This section revisits the relational learning theory, introduces the DCL approach and compares it to related concept-search approaches.

17.3.1 *Relational learning setting*

We consider the machine learning problem as defined in [Mitchell (1982)]. A (single) concept learning problem is defined as follows. Given (i) a training set $E = E^+ \cup E^-$ of positive and negative examples drawn from an example language $\mathcal{L}_e$, (ii) a hypothesis language $\mathcal{L}_h$, (iii) optionally, some background knowledge B described in a relational language $\mathcal{L}_b$ and (iv) a generality relation $\geq$ relating formulas of $\mathcal{L}_e$ and $\mathcal{L}_h$, learning is defined as search in $\mathcal{L}_h$ for a hypothesis h such that h is consistent with E. A hypothesis h is consistent with a training set E if and only if it is both complete ($\forall e^+ \in E^+, h, B \geq e^+$) and correct ($\forall e^- \in E^-, h, B \not\geq e^-$). In an ILP setting, $\mathcal{L}_e$, $\mathcal{L}_b$ and $\mathcal{L}_h$ are Datalog languages, and most often, examples are ground facts or clauses, background knowledge is a set of ground facts or clauses and the generality relation is a restriction of deduction. As explained in [Mitchell (1982)], there are two main strategies for searching $\mathcal{L}_h$: either generate-and-test or data-driven, and following any of those strategies, algorithms may proceed either top-down or bottom-up, or any combination of those. We used in our experiments the well-known Aleph system, because of its ability to handle rich background knowledge, made of both facts and rules. Aleph follows a top-down generate-and-test approach.

It takes as input a set of examples, represented as a set of Prolog facts and background knowledge as a Datalog program. It also enables the user to express additional constraints C on the admissible hypotheses. Aleph tries to find a hypothesis $h \in \mathcal{L}_h$, such that h satisfies the constraint C, which is complete and partially correct. We used Aleph default mode; in this mode, Aleph uses a simple greedy set cover procedure and constructs a theory H step by step, one clause at a time. To add a clause to the current target concept, Aleph selects an uncovered example as a seed, builds a most specific clause from this seed as the lowest bound of its search space and then performs an admissible search over the space of clauses that subsume this lower bound according to the user clause length bound. In the next section, we show the reduction of the source model, the target model and the mapping between them as an ILP problem.

17.3.2 *Dependent concept learning problem*

Let $\{c_1, c_2, \ldots, c_n\}$ be a set of concepts to be learned in our problem. If we consider all the concepts independently, each concept c_i defines an independent ILP problem, i.e., all concepts have independent training sets E_i and share the same hypothesis language L_h and the same background knowledge B. We refer to this framework as the *Independent-Concept Learning* (ICL). The second framework, DCL, takes into account a pre-order relation[4] $\preceq$ between concepts to be learned such that $c_i \preceq c_j$ if the concept c_j depends on the concept c_i or in other term, if c_i is used to define c_j (Definition 5). More formally, a concept c_j is called *parent* of the concept c_i (or c_i is the *child or offspring* of c_j) if and only if $c_i \preceq c_j$ and there exists no concept c_k such that $c_i \preceq c_k \preceq c_j$. $c_i \preceq c_j$ denotes that c_j depends on c_i for its definition. A concept c_i is called *root* concept if there exists no concept c_k such that $c_k \preceq c_i$ (in other words, a root concept c_i does not depend on any concept c_k, for $k \neq i$). The DCL framework uses the idea of decomposing a complex learning problem into a number of simpler ones. Then, it adapts this idea to the context of ILP multi-predicate learning.

A dependent-concept ILP learning algorithm is an algorithm that accepts a pre-ordered set of concepts, starts with learning root concepts, then child (or offspring) concepts, and propagates the learned rules to the background knowledge of their parent concepts and continues recursively the learning process until all dependent-concepts have been learned. Within this approach, we benchmark two settings: (i) the background knowledge B_j of a dependent-concept (parent) c_j is extended with the child concept instances (as a set of facts — this framework is referred to as DCLI) and (ii) B_j is extended with child concept intensional definitions: all child concepts are learned as sets of rules and are added to B_j — this framework is referred to as DCLR in the following sections. In both cases, DCLI or DCLR, all predicates representing child of c_j can be used in the body of c_j's definition. Our claim here is that the quality of the c_j's theory substantially improves if all its child concepts are known in B_j, extensionnally or intensionnally. Section 17.4 provides results concerning the impact of child concepts' representation (extensional vs. intensional) on the quality of the c_j. Finally, the task of empirical DCL in ILP, which is concerned with learning a set of concepts based on a dependency graph and given a set of examples and background knowledge, can be formulated as follows:

[4] A pre-order is a reflexive and transitive binary relationship.

Given: A dependency graph $G_d = (C_d, E_d)$ where $Cd = \{c_1, c_2, \ldots, c_n\}$ the set of concepts to learn such that $\forall c_i \in C_d$:

- A set of transformation examples (i.e., examples) $E = \{E_1, E_2, \ldots, E_n\}$ is given; and defined as (where $|TM|$ is the number of training models):
$$E_i = \{R_i^j(M^j, N^j) \mid R^j(M^j, N^j) \subseteq \mathbb{P}(M^j) \times \mathbb{P}(N^j),\ j \leq |TM|\}$$
- Background knowledge B which provide additional information about the examples and defined as:
$$B = \{\mathbb{P}(M^j) \cup \mathbb{P}(N^j) \mid M^j\ conformsTo\ MM,\ N^j\ conformsTo\ MN)\}$$

Find: $\forall c_i \in C_d$, based on E_d and following a *BFS* strategy,[5] learn a transformation rule $R_i(MM, MN) \subseteq \mathbb{P}(MM) \times \mathbb{P}(MN)$; where MM is the reference source-metamodel and MN is the reference target-metamodel.

17.3.3 *Comparison with related concept search problems*

Stone *et al.* introduce in [Stone and Veloso (2000)] the *layered learning* machine learning paradigm. In [Nguyen *et al.* (2004)] the authors study the problem of constructing the approximation of higher-level concepts by composing the approximation of lower-level concepts. Authors in [Gustafson and Hsu (2001); Jackson and Gibbons (2007)] present an alternative to standard genetic programming that applies layered learning techniques to decompose a problem. The layered learning approach presented by Muggleton in [Muggleton (1993)] aims at the construction of a large theory in small pieces. Compared to layered learning, the DCL approach aims to find all concept theory using the theories of concepts on which they depend. Then, while the layered learning approach exploits a bottom-up, hierarchical task decomposition, the DCL algorithm exploits the dependency relationships between specific concepts of the given dependency graph. The dependency structure in [Stone and Veloso (2000)] is a hierarchy, whereas our dependency structure is a *directed acyclic graph.* A breadth-first search algorithm is used to explore the dependency graph.

Within the field of ILP the term *Predicate Invention* is introduced [Muggleton (1991)] and it involves the decomposition of predicates being learned into useful sub-concepts. Muggleton [Muggleton and Road (1994)] defines Predicate Invention as the augmentation of a given theoretical vocabulary to allow finite axiomatization of the observational predicates. In [Stahl

[5] Start by an offspring and non-dependent concept (i.e., a root concept), then follow its parent dependent-concepts.

(1994, 1995)], Stahl studies the utility of predicate invention task in ILP and its capabilities as a bias shift operation. Rios *et al.* investigate in [Rios and Matwin (1998)] on specification language extension when no examples are explicitly given of the invented predicate. The DCL and Predicate Invention approaches share the fact they correspond to the process of introducing new theoretical relationships. However, in the case of Predicate Invention, the approach is usually based on decomposition of the theory to learn simple sub-theories. The DCL approach is based on the composition of a theory from the learned theories.

In [Gama and Brazdil (2000)], authors introduces the *Cascade Generalization* method. This approach is compared to other approaches that generate and combine different classifiers like the *Stacked Generalization* approach [Ting and Witten (1997, 1999); Wolpert (1992)]. In [Xie (2006)], Xie proposes several speed-up variants of the original cascade generalization and shows that the proposed variants are much faster than the original one. As with Cascade Generalization, the DCL approach extends the background knowledge at each level by the information on concepts of the sub-level (according to the dependency graph). But, within the proposed DCL, we use the same classifiers for all iterations. In our experiments, we report the results of the extension of the background knowledge by instances (first setting named DCLI) and the learned theory (second setting named DCLR).

The model transformation by example approach aims to find contextual patterns in the source model that map contextual patterns in the target model. This task is defined as *Context Analysis* in [Varró (2006)]. The machine learning approaches that exploit context to synthesize concepts are proposed in [Bieszczad and Bieszczad (2006); Turney (1993)]. In [Turney (1993)] the author provides a precise, formal definition of context and lists four general strategies for exploiting contextual information. Authors in [Bieszczad and Bieszczad (2006)] introduce an enhanced architecture that enables contextual learning in the *Neurosolver* (a problem-solving system). Nevertheless, the notion of context is different in DCL. In fact, in DCL, contextual information is the result of the learning process (which will form the transformation rule); while within the *Contextual Learning* strategy the context is part of input information that improves the performance of the learner.

17.4 Empirical Results

This section describes the experimental setup and compares the results of the two tested methods: ICL and DCL.

17.4.1 *Materials and methods*

For the experimentations presented in [Essaidi *et al.* (2011)], we use a set of real-world data models provided by an industrial partner. Concerning the experimentations of this chapter, we used the Microsoft AdventureWorks 2008R2 sample database family[6] reference databases. The AdventureWorksOLTP is a sample operational database used to define the source model (i.e., DSPIM). The AdventureWorksDW is a sample data warehouse schema used as target model (i.e., MDPIM). AdventureWorksOLTP, AdventureWorksDW and the mapping between them (evaluated by the expert) is considered as a reference project trace. This will allow us to benchmark our approach on a new extended schema (that generates more examples) and a new dependency graph. The database elements (i.e., classes, properties and associations) are encoded as background knowledge (B) and the mapping instances between their elements allows us to define positive (E^+) and negative (E^-) examples. Concerning the number of examples, we have $\|E_{ClassToCube}\| = 71$ denoting the number of examples (positives and negatives) used to learn *ClassToCube* concept, $\|E_{PropertyToMeasure}\| = 249$, $\|E_{PropertyToDimension}\| = 245$, $\|E_{RelationShipToDimension}\| = 93$, $\|E_{ElementToHierarchyPath}\| = 338$, and $\|E_{ElementToDimensionLevel}\| = 338$.

We used the Aleph ILP engine to learn first-order rules. We ran Aleph in the default mode, except for the *minpos* and *noise* parameters: *:- set(minpos, p)* establishes as p the minimum number of positive examples covered by each rule in the theory (for all experiments we fix $p = 2$); and *:- set(noise, n)* is used to report learning performance by varying the number of negative examples allowed to be covered by an acceptable clause (we use two setting $n = 5$ and $n = 10$). Then, a Prolog compiler is needed to run Aleph. We use YAP (Yet Another Prolog),[7] an optimized open-source Prolog platform. We propose to compare the following approaches:

(1) The ICL approach, which proposes to learn the set of considered concepts independently.
(2) The DCL approach, which considers a dependency graph to learn the concepts. Within this approach, we benchmark two settings: (i) the background knowledge B of dependent-concepts (parent concepts) is updated with their child instances (denoted DCLI); and (ii) with their child intensional definitions (denoted DCLR). We identify the concept

[6] `http://msftdbprodsamples.codeplex.com/`
[7] `http://www.dcc.fc.up.pt/~vsc/Yap/`

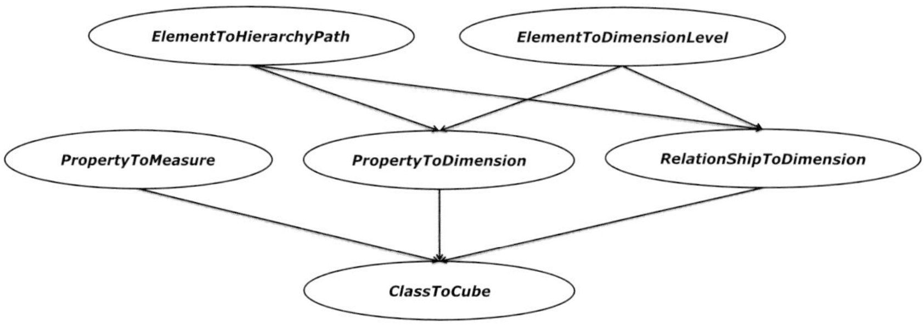

Fig. 17.1 The considered dependency graph.

dependencies illustrated by the graph in Fig. 17.1:

- *ClassToCube* $\preceq$ *PropertyToMeasure*: The *PropertyToMeasure* concept depends on the concept *ClassToCube*. In general, the context of transforming *properties* depends on contextual information of transforming *classes*, and the context of obtaining *measures* is part of the context of obtaining *cubes*. In fact, *Properties* that become *Measures* are numeric *properties* of *classes* that become *cubes*. So, we need information about the context of *ClassToCube* transformation in order to find the context of *PropertyToMeasure*.
- *ClassToCube* $\preceq$ *PropertyToDimension*: This defines dependency between *classes* transformed into *cubes* and their *properties* that can be transformed into *dimensions*. Regarding the UML CORE metamodel, we find a structural dependency between *Class* and *Property* elements (a *Class* includes attributes, represented by the *ownedAttribute* role that defines a set of *properties*). Then regarding the CWM OLAP metamodel, we have a structural dependency between the *Cube* and *Dimension* elements. Current experiments confirm that structural dependencies in the metamodel act on ways to perform learning.
- *ClassToCube* $\preceq$ *RelationShipToDimension*: Indeed, *dimensions* are also obtained from *relationships* of the *Class* that is transformed into *Cube*. The *CubeDimensionAssociation* meta-class relates a *Cube* to its defining dimensions as shown by the CWM OLAP metamodel in [Essaidi *et al.* (2011)]. These relationships define the axes of analysis in the target multidimensional schema [Wrembel and Koncilia (2007)].
- (*PropertyToDimension*, *RelationShipToDimension*) $\preceq$ *ElementToHierarchyPath*: A *Dimension* has zero or more hierarchies.

A *Hierarchy* is an organizational structure that describes a traversal pattern through a *Dimension*, based on parent/child relationships between members of a *Dimension*. Then, elements that are transformed into dimensions (*properties* and *relationships*) extend the background knowledge used to find hierarchy paths.

- (*PropertyToDimension*, *RelationShipToDimension*) $\preceq$ *ElementToDimensionLevel*: A *LevelBasedHierarchy* describes hierarchical relationships between specific levels of a *Dimension* (e.g., *Day*, *Month*, *Quarter* and *Year* levels for the *Time* dimension). So, rules of transforming elements into *Dimension* are used to find rules of obtaining the levels.

17.4.2 *Results and discussion*

The first goal of this benchmark is to examine how the number of training models and examples influence the performances. Accuracy is commonly used for comparing the performances in machine learning and it is defined as $Accuracy = \frac{TP+TN}{P+N}$, where P (N) is the number of examples classified as positive (negative), and TP (TN) is the number of examples classified as positive (negative) that are indeed positive (negative). In [Essaidi *et al.* (2011)], we examined the accuracy of the learned rules to show the impact of the number of training models and examples. We reported the obtained test accuracy curves for *ClassToCube* and *PropertyToDimension*. The accuracy of current experiments based on the new dataset (of AdventureWorks) confirm the results reported in [Essaidi *et al.* (2011)].

The second goal of the analysis is to study the performances of the DCL approach (with the two settings DCLI and DCLR) compared to the ICL approach. The *Receiver-Operating-Characteristics* (ROC) graphs are a useful technique for visualizing, organizing and selecting classifiers based on their performance [Fawcett (2004)]. We report in this section the ROC curves of the tested approaches (ICL, DCLI and DCLR) based on the new dataset and the new enhanced dependency graph. The following metrics are used to report the ROC graphs: The $true-positive-rate$ (also called hit rate and recall = sensitivity) is estimated as $tp\ rate = \frac{TP}{P}$ and the $false-positive-rate$ (also called false alarm rate = 1 − specificity) as $fp\ rate = \frac{FP}{N}$. ROC graphs are two-dimensional graphs in which $tprate(sensitivity)$ is plotted on the Y axis and $fprate(1-specificity)$ is plotted on the X axis. In order to assess the impact of a child concept rule's quality on the learning performances of a parent concept, we experiment the case where the child concept is noisy. This experiment is made within the DCL approach. We add noise to the non-dependent concept (i.e., *ClassToCube*) and we observe results of learning dependent-concepts with different acceptable noise settings ($n = 5$ and $n = 10$). We report the cases where 10% (denoted N-DCLI and N-DCLR) and 20% (denoted N2-DCLI and N2-DCLR) of the examples are noisy (to add noise, we swap positive and negative examples).

The area under the ROC curve, abbreviated AUC, is the common measure used to compare the tested methods. The AUC represents, also, a measure of accuracy (results are reported by Figs. 17.2, 17.3, 17.4, 17.5

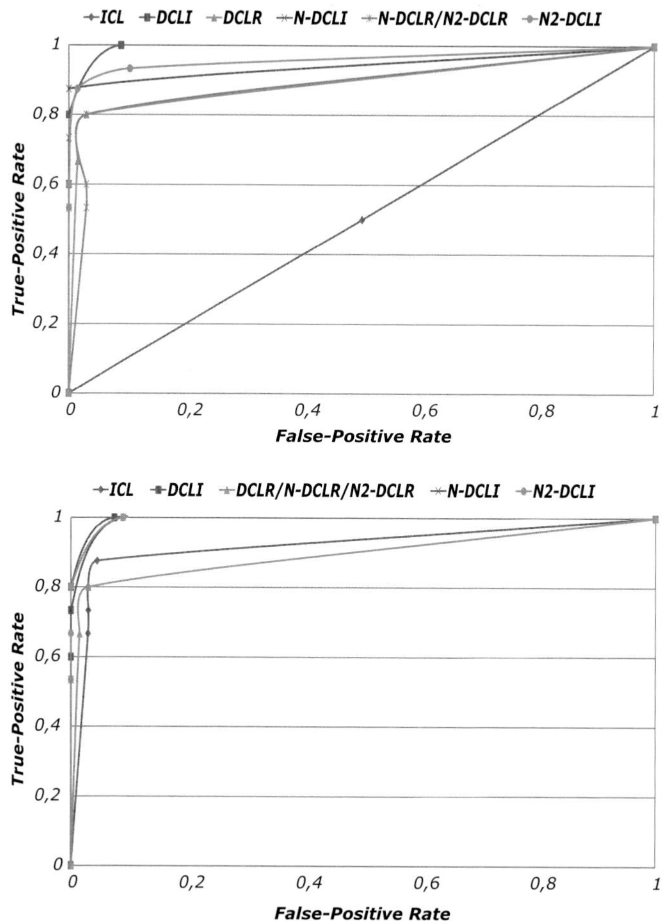

Fig. 17.2 Learning *PropertyToMeasure* ($n = 5$ for left) and ($n = 10$ for right).

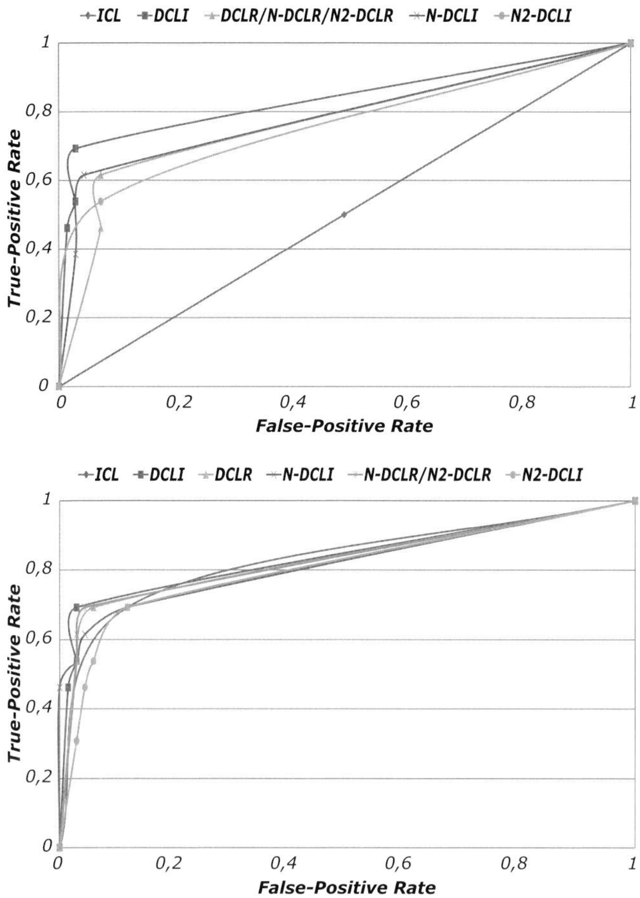

Fig. 17.3 Learning *PropertyToDimension* ($n = 5$ for left) and ($n = 10$ for right).

and 17.6). Figures show that the $n = 10$ setting (right-hand part of each figure) gives best performances compared to $n = 5$. This confirms that the choice of this parameter is important to deal with noisy information of database models in general. Comparing ICL, DCLI and DCLR approaches, results show that the DCLI has greater AUC than other tested methods. The DCLI curves follow almost the upper-left border of the ROC space. Therefore, it has better average performance compared to the DCLR and ICL ($AUC_{DCLI} > AUC_{DCLR} > AUC_{ICL}$). The ICL curves almost follow the 45-degree diagonal of the ROC space, which represents a random classifier. The DCLR setting exhibits good results with respect to the ICL

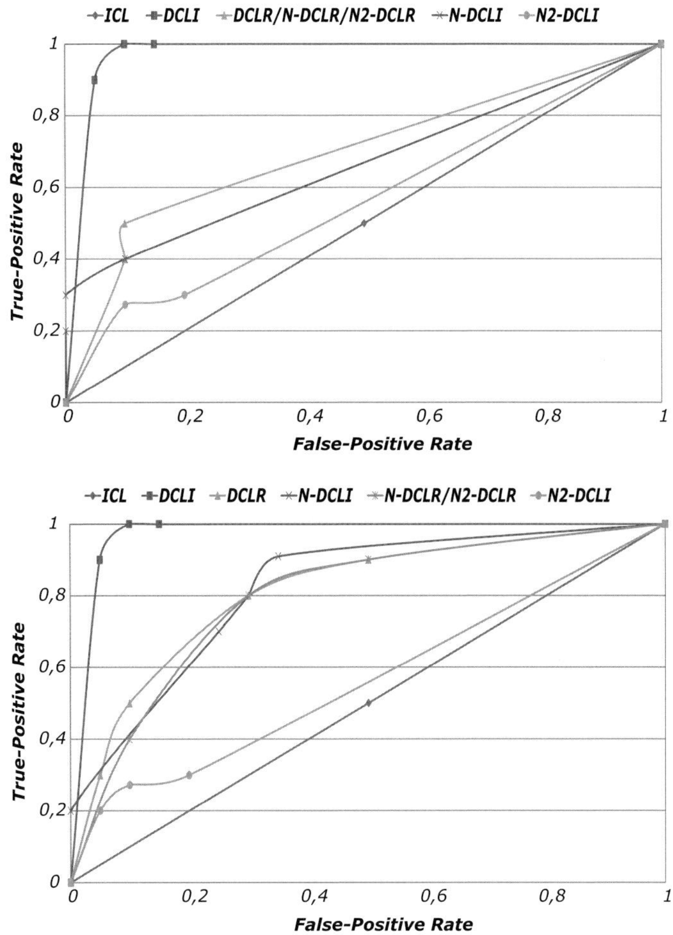

Fig. 17.4 Learning *RelationshipToDimension* ($n = 5$ for left) and ($n = 10$ for right).

approach, which are nevertheless slightly worse than results of the DCLI setting.

The $AUC_{DCLI} > AUC_{DCLR} > AUC_{ICL}$ result is expected, because the DCLI configuration, when learning a parent concept, uses in its background knowledge offspring concepts as a set of facts (extensional definition), as opposed to DCLR, which previously learns, as sets of rules, a definition for offspring concepts. In case lower-level concepts (i.e., offspring concepts) are not perfectly identified, the errors for offspring concepts

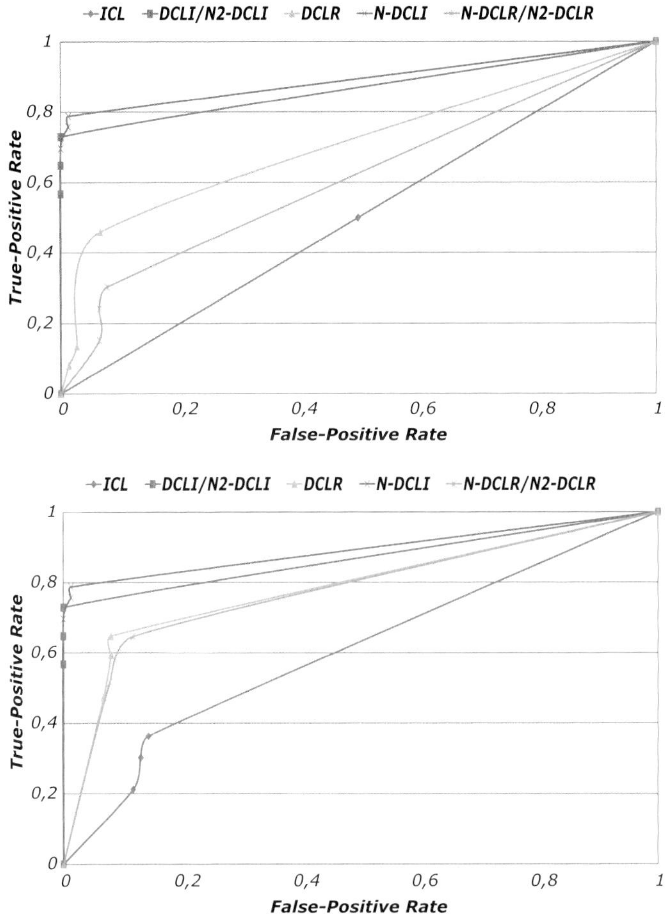

Fig. 17.5 Learning *ElementToHierarchyPath* ($n = 5$ for left) and ($n = 10$ for right).

propagate to parent concepts. We assume here that examples are noise free, which explains why DCLI has a better behavior than DCLR. Thus, for *PropertyToMeasure*, *PropertyToDimension* and *RelationshipToDimension*, results integrate the error rate from *ClassToCube* learned rules. For the parent concepts *ElementToHierarchyPath* and *ElementToDimensionLevel* that depend on *(PropertyToDimension and RelationshipToDimension)*, results are influenced by the error rate propagation from learning *ClassToCube* and then *PropertyToDimension* and *RelationshipToDimension*.

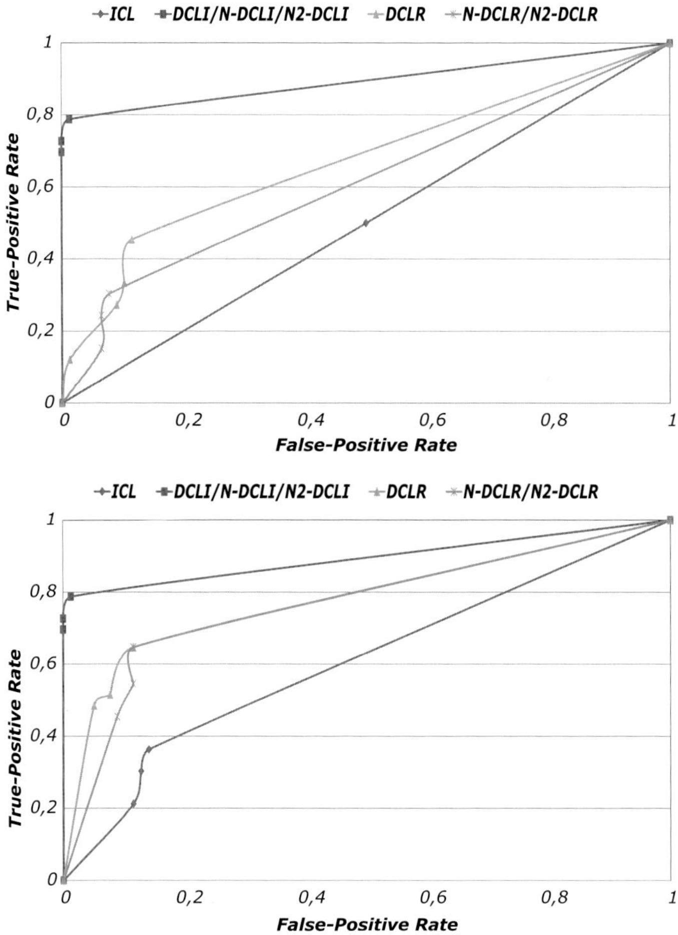

Fig. 17.6 Learning *ElementToDimensionLevel* ($n = 5$ for left) and ($n = 10$ for right).

Then, considering the N-DCLI/N2-DCLI and N-DCLR/N2-DCLR, we have mainly: $AUC_{N-DCLI} > AUC_{N2-DCLI}$ and $AUC_{N-DCLR} > AUC_{N2-DCLR}$. Curves show that the obtained performances depend on the concept to learn and its degree of dependence on *ClassToCube* (the noisy non-dependent concept of this configuration). For instance, in Figs. 17.3 and 17.4, *PropertyToDimension* and *RelationshipToDimension* are more impacted than *PropertyToMeasure* (in Fig. 17.2). The *PropertyToDimension* and *RelationshiptoDimension* concepts are highly dependent on *ClassToCube*. This can be observed on most schemas (remarks provided in [Essaidi *et al.* (2011)]) and is confirmed by the expert point of view. For example, in the case of *RelationshipToDimension*, the N2-DCLI curve seems to reach the 45-degree diagonal. This gives us an idea on the noise that we can accept when learning specific dependency relationships. The *ElementToHierarchyPath* and *ElementToDimensionLevel* concepts are impacted by the noisy data of *ClassToCube*, but less than *PropertyToDimension* and *RelationshipToDimension*. We observe that *ElementToHierarchyPath* and *ElementToDimensionLevel* are not in direct dependence with *ClassToCube*.

17.5 Conclusion

This chapter studies a real complex machine learning application: model-driven data warehouse automation using machine learning techniques. It includes the use of standard algorithms and a design of architecture to limit the impact of machine learning to the regions where learning from experience is needed. In addition, from our application needs, we found an interesting machine learning problem: learning dependent-concept. Experimental results show that the proposed DCL approach to derive transformation rules in context of model-driven data warehouse gives significant performance improvement compared to the standard approach. From the business point of view, the learned theories are, in general, close to the ones given by human experts. Our future work will experiment the case when a business goals model is considered during transformations. For example, the derivation of the MDPIM from the pair (DSPIM, MDCIM), where MDCIM defines the organization requirements/goals. We plan also to extend the approach to new application domains that provide a large dependency graph (for example, the *Extraction, Transformation and Loading* process in the data warehousing architecture).

Bibliography

Z. Balogh and D. Varró. Model transformation by example using inductive logic programming. *Software and System Modeling*, **8(3)**, 347–364. 2009.

J. Bézivin. On the unification power of models. *Software and System Modeling*, **4(2)**, 171–188. 2005.

J. Bézivin. Model driven engineering: An emerging technical space. *Generative and Transformational Techniques in Software* Engineering, LNCS, vol. 4143. Springer, Berlin, pp. 36–64. 2006.

A. Bieszczad and K. Bieszczad. Contextual learning in the neurosolver. In S. Kollis, A. Stafylopatis, W. Duch and E. Oja (eds). *Artifial Neural Networks: Proceedings of the 16th International Conference on Artificial Neural Networks 2006*. Springer, Berlin, pp. 474–484. 2006.

K. Czarnecki and S. Helsen. Feature-based survey of model transformation approaches. *IBM Syst. J.*, **45**, 621–645. 2006.

Z. Diskin and U. Wolter. A diagrammatic logic for object-oriented visual modeling. *Electr. Notes Theor. Comput. Sci.*, **203(6)**, 19–41. 2008.

X. Dolques, M. Huchard and C. Nebut. From transformation traces to transformation rules: Assisting model driven engineering approach with formal concept analysis. In *Proceedings of the 17th International Conference on Conceptual Structures*, pp. 93–106. ICCS 2009: Moscow, 26–31 July 2009.

F. Esposito, G. Semeraro, N. Fanizzi and S. Ferilli. Multistrategy theory revision: Induction and abduction in inthelex. *Mach. Learn.*, **38(1–2)**, 133–156, 2000.

M. Essaidi and A. Osmani. Model driven data warehouse using MDA and 2TUP. *J. Comput. Methods Sci. Eng.*, **10**, 119–134. 2010a.

M. Essaidi and A. Osmani. Towards model-driven data warehouse automation using machine learning. *Proceedings of the International Conference on Evolutionary Computation*, pp. 380–383. 2010b. ICEC 2010: Valencia, 24–26 October 2010.

M. Essaidi, A. Osmani, and C. Rouveirol. Transformations learning in context of model-driven data warehouse: An experimental design based on inductive logic programming. *Proceedings of the 23rd IEEE International Conference on Tools with Artificial Intelligence*, pp. 693–700. 2011. ICTAI 2011: Boca Raton, Florida, 7–9 November 2011.

T. Fawcett. *Roc graphs: Notes and practical considerations for researchers.* Technical report, HP Laboratories, 2004.

J. A. Gama and P. Brazdil. Cascade Generalization. *Mach. Learn.*, **41**, 315–343. 2000.

I. García-Magariño, J. J. Gómez-Sanz and R. Fuentes-Fernández. Model transformation by-example: An algorithm for generating many-to-many transformation rules in several model transformation languages. In A. Vallecillo, J. Gray and A. Pierantonio (eds). *Proceedings of the First International Conference on Theory and Practice of Model Transformations*, LNCS, vol. 5063. Springer, Berlin, pp. 52–66. 2009.

A. Gerber, M. Lawley, K. Raymond, J. Steel and A. Wood. Transformation: The missing link of mda. In A. Corradini, H. Ehrig, H. -J. Kreowski, and G. Rozenberg, G. (eds). *Proceedings of the 1st International Conference on Graph Transformation*, LNCS, vol. 2505. Springer, Berlin, pp. 90–105. 2002.

S. M. Gustafson and W. H. Hsu. Layered Learning in Genetic Programming for a Cooperative Robot Soccer Problem. *Proceedings of the 4th European Conference on Genetic Programming*, pp. 291–301. EuroGP 2001: Milan, 18–20 April 2001.

D. Jackson and A. P. Gibbons. Layered learning in boolean GP problems. In M. Ebner, M. O'Neill, A. Ekárt, L. Vanneschi and A. Esparcia-Alcázar (eds.). *Proceedings of the 10th European Conference on Genetic Programming*, LNCS, vol. 4445. Springer, Berlin, pp. 148–159. 2007.

F. Jouault and J. Bézivin. KM3: A DSL for Metamodel Specification. *Proceedings of the 8th IFIP International Conference on Formal Methods for Open Object-Based Distributed Systems*, pp. 171–185. FMOODS 2006: Bologna, 14–16 June 2006.

M. Kessentini, M. Wimmer, H. Sahraoui and M. Boukadoum. Generating transformation rules from examples for behavioral models. *Proceedings of the Second International Workshop on Behaviour Modelling: Foundation and Applications*, pp. 2:1–2:7. 2010. BM-FA 2010: Paris, 14 June 2010.

N. Lavrac and S. Dzeroski. *Inductive Logic Programming: Techniques and Applications.* Ellis Horwood, New York. 1994.

J.-N. Mazón and J. Trujillo. An mda approach for the development of data warehouses. *Decis. Support Syst.*, **45**, 41–58. 2008.

T. M. Mitchell. Generalization as search. *Artif. Intell.*, **18**, 203–226, 1982.

S. H. Muggleton. Inductive Logic Programming. *New Generat. Comput.*, **8**, 295–318. 1991.

S. H. Muggleton. Optimal layered learning: A PAC approach to incremental sampling. *Proceedings of the 4th Conference on Algorithmic Learning Theory*, pp. 37–44. ALT 1993: Tokyo, 8–10 November 1993.

S. H. Muggleton and L. De Raedt. Inductive logic programming: Theory and methods. *J. Log. Program.*, **19/20**, 629–679. 1994.

S. H. Muggleton and K. Road. Predicate invention and utilisation. *J. Exp. Theor. Artif. In.*, **6**, 6–1. 1994.

S. H. Nguyen, J. G. Bazan, A. Skowron and H. S. Nguyen. Layered learning for concept synthesis. *T. Rough Sets*, **3100**, 187–208. 2004.

R. Rios and S. Matwin. Predicate invention from a few examples. In R. E. Mercer and E. Neufeld (eds). *Advances in Artificial Intelligence: Proceedings of the 12th Biennial Conference of the Canadian Society for Computational Studies of Intelligence*, LNCS, vol. 1418. Springer-Verlag, Berlin, pp. 455-466. 1998.

A. Rutle, A. Rossini, Y. Lamo and U. Wolter. A diagrammatic formalisation of mof-based modelling languages. *TOOLS*, **47**, 37–56. 2009.

A. Rutle, U. Wolter, and Y. Lamo. A diagrammatic approach to model transformations. *Proceedings of the 2008 Euro American Conference on Telematics and Information Systems.* EATIS 2008: Aracaju 10–12 September 2008.

I. Stahl. On the utility of predicate invention in inductive logic programming. In F. Bergadano and L. De Raedt (eds). *Proceedings of the European Conference on Machine Learning*, LNCS, vol. 784. Springer, Berlin, pp. 272–286. 1994.

I. Stahl. The appropriateness of predicate invention as bias shift operation in ILP. *Mach. Learn.*, **20**, 95–117. 1995.

P. Stevens. Bidirectional model transformations in QVT: semantic issues and open questions. *Software and System Modeling*, **9(1)**, 7–20. 2010.

P. Stone and M. M. Veloso. Layered learning. In R. López de Mántaras and E. Plaza (eds). *Proceedings of the 11th European Conference on Machine Learning*, LNCS, vol. 1810. Springer-Verlang, Berlin, pp. 369–381. 2000.

M. Strommer and M. Wimmer. A framework for model transformation by-example: Concepts and tool support. *Proceedings of the 46th International Conference, TOOLS EUROPE 2008*, pp. 372–391. 2008. TOOLS 2008: Zurich, 30 June–4 July 2008.

K. M. Ting and I. H. Witten. Stacked generalization: when does it work? *Proceedings of the Fifteenth International Joint Conference on Artificial Intelligence*, pp. 866–871. 1997. IJCAI 1997: Nagoya, 23–29 August 1997.

K. M. Ting and I. H. Witten. Issues in stacked generalization. *J. Artif. Intell. Res.*, **10**, 271–289. 1999.

P. D. Turney. Exploiting context when learning to classify. In P. Brazdil (ed.). *Proceedings of the European Conference on Machine Learning*, LNCS, vol. 667. Springer-Verlag, Berlin, pp. 402–407. 1993.

D. Varró. Model transformation by example. In O. Nierstrasz, J. Whittle, D. Harel and G. Reggio (eds.). *Proceedings of the 9th International Conference Model Driven Engineering Languages and Systems*, LNCS, vol. 4199. Springer-Verlag, Berlin, pp. 410–424. 2006.

D. H. Wolpert. Stacked Generalization. *Neural Networks*, **5**, 241–259. 1992.

R. Wrembel and C. Koncilia. *Data Warehouses and OLAP: Concepts, Architectures and Solutions.* IGI Global, Hershey, Pennsylvania. 2007.

Z. Xie. Several speed-up variants of cascade generalization. In L. Wang, L. Jiao, G. Shi, X. Li, J. Liu (eds). *Proceedings of the Third International Conference on Fuzzy Systems and Knowledge Discovery*, LNCS, vol. 4223. Springer-Verlag, Verlin, pp. 536–540. 2006.

L. Zepeda, M. Celma and R. Zatarain. A mixed approach for data warehouse conceptual design with MDA. In O. Gervasi, B. Murgante, A. Laganà, D. Taniar and Y. Mun (eds). *Proceedings of the International Conference on Computational Science and Its Applications*, LNCS, vol. 5072. Springer-Verlag, Berlin, pp. 1204–1217. 2008.

Chapter 18

Graph Contraction Pattern Matching for Graphs of Bounded Treewidth

Takashi Yamada and Takayoshi Shoudai

Department of Informatics, Kyushu University, Japan

A *graph contraction pattern* is a triplet $h = (V, E, U)$ where (V, E) is a connected graph and U is a distinguished subset of V. The graph contraction pattern matching problem is defined as follows. Given a graph contraction pattern $h = (V, E, U)$ and a graph G, can G be transformed to (V, E) by edge contractions so that for any $v \in V \backslash U$, only one vertex in G can be mapped to v? We show that this problem is solvable in polynomial time if (1) (V, E) is of bounded treewidth, (2) U is an independent set of (V, E), and (3) all vertices in U are of bounded degree.

18.1 Introduction

Large amounts of data with graph structures — such as map data, CAD, biomolecular, chemical molecules, the World Wide Web — are stored in databases. Almost all chemical compounds stored in the NCI chemical dataset[1] are known to be expressed by outerplanar graphs. Horváth *et al.* [Horváth *et al.* (2010)] proposed an efficient frequent subgraph mining algorithm for a dataset expressed by outerplanar graphs. We have developed general graph patterns with structured variables which can be replaced with arbitrary connected graphs, in order to represent expressive patterns appearing in a given dataset of graphs. In [Yamasaki *et al.* (2009)], we introduced a general concept of block-preserving graph patterns and presented a frequent graph pattern mining algorithm on outerplanar graphs.

[1] `http://cactus.nci.nih.gov`.

Toward a graph mining on more general classes of graphs, Horváth and Ramon proposed a frequent subgraph mining algorithm for a dataset of graphs of bounded treewidth [Horváth and Ramon (2010)]. Some NP-completeness problems on graphs are solvable in polynomial time if the input can be restricted to graphs of bounded treewidth. From a practical viewpoint, 99.97% of 250, 251 chemical compounds in the NCI chemical dataset are expressed by graphs of treewidth at most three [Horváth and Ramon (2010)]. We proposed a graph pattern of bounded treewidth and a polynomial time pattern matching algorithm on the graph patterns [Yamada and Shoudai (2011)]. On the other hand, the pattern matching problem on graph patterns is computationally expensive unless a graph pattern is essentially two-connected [Miyahara *et al.* (2000)]. In this paper, in order to discover more than two-connected graph patterns in a target dataset, we define a new graph pattern expression, called a graph contraction pattern, by using a concept of edge contractions on connected graphs.

The H-contractibility problem takes as input two graphs G and H, and asks whether G can be transformed into H by edge contractions. Based on the H-contractibility problem, we define a graph contraction pattern as a triplet $h = (V, E, U)$ where (V, E) is a connected graph and U is a distinguished subset of V. The graph contraction pattern matching problem is defined as follows. Given a graph contraction pattern $h = (V, E, U)$ and a graph G, can G be transformed to (V, E) by edge contractions so that for any $v \in V \setminus U$, only one vertex in G can be mapped to v? In Fig. 18.1, G_1 is transformed to (V, E) by edge contractions so that only one vertex in G_1 is mapped to each vertex in $V \setminus U$. G_2 is also transformed to (V, E) in such a way. In this chapter, we show that this problem is solvable in polynomial time if (1) (V, E) is of bounded treewidth, (2) U is

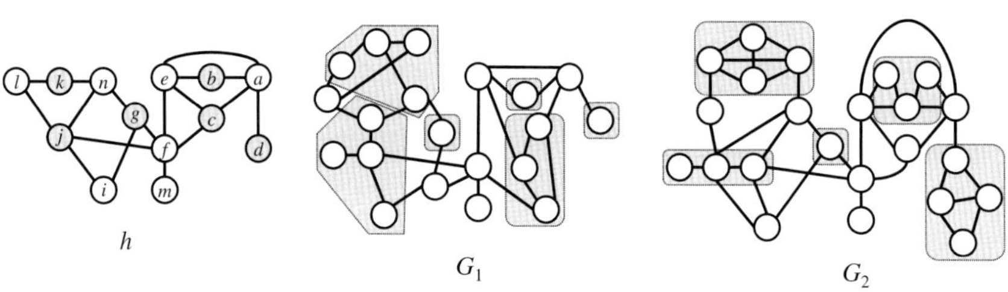

Fig. 18.1 Let $h = (V, E, U)$ be a graph contraction pattern, where (V, E) is a connected graph of treewidth 2 and $U = \{b, c, d, g, j, k\}$. h is a common pattern of G_1 and G_2.

an independent set of (V, E), and (3) all vertices in U are of bounded degree.

18.2 Preliminaries

18.2.1 *Normalized tree decomposition*

All graphs in this chapter, are simple and loopless. For a graph G, we denote by $V(G)$ and $E(G)$ the vertex set and the edge set of G, respectively. We denote by $N(v)$ the set of neighbors of a vertex v. For $U_1, U_2 \subseteq V(G)$, we say that U_1 and U_2 are adjacent if there is an edge $\{v, w\}$ such that $v \in U_1$ and $w \in U_2$. For $U \subseteq V(G)$, we denote by $G[U]$ the subgraph of G induced by U.

A *tree-decomposition* of a graph G is a 2-tuple $(T, \mathcal{X})$ where T is a tree and $\mathcal{X} = \{\mathcal{X}(\alpha) \mid \mathcal{X}(\alpha) \subseteq V(G) \text{ for all } \alpha \in V(T)\}$ that satisfies the following three conditions: (1) $\bigcup_{\alpha \in V(T)} \mathcal{X}(\alpha) = V(G)$, (2) $\forall v, w \in V(G)\ [\{v, w\} \in E(G) \Rightarrow \exists \alpha \in V(T)\ [\{v, w\} \subseteq \mathcal{X}(\alpha)]]$, and (3) $\forall \alpha, \beta, \gamma \in V(T)\ [\beta$ is on the path from α to γ in $T \Rightarrow \mathcal{X}(\alpha) \cap \mathcal{X}(\gamma) \subseteq \mathcal{X}(\beta)]$. The width of a tree-decomposition $(T, \mathcal{X})$ is $\max_{\alpha \in V(T)} |\mathcal{X}(\alpha)| - 1$. The treewidth of a graph G is the minimum width over all possible tree-decompositions of G. We say that a tree-decomposition of a graph G is optimal if its width equals to the treewidth of G.

Thereafter, to distinguish from a vertex of graph G, we call a vertex of T a node. Below we assume that the tree T of a tree-decomposition $(T, \mathcal{X})$ is a rooted tree by specifying a node of T. For a tree-decomposition $(T, \mathcal{X})$, we denote by $T^{\downarrow a}$ the maximal subtree rooted at a node $\alpha \in V(T)$, by $\mathcal{X}(T^{\downarrow \alpha})$ the union of elements of nodes of $T^{\downarrow \alpha}$, i.e., $\mathcal{X}(T^{\downarrow \alpha}) = \bigcup_{\beta \in V(T^{\downarrow \alpha})} \mathcal{X}(\beta)$.

A tree-decomposition $(T, \mathcal{X})$ is smooth if $\forall \{\alpha, \beta\} \in E(T)[|\mathcal{X}(\alpha) \backslash \mathcal{X}(\beta)| = |\mathcal{X}(\beta) \backslash \mathcal{X}(\alpha)| = 1]$. A tree-decomposition $(T, \mathcal{X})$ has a *subtree connected characteristic* if $\forall \{\alpha, \beta\} \in E(T)[\beta$ is a child of α and $G[\mathcal{X}(T^{\downarrow \beta}) \backslash \mathcal{X}(\alpha)]$ is connected]. A tree-decomposition $(T, \mathcal{X})$ is normalized if it satisfies the following three conditions: (1) $(T, \mathcal{X})$ is optimal, (2) $(T, \mathcal{X})$ is smooth, and (3) T is a rooted tree and $(T, \mathcal{X})$ has a subtree connected characteristics. Nagoya *et al.* [Nagoya *et al.* (2002)] gave a polynomial time algorithm for constructing a normalized tree-decomposition from any tree-decomposition.

Theorem 18.1. [Nagoya *et al.* (2002)] *A normalized tree-decomposition of G of treewidth k is obtained from any optimal tree-decomposition of G in $O(kn^2)$ time, where $n = |V(G)|$.*

18.2.2 *Graph contraction pattern*

Let G and H be connected graphs. An H*-witness structure* $\mathcal{W} = \{W(u)|u \in V(H)\}$ is a partition of $V(G)$ satisfying the following conditions: (1) $\forall W(u) \in \mathcal{W}$ [$G[W(u)]$ is connected], and (2) $\forall u, u' \in V(H)[\{u, u'\} \in E(H) \Leftrightarrow \exists\{v, w\} \in E(G)[v \in W(u), w \in W(u')]]$. We call each set $W(u) \in \mathcal{W}$ the H*-witness set* of u. When G has an H-witness structure, G can be transformed to H by contracting each of H-witness sets into one vertex by edge contractions.

A graph contraction pattern h (*GC-pattern*, for short) is a triplet $h = (V, E, U)$ where (V, E) is a connected graph and U is a subset of V. We denote by $V(h)$ and $E(h)$ the vertex set and the edge set of h, respectively. And for $V' \subseteq V(h)$, we denote by $h[V']$ the graph contraction subpattern (GC-subpattern, for short) induced by V', i.e., $h[V'] = (V', E(h) \cap \{\{v, w\}|v, w \in V'\}, U \cap V')$.

We say that a GC-pattern h matches a graph G if G has a $(V(h), E(h))$-witness structure $\mathcal{W} = \{W(u)|u \in V(h)\}$ satisfying $\forall v \in V(h) \setminus U$ $[|W(v)| = 1]$. We call an element of U a *contractible vertex*, and an element of $V(h) \setminus U$ an *uncontractible vertex*. And for a GC-pattern h, a $(V(h), E(h))$-witness structure of h is called an h*-witness structure*.

18.2.3 *Main results*

The graph contraction pattern matching problem is to decide whether or not a given GC-pattern h matches a given graph G. Our main result is the following theorem.

Theorem 18.2. *Given a GC-pattern $h = (V, E, U)$ and a graph G, the GC-pattern matching problem is solvable in polynomial time if h satisfies the following three conditions*: (1) (V, E) *is of bounded treewidth,* (2) U *is an independent set of* (V, E), *and* (3) *all vertices in* U *are of bounded degree.*

U is an independent set of $(V(h), E(h))$	F [Brouwer and Veldman (1987)]	*	T	
All vertices in U are of bounded degree	*	F [this paper]	T	
$(V(h), E(h))$ is of a bounded treewidth	*	*	F	T
Time Complexity	NP-complete		GI-hard	P [this paper]

We show a polynomial time algorithm that solves this problem in the next section. Our algorithm is based on the idea of the graph isomorphism algorithm for a graph with bounded treewidth in [Nagoya *et al.* (2002)]. A GC-pattern matching problem becomes intractable if it does not satisfy the condition of Theorem 18.2.

Theorem 18.3. *For inputs G and h, the GC-pattern matching problem is NP-complete if the degree of a vertex in U is not bounded by a fixed constant.*

Moreover, we can show the time complexities of this problem in the cases whether or not each condition of Theorem 18.2 is satisfied. We summarize them in the next table. "T" means that the condition is satisfied and "F" means not satisfied. And "*" may be either "T" or "F". The class GI is the set of problems with a polynomial-time reduction to the graph isomorphism problem.

18.3 A Pattern Matching Algorithm for GC-Patterns

We assume that a given GC-pattern h satisfies the conditions of Theorem 18.2. And let $(T, \mathcal{X})$ be a normalized tree-decomposition of $(V(h), E(h))$.

In our algorithm, we construct a whole witness structure from a union of partial witness structures. So we need the following definition.

Definition 18.1. For two GC-subpatterns h_1, h_2 of h, let $\mathcal{W}_1$ and $\mathcal{W}_2$ be h_1- and h_2-witness structures, respectively. Then, we say that $\mathcal{W}_1$ *does not contradict* $\mathcal{W}_2$ if it satisfies the following conditions. (1) $W_1(v) = W_2(v)$ for any $v \in V(h_1) \cap V(h_2)$, (2) for any $u \in V(h_i)$ and $v \in V(h_2)$, $\{u, v\} \in E(h) \Leftrightarrow W_1(u)$ and $W_2(v)$ are adjacent.

And, we construct a partial witness structure from an injection.

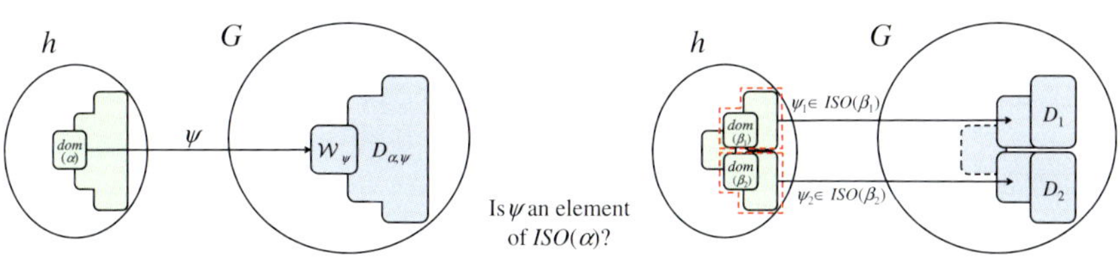

Fig. 18.2 The algorithm incrementally decides whether a node mapping ψ is an element of $ISO(\alpha)$ or not.

Definition 18.2. Let *dom* be a set of contractible vertices, all of those neighbors, and some uncontractible vertices of h. Then, for an injection $\psi : dom \to V(G)$, we construct a *ψ-structure* $\mathcal{W}_\psi = \{W_\psi(v) | v \in dom\}$ as follows: (1) $W_\psi(v) = \{\psi(v)\}$ if v is uncontractible, (2) otherwise, $W_\psi(v)$ is the vertex set of the connected component in $G[V(G) \setminus \psi(N(v))]$ that includes $\psi(v)$.

If ψ is suitable, then $\mathcal{W}_\psi$ becomes one of $h[dom]$-witness structures.

Definition 18.3. For a node $\alpha \in T$, let $dom(\alpha)$ be a vertex set $\mathcal{X}(\alpha) \cup \{N(v) | v \in \mathcal{X}(\alpha) \cap U\}$. And, we say that a mapping $\psi : dom(\alpha) \to V(G)$ is a *node mapping* of α if $\mathcal{W}_\psi$ is an $h[dom(\alpha)]$-witness structure.

Let α' be the parent node of α. Then $h[\mathcal{X}(T^{\downarrow\alpha}) \backslash \mathcal{X}(\alpha')]$ is connected. We define $D_{\alpha,\psi}$ corresponding to $h[\mathcal{X}(T^{\downarrow\alpha}) \setminus \mathcal{X}(\alpha')]$ as follows. $D_{\alpha,\psi}$ is the connected component in the graph obtained from G by removing $W_\psi(h)$ for each $h \in \mathcal{X}(\alpha) \cap \mathcal{X}(\alpha')$ that includes $W_\psi(v)$ where $v \in \mathcal{X}(\alpha) \setminus \mathcal{X}(\alpha')$. Moreover we define $ISO(\alpha)$ as the set of all node mappings ψ satisfying the following condition. $G[V(D_{\alpha,\psi}) \cup \bigcup_{v \in dom(\alpha)} W_\psi(v)]$ has an $h[\mathcal{X}(T^{\downarrow\alpha}) \cup dom(\alpha)]$-witness structure such that does not contradict $\mathcal{W}_\psi$. From these definitions, we can easily see the following lemma.

Lemma 1. *A GC-pattern h matches a graph G if and only if $ISO(r_T) \neq \emptyset$ where r_T is the root of T.*

Let $\beta_1, \ldots, \beta_m$ be the children of α. Then the GC-pattern obtained from $h[\mathcal{X}(T^{\downarrow\alpha}) \setminus \mathcal{X}(\alpha')]$ by removing $\mathcal{X}(\alpha)$ has m connected components. Similarly, the graph obtained from $D_{\alpha,\psi}$ by removing $W_\psi(v)$ for each $v \in \mathcal{X}(\alpha)$ has m' connected components D_i ($i = 1, \ldots, m'$). If $m \neq m'$, G has no h-witness structure that does not contradict $\mathcal{W}_\psi$. Afterwards, we assume that $m = m'$. For each β_i, we assume that there is a node mapping $\psi_{\beta_i} \in ISO(\beta_i)$ such that $\mathcal{W}_{\psi_{\beta_i}}$ does not contradict $\mathcal{W}_\psi$. Let $\mathcal{W}_{\beta_i}$ be a witness structure that makes ψ_{β_i} an element of $ISO(\beta_i)$. Then we construct a witness structure $\mathcal{W}$ as the union of $\mathcal{W}_\psi$ and each $\mathcal{W}_{\beta_i}$. Then, the constructed $\mathcal{W}$ makes ψ an element of $ISO(\alpha)$ (Fig. 18.1).

Lemma 2. *$\psi \in ISO(\alpha)$ if and only if there is an injection from $\beta_1, \ldots, \beta_m$ to $D_1, \ldots, D_m$ satisfying the following condition. If β_i is mapped to D_j,* *there is a node mapping ψ_{β_i} of β_i such that $\mathcal{W}_{\psi_\beta}$ does not contradict $\mathcal{W}_\psi$ and $(D_{\beta_i,\psi_i} = D_j) \wedge (\psi_{\beta_i} \in ISO(\beta_i))$.*

For deciding whether $\psi \in ISO(\alpha)$ or not, we construct a bipartite graph defined as follows and solve the perfect matching problem on the bipartite graph.

Definition 18.4. For node α, let B be the set of all children of α. And let C be the set of all connected components of the graph obtained from $D_{\alpha,\psi}$ by removing $W_\psi(h)$ for each $h \in \mathcal{X}(\alpha)$. And, let $E = \{\{\beta, D\} | (\beta \in B) \wedge (D \in C) \wedge (\exists \psi_\beta \in ISO(\beta, G)[(\mathcal{W}_{\psi_\beta}$ does not contradict $\mathcal{W}_\psi) \wedge (D = D_{\beta,\psi_\beta})]\}$. Then we define a bipartite graph $Q(\alpha, \psi) = (B, C, E)$.

Lemma 3. *The bipartite graph $Q(\alpha, \psi)$ has a perfect matching if and only if $\psi \in ISO(\alpha)$.*

We give a formal description of our algorithm in Fig. 18.3. The correctness of our algorithm is shown from Lemmas 1 and 3. Our algorithm runs in $O(N^{k(d+1)+1.5})$ time, where N is the number of vertices of G and d is the maximum degree of the vertices of U. Then we can show Theorem 18.2.

Algorithm CONTRACTION_PATTERN_MATCHING;
Input: A GC-pattern h, a graph G,
  a normalized tree-decomposition $(T, \mathcal{X})$ of $(V(h), E(h))$;
begin
  forall $\alpha \in V(T)$ **do** $ISO(\alpha) := \emptyset$; // *Initialization.*
  while $\exists \alpha \in V(T)$ $[ISO(\beta) \neq \emptyset$ for all children β of $\alpha]$ **do** // *Main Processes.*
    forall node mappings ψ of α **do**
      if NODE_MAPPING_EXTENSION$(h, (T, \mathcal{X}), \alpha, G, \psi)$ returns *yes* **then**
        $ISO(\alpha) := ISO(\alpha) \cup \{\psi\}$;
  if $ISO(r_T) \neq \emptyset$ **then return** *yes* **else return** *no* // *Decision.*
end;

Procedure NODE_MAPPING_EXTENSION$(h, (T, \mathcal{X}), \alpha, G, \psi)$;
Input: a GC-pattern h, a normalized tree-decomposition $(T, \mathcal{X})$,
  a node $\alpha \in V(T)$, a graph G, and a node mapping ψ of α;
begin
  Construct a bipartite graph $Q(\alpha, \psi)$ from h, $(T, \mathcal{X})$, α, G, and ψ;
  if $Q(\alpha, \psi)$ has a perfect matching **then return** *yes* **else return** *no*
end;

Fig. 18.3 GC-pattern matching algorithm.

Bibliography

A. E. Brouwer and H. J. Veldman. Contractibility and NP-completeness. *J. Graph Theor.*, **11**, 71–79. 1987.

T. Horváth and J. Ramon. Efficient frequent connected subgraph mining in graphs of bounded tree-width. *Theor. Comput. Sci.*, **411(31–33)**, 2784–2797. 2010.

T. Horváth, J. Ramon and S. Wrobel. Frequent subgraph mining in outer-planar graphs. *Data Min. Knowl. Disc.*, **21(3)**, 472–508. 2010.

T. Miyahara, T. Shoudai, T. Uchida, K. Takahashi and H. Ueda. Polynomial time matching algorithms for tree-like structured patterns in knowledge discovery. In T. Terano, H. Liu and A. L. P. Chen (eds). *Proceedings of the Fourth European Conference on Principles and Practice of Knowledge Discovery in Databases*, LNAI vol. 1805. Springer, Berlin, pp. 5–16. 2000.

T. Nagoya, S. Tani and S. Toda. A polynomial-time algorithm for counting graph isomorphisms among partial k-trees (in Japanese). *IEICE T. Inf. Syst.*, **J85-D1(5)**, 424–435. 2002.

T. Yamada and T. Shoudai. Efficient pattern matching on graph patterns of bounded treewidth. *Electron. Notes Discrete Math.*, **37**, 117–122. 2011.

H. Yamasaki, Y. Sasaki, T. Shoudai, T. Uchida and Y. Suzuki. Learning block-preserving graph patterns and its application to data mining. *Mach. Learn.*, **76(1)**, 137–173. 2009.

Chapter 19

mLynx: Relational Mutual Information

Nicola Di Mauro, Teresa M.A. Basile,
Stefano Ferilli and Floriana Esposito
Department of Computer Science,
LACAM laboratory University of Bari "Aldo Moro", Italy

This paper represents a further steps in combining Information Theory tools with relational learning. We show how mutual information can be used to find relevant relational features.

19.1 Introduction

According to Tishby *et al.* [Tishby *et al.* (1999)], Information Theory provides a natural quantitative approach to the question of *relevant information* and an alternative view for Machine Learning because of the abstract and principled concept of *mutual information* (MI). For instance, they provided the Information Bottleneck (IB) method taking in mind that any learning process has to deal with the basic tradeoff between the complexity of the available data representation and the best accuracy that this complexity enables. The first approach using the IB method for Statistical Relational Learning (SRL) [Getoor and Taskar (2007)] has been proposed in [Riguzzi and Di Mauro (2012)] and this chapter is a new step forward for information theoretic relational learning. We use the MI descriptor from Information Theory to propose an SRL method that learns the model by finding the most relevant features. Given a training dataset $\mathcal{D} = \{\mathbf{x}_i, c_i\}_{i=1}^n$ of n relational examples, characterized by a set of m relational features

$X = \{f_i\}_{i=1}^m$, and a target discrete random variable c, generating class labels c_i, the aim of this chapter is to find a subset of X that optimally characterizes the variable c, minimizing the classifier's probability error. We want to find the maximal statistical dependency of the target class c on the data distribution in the selected subspace (*maximal dependency*), that usually corresponds to the *maximal relevance* of the features to the target class c.

Most of the Inductive Logic Programming (ILP) learning approaches build models by searching for *good* relational features guided by a scoring function, such as in FOIL. In many SRL systems this *feature construction* process is combined with a discriminative/generative probabilistic method in order to deal with noisy data and uncertainty, such as in `kFOIL` [Landwehr *et al.* (2006)], `rsLDA` [Taranto *et al.* (2011)], and Markov Logic Networks (MLNs) [Richardson and Pedro (2006)]. The combination may be *static* or *dynamic*. In the former case (*static propositionalization*), the constructed features are usually considered as boolean features and used offline as input to a propositional statistical learner; while in the latter case (*dynamic propositionalization*), the feature construction and probabilistic model selection are combined into a single process. We propose the `mLynx` system that, after a feature construction phase, stochastically searches, guided by the mutual information criterion, the set of the most relevant features, minimizing a Bayesian classifier's probability error.

19.2 Feature Construction and Classification

This section reports the first components of the `mLynx` system, extending `Lynx` [Di Mauro *et al.* (2011)], that implements a probabilistic query-based classifier based on mutual information. Specifically, we start to report its feature construction capability and the adopted query-based classification model. The adopted mutual information feature selection approach will be presented in Section 19.3.

The first step of `mLynx` carries out a feature construction process by mining frequent Prolog queries (relational features), adopting an approach similar to that reported in [Kramer and De Raedt (2001)]. The algorithm for frequent relational query mining is based on the same idea as the generic level-wise search method, performing a breadth-first search in the lattice of queries ordered by a specialization relation $\preceq$. The algorithm starts with the most general Prolog queries. At each step it tries to specialize all the candidate frequent queries, discarding the non-frequent ones and storing those whose length is less or equal to a user-specified input parameter. Furthermore, for each new refined query, semantically equivalent patterns are detected, by using the θ_{OI}-subsumption relation, and discarded. In the specialization phase the specialization operator, basically, adds atoms to the query.

Now, having a set of relational features, we need a way to use them in order to correctly classify unseen examples. Given the training set $\mathcal{D} = \{\mathbf{x}_i, c_i\}_{i=1}^n$ of n relational examples, where c denotes the discrete class random variables taking values from $\{1, 2, \ldots, Q\}$, the goal is to learn a function $h : x \rightarrow c$ from $\mathcal{D}$ that predicts the label for each unseen instance. Let $\mathcal{Q}$, with $|\mathcal{Q}| = d$, be the set of features obtained in the first step of the `mLynx` system (the queries mined from $\mathcal{D}$). For each example $\mathbf{x}_k$ we can build a d-component vector-valued $\mathbf{x}_k = (x_k^1, x_k^2, \ldots, x_k^d)$ random variable where each $x_k^i \in \mathbf{x}_k$ is 1 if the query $q_i \in \mathcal{Q}$ subsumes example $\mathbf{x}_k$, and 0 otherwise, for each $1 \leq i \leq d$.

Using the Bayes' theorem, if $p(c_j)$ describes the prior probability of class c_j, then the posterior probability $p(c_j|\mathbf{x})$ can be computed from $p(\mathbf{x}|c_j)$ as

$$p(c_j|\mathbf{x}) = \frac{p(\mathbf{x}|c_j)p(c_j)}{\sum_{i=1}^{Q} p(\mathbf{x}|c_i)p(c_i)}.$$

Given a set of discriminant functions $\{g_i(\mathbf{x})\}_{i=1}^{Q}$, a classifier is said to assign the vector $\mathbf{x}$ to class c_j if $g_j(\mathbf{x}) > g_i(\mathbf{x})$ for all $j \neq i$. Taking $g_i(\mathbf{x}) = P(c_i|\mathbf{x})$, the maximum discriminant function corresponds to the *maximum a posteriori* (MAP) probability. For minimum error rate classification, the following discriminant function will be used: $g_i(\mathbf{x}) = \ln p(\mathbf{x}|c_i) + \ln p(c_i)$. Given $\mathbf{x} = (x_1, \ldots, x_d)$, we define $p_{ij} = \mathrm{Prob}(x_i = 1|c_j)$ with the components of $\mathbf{x}$ being statistically independent for all $x_i \in \mathbf{x}$. The estimator $\hat{p}_{ij}$ of the factor p_{ij} corresponds to the frequency counts on the training examples: $\hat{p}_{ij} = \eta_{i,j}(\mathcal{D}, \mathcal{Q}) = |\{\mathbf{x}_k, c_k \in \mathcal{D}|c_k = j \wedge q_i \in \mathcal{Q} \text{ subsumes } \mathbf{x}_k\}|/\eta_j(\mathcal{D})$, where $\eta_j(\mathcal{D}) = |\{\mathbf{x}_k, c_k \in \mathcal{D}|c_k = j|$. The estimator $\hat{p}(c_j)$ of $p(c_j)$ is $\eta_j(\mathcal{D})/|\mathcal{D}|$. By assuming conditional independence $p(\mathbf{x}|c_j) = \prod_{i=1}^{d}(p_{ij})^{x_i}(1 - p_{ij})^{1-x_i}$, yielding the discriminant function

$$g_j(\mathbf{x}) = \ln p(\mathbf{x}|c_j) + \ln p(c_j) = \sum_{i=1}^{d} x_i \ln \frac{p_{ij}}{1 - p_{ij}} + \sum_{i=1}^{d} \ln(1 - p_{ij}) + \ln p(c_j).$$

The minimum probability error is achieved by deciding c_k if $g_k(\mathbf{x}) \geq g_j(\mathbf{x})$ for all j and k.

19.3 Mutual Information Feature Selection

A formalization of the uncertainty of a random variable is the Shannon's entropy. Let x be a discrete random variable and $p(x)$ its probabilistic density function, then the entropy of x, a measure of uncertainty, is defined as usual by $H(x) = \mathbb{E}(I(x)) = \sum_i p(x_i)I(x) = -\sum_i p(x_i)\log p(x_i)$, assuming $p(x_i)\log p(x_i) = 0$ in case of $p(x_i) = 0$. For two random variables x and y, their joint entropy is defined as $H(x,y) = -\sum_{i,j} p(x_i,y_j)\log p(x_i,y_j)$, and the conditional entropy is defined as $H(x|y) = -\sum_{i,j} p(x_i,y_j)\log p(x_i|y_j)$. From the last definition, the chain rule for conditional entropy is $H(x,y) = H(x) + H(y|x)$.

The *mutual information* $I(x;y)$ measures how much (on average) the realization of the random variable y tells about the realization of x:

$$I(x;y) = H(x) - H(x|y) = \sum_{i,j} p(x_i,y_j)\log\frac{p(x_i,y_j)}{p(x_i)p(y_j)}. \qquad (19.1)$$

Given a set X of M features, mutual information feature selection corresponds to find a set $S = \{f_i\}_{i=1}^m \subset X$ whose elements jointly have the largest dependency on the class c, corresponding to optimize the *maximum dependency* condition:

$$\max_{S\subset X} I(S;c). \qquad (19.2)$$

Directly computing (19.2) has some difficulties [Peng *et al.* (2005)], and different approaches to approximate it have been proposed. The approach we used in this chapter is the *minimal redundancy and maximal relevance* criterion (mRMR) [Peng *et al.* (2005)]. An approximation of (19.2) can be obtained by optimizing the *maximal relevance* criterion:

$$\max_{S\subset X}\frac{1}{|S|}\sum_{f_i\in S} I(f_i;c). \qquad (19.3)$$

In maximizing the relevance, the selected features f_i are required to have the largest mutual information $I(f_i;c)$ with the class c (i.e., the largest dependency on the class). Combinations of individually good features do not necessarily lead to good classification performance. Selecting features according to (19.3) could lead to a set containing high redundant features. Hence, in order to have mutually exclusive features the criterion of *minimal redundancy* should be optimized:

$$\min_{S\subset X}\frac{1}{|S|^2}\sum_{f_i,f_j\in S} I(f_i;f_j). \qquad (19.4)$$

The mRMR combines these two last criteria by simultaneously optimizing (19.3) and (19.4). A possible technique may be to *incrementally search* near-optimal features as follows. Assume S is the subset of m features already selected. The incremental algorithm selects the next feature $f_j \in X \backslash S$ to be added to S by optimizing the following condition:

$$\max_{f_j \in \mathcal{X} \backslash S} \left(I(f_j; c) - \frac{1}{|S|} \sum_{f_i \in S} I(f_j; f_i) \right). \tag{19.5}$$

Starting from an empty set and using (19.5) to incrementally select the features to add, a first problem is how to determine the optimal number of features m. Furthermore, even fixing in advance the number m of features to be selected, another problem is that this incremental approach does not assure to find the global optimal solution, and repeated executions could lead the search to be trapped in the same local optimum solution.

One way to decrease the probability of being stuck in a local maximum and avoiding to test all the $2^M - 1$ possible subset solutions, is to consider the use of a *stochastic local search* (SLS) procedure. In this paper we propose a new SLS procedure, similar to the Randomized Iterative Improvement method, able to solve the above problems, as reported in Fig. 19.1. Given X the set of available features, the algorithm starts by randomly selecting a feature $f_s \in X$, and setting $S = \{f_s\}$. Then, it iteratively adds a new feature $f_i \in X \backslash S$ to S according to (19.5) until the new information for the class variable c contributed by the feature f_j given S is greater than a threshold α. This helps the search to be immunized against noisy data, to overcome over-fitting problems, and to solve the problem of how to choose the number m of features to be selected. Furthermore, to implement diversification in the algorithm, the iterative construction phase can choose to make a random walk (by adding a random feature) with a walking probability wp.

After each construction phase, the found solution is evaluated according to the classifier's probability error, and the process is restarted hoping to find a better solution. Given S the selected features, for each example e_j we let the classifier find the MAP hypothesis $\widehat{h}_P(\mathbf{x}_j) = \arg\max_i g_i(\mathbf{x}_j)$ according to the Bayesian discriminant function reported in Section 19.2 where $\mathbf{x}_j$ is the feature-based representation of the example e_j obtained using the queries in S. Hence the optimization problem corresponds to minimize the expectation $\mathbb{E}[\mathbf{1}_{\widehat{h}_P(\mathbf{x}_i) \neq c_i}]$ where $\mathbf{1}_{\widehat{h}_P(\mathbf{x}_i) \neq c_i}$ is the characteristic function

Algorithm 1: Randomized sequential forward feature selection

input : X: input features; wp: walking probability; $restarts$: number of restarts; α: threshold
output: $\hat{S}$: the optimal subset

$S = \emptyset$; $i = 0$; $bestValue = \infty$;
while $i < restarts$ **do**
  randomly select a feature f_s from X;
  $S = \{f_s\}$; $improve =$ true;
  while $improve$ **and** $|S| \neq |\mathcal{X}|$ **do**
    if $wp <$ `rand(0,1)` **then**
      $\max_{f_j \in \mathcal{X} \setminus S} \mathrm{mRMR}(f_j, c, S) = \max_{f_j \in \mathcal{X} \setminus S} \left(I(f_j; c) - \frac{1}{|S|} \sum_{f_i \in S} I(f_j; f_i) \right)$;
      if $\mathrm{mRMR}(f_j, c, S) > \alpha$ **then**
        $S = S \cup \{f_j\}$;
      else
        $improve =$ false;
    else
      randomly select $f_j \in \mathcal{X} \setminus S$;
      $S = S \cup \{f_j\}$;
  if $err_D(S) < bestValue$ **then**
    $\hat{S} = S$; $bestValue = err_D(S)$;
  $i = i + 1$;
return $\hat{S}$

Fig. 19.1 The learning framework.

of the training example e_i returning 1 if $\widehat{h}_P(\mathbf{x}_i) \neq c_i$, and 0 otherwise. Finally, the number of classification errors made by the Bayesian classifier using the queries S is $err_{\mathcal{D}}(S) = |\mathcal{D}|\mathbb{E}[\mathbf{1}_{\widehat{h}_P(\mathbf{x}_i) \neq c_i}]$.

19.4 Experiments

We tested the proposed `mLynx` approach on the well-known Mutagenesis ILP dataset, and on the widely used UW-CSE SRL dataset [Parag and Pedro (2005)]. The Mutagenesis dataset regards the problem to predict the mutagenicity of a set of compounds. As in [Landwehr *et al.* (2006)] we used atom and bond information only. `mLynx` has been compared to `kFOIL` [Landwehr *et al.* (2006)], whose results with a tenfold cross validation are listed in Table 19.1. For `mLynx` we set $\alpha = 10^{-2}$, $restarts = 100$, and $wp = 0.05$. The accuracy obtained with `mLynx` is higher than that obtained

Table 19.1 Average accuracy on the Mutagenesis dataset for `mLynx` and `kFOIL`.

Dataset	`mLynx`	`kFOIL`
Mutagenesis r.f.	83.94 ± 6.2	77.64 ± 6.5
Mutagenesis r.u.	80.90 ± 15.7	77.50 ± 18.44

Table 19.2 AUC for ROC and PR on the UW-CSE dataset for `mLynx` and `Alchemy`.

	`mLynx`		`Alchemy`	
	AUC ROC	AUC PR	AUC ROC	AUC PR
ai	0.929	0.295	0.903	0.286
graphics	0.960	0.697	0.967	0.313
language	0.980	0.797	0.823	0.188
systems	0.933	0.252	0.914	0.224
theory	0.922	0.427	0.867	0.184
mean	0.945	0.494	0.895	0.239

with `kFOIL` with a difference that is statistically significant with p-value of 0.0455 for the Mutagenesis r.f. dataset.

The UW-CSE dataset [Parag and Pedro (2005)] regards the Department of Computer Science and Engineering at the University of Washington, describing relationships among professors, students, courses and publications with 3,212 true ground atoms over 12 predicates. The task is to predict the relationship `advisedBy(X,Y)` using in turn four of the five research areas (ai, graphics, language, theory and systems) for training and the remaining one for testing as in [Parag and Pedro (2005)]. For `mLynx` we set $\alpha = 10^{-4}$, $restarts = 100$, and $wp = 0.05$. For Alchemy [Richardson and Pedro (2006)] we used the hand-coded MLN reported in [Parag and Pedro (2005)] including formulas stating regularities, and the applying Alchemy to discriminative learn the weights and testing the resulting MLN on the testing set using the MC-SAT. Table 19.2 shows the AUC for ROC and Precision-Recall (PR) for `mLynx` and `Alchemy`. The results show that `mLynx` generally improves on `Alchemy` with a difference that is statistically significant with p-value of 0.095 for ROC and with p-value 0.052 for PR.

Bibliography

N. Di Mauro, T. M. A. Basile, S. Ferilli and F. Esposito. Optimizing probabilistic models for relational sequence learning. *19th International Symposium on Methodologies for Intelligent Systems*, LNAI, vol. 6804 pp. 240–249. 2011. ISMIS 2011: 28–30 June 2011.

L. Getoor and B. Taskar. *Introduction to Statistical Relational Learning (Adaptive Computation and Machine Learning)*. The MIT Press, Cambridge, Massachusetts. 2007.

S. Kramer and L. De Raedt. Feature construction with version spaces for biochemical applications. In C. E. Brodley and A. P. Danyluk (eds). *Proceedings of the 18th International Conference on Machine Learning*, pp. 258–265. Morgan Kaufmann, Burlington, Massachusetts. 2001.

N. Landwehr, A. Passerini, L. De Raedt and P. Frasconi. kFOIL: Learning simple relational kernels. In A. Cohn (ed.). *Proceedings of the Twenty-First National Conference on Artificial Intelligence*. AAAI Press, Boston, Massachusetts, pp. 389–394. 2006.

H. Peng, F. Long and C. Ding. Feature selection based on mutual information: criteria of max-dependency, max-relevance, and min-redundancy. *IEEE T. Pattern Anal.*, **27(8)**, 1226–1238. 2005.

M. Richardson and P. Domingos. Markov logic networks. *Mach. Learn.*, **62(1–2)**, 107–136. 2006.

F. Riguzzi and N. Di Mauro. Applying the information bottleneck to statistical relational learning. *Mach. Learn.*, **86**, 89–114. 2012.

P. Singla and P. Domingos. Discriminative training of Markov logic networks. *Proceedings of the Twentieth National Conference on Artificial Intelligence*. AAAI Press, Boston, Massachusetts, pp. 868–873. 2005.

C. Taranto, N. Di Mauro and F. Esposito. rsLDA: A Bayesian hierarchical model for relational learning. In J. Zhang and G. Livraga (eds). *Proceedings of the 23rd International Conference on Data and Knowledge Engineering*. IEEE Press, New York, pp. 68–74. 2011.

N. Tishby, F. C. Pereira and W. Bialek. The information bottleneck method. In B. Hajek and R. S. Sreenivas (eds). *Proceedings of the 37th Annual Allerton Conference on Communication, Control, and* Computing. University of Illinois Press, Chicago, Illinois, pp. 368–377. 1999.

PART 4
Theory

Chapter 20

Machine Learning Coalgebraic Proofs

Ekaterina Komendantskaya

Department of Computing, University of Dundee, UK[1]

This chapter argues for a novel method to machine learn patterns in formal proofs using statistical machine learning methods. The method exploits coalgebraic approach to proofs. The success of the method is demonstrated on three applications allowing to distinguish well-formed proofs from ill-formed proofs, identify families of proofs and even families of potentially provable goals.

20.1 Background

Research in formal logic has always aspired to design a formal theory based upon a language expressive enough to allow formalisation of complex mathematical theories and (later) programming tasks. Once a given problem is formulated in the language of such a theory, one can use the theory to prove or verify various statements, theorems and properties.

One of the major steps towards this goal was made in the mid 1960s, when *Logic Programming* — a family of programming languages based upon first-order logic — was designed and implemented. The two major methods used in logic programming were first-order unification and resolution [Robinson (1965)]; first-order unification is decidable and SLD-resolution based on it yields efficient implementations. Many state-of-the art tools currently used in formal methods are based on this methodology.

[1]The work was supported by the Engineering and Physical Sciences Research Council, UK; Postdoctoral Fellow research grant EP/F044046/2.

Over the past decade, higher-order proof assistants (also called Interactive Theorem Provers, or ITPs), such as ACL2, AGDA, Coq and Isabelle(HOL) have proven to be suitable for expressing and solving sophisticated mathematical problems (e.g. verification of the Four-Colour Theorem in Coq), and industrial-scale verification of very complex computer systems (e.g. verification of computer micro-processors in ACL2).

However, currently, ITPs require considerable programming skills, constant interaction between the prover and the programmer, and overall are time-consuming and hence expensive. Some aspects of higher-order theorem proving may never be fully automated due to their hardness: for example, higher-order unification is undecidable; termination of functions cannot be automatically decided in the general case due to the Halting Problem.

Programs in ITPs contain thousands of lemmas and theorems of variable sizes and complexities; each proof is constructed by combining a finite number of tactics. Some proofs may yield the same pattern of tactics, and can be fully automated, and others may require programmer's intervention. In this case, a manually found proof for one problematic lemma may serve as a template for several other lemmas needing a manual proof. Automated discovery of common proof-patterns using tools of statistical machine learning is the goal of the method ML-CAP (for *Machine-Learning Coalgebraic Automated Proofs*).

Another feature of theorem proving is that unsuccessful attempts at proofs, although discarded when the correct proof is found, play an important role in proof discovery. This kind of "negative" information finds no place in mathematical textbooks or libraries of automated proofs. Conveniently, analysis of both positive and negative examples is inherent in statistical machine learning [Bishop (2006); Duda *et al.* (2001)]; and the ML-CAP method we propose exploits this.

Figure 20.1 shows other AI methods that may eventually serve for various automation or optimisation tasks in ITPs. ML-CAP is one possible *proof-pattern recognition* method in this figure.

Many related attempts to exploit the inductive nature of formal reasoning are related to methods of *Inductive Logic*, (e.g. [Basin *et al.* (2005); Colton (2002); Ireland *et al.* (2010); Johansson *et al.* (2010); Kersting *et al.* (2006); Sorge *et al.* (2008); De Raedt (2008)]). In contrast to them, we propose to enrich the inductive logic methods with the tools of statistical machine learning [Bishop (2006); Duda *et al.* (2001)], such as neural

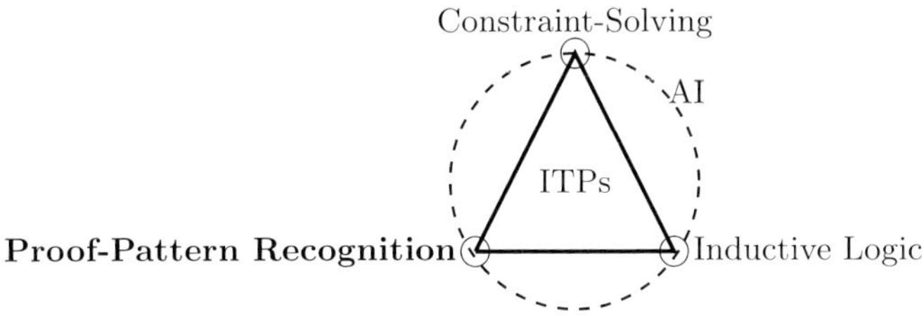

Fig. 20.1 Possible extensions of formal methods coming from AI.

networks or kernels/SVMs, known for applications in statistical pattern recognition.

Unlike logic programming that has been successfully adapted to AI purposes, higher-order theorem proving and ITPs are commonly seen as areas completely disjointed from AI. Our ML-CAP method is intended to fill this gap. A related attempt to apply machine learning methods in higher-order logics was the application of *kernel methods* to manipulate terms of λ-calculus [Gartner *et al.* (2004); Lloyd (2003); Passerini *et al.* (2006)].

20.2 Methodology

The method *ML-CAP* we propose here is a pilot attempt to advance implementation of formal proofs by employing methods from Machine Learning and Coalgebra; see Fig. 20.2.

There are some serious constraints on merging machine-learning and formal methods. The first constraint is zero-tolerance to "noise" in the syntax of ITPs (which made them so valuable for formal verification), whereas noise is part of statistical approximation and is endemic in machine learning methods. This makes for a clash in approaches to the syntax. Neuro-symbolic systems often solve this problem by "propositionalising" the syntax and working with (vectors of) truth values instead. This solution, however, does not work for some fragments of first-order logics or for higher-order logics.

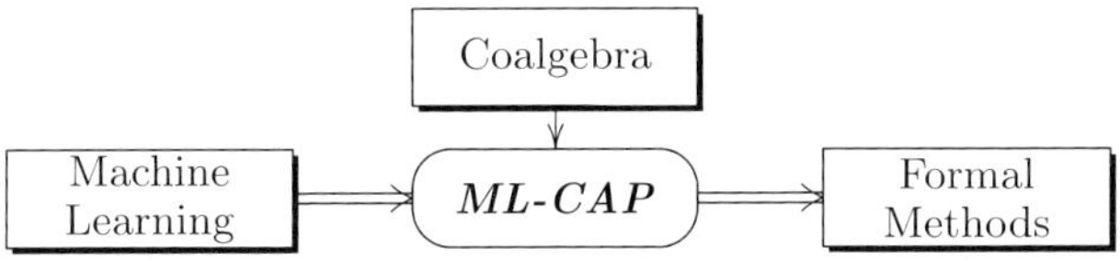

Fig. 20.2 Methods used in ML-CAP.

The second obstacle is that many conventional algorithms used in formal methods and involving variable dependencies tend to be implemented sequentially, while statistical machine learning lends itself to concurrency, with many algorithms coming from linear algebra.

These two obstacles can be avoided if we use coalgebraic representation of proofs, [Komendantskaya and Power (2011a,b)]. Coalgebraic representation of formal proofs facilitates extraction of important proof features that can be classified and "learned" using statistical machine learning methods, see also Fig. 20.2.

Coalgebraic methods occur in different areas of computer science, and range from categorical (structural) semantics of programming languages, [Jacobs and Rutten (1997); Komendantskaya and Power (2011a,b); Plotkin (2004); Rutten (2000); Turi and Plotkin (1997)] and models of concurrent systems [Milner (1989)] to programming with infinite data-structures in Type Theory [Bertot and Komendantskaya (2008); Coquand (1994)] or in Logic Programming [Gupta *et al.* (2007); Simon *et al.* (2007); Komendantskaya and Power (2011a,b)]. However, the potential of coalgebraic methods in statistical machine learning has not yet received equal attention. See [Chaput *et al.* (2009)] for a relation between coalgebra and probabilistic systems.

Generally, the coalgebraic approach to computation brings two advantages: coinductive proofs and programs are often concurrent and/or potentially infinite. Coalgebraic methods offer ways to reform the classical approach to (semantics of) computations in terms of input/output in favour of an approach that pays attention to structure, repeating patterns in computations, and observables of program execution. The main hypothesis of the ML-CAP method is that these properties of coalgebraic methods make it possible to tackle some problematic aspects of formal reasoning using machinery developed by statistical pattern recognition [Bishop (2006); Duda *et al.* (2001)].

The method ML-CAP arose from the work on coalgebraic semantics for logic programming [Komendantskaya and Power (2011a)], which gave rise to the novel algorithm for performing coinductive concurrent derivations in logic programs [Komendantskaya and Power (2011b)]. Our recent experiments have shown that these coalgebraic proofs yield excellent results in statistical pattern recognition. All experiments we report here concern first-order logic programs corresponding to inductive and coinductive types in ITPs.

20.3 Agenda and Preliminary Results

In this section, we summarise some of the results concerning data-mining proofs in logic programming. When working with automated proofs, we use their representation as coinductive proof trees, [Komendantskaya and Power (2011a)]. We have identified four benchmark problems for machine learning formal proofs, as follows.

Problem 1. Classification of well-formed and ill-formed proofs. *Given a set of examples of well-formed and ill-formed coinductive trees, classify any new example of a coinductive tree in either of the two classes.*

This task is one of the most difficult for pattern recognition (see Table 20.1), and at the same time, perhaps the least significant for practical purposes, as automated proof methods already work well for such tasks.

A more interesting task in practical terms is recognition of various proof families among well-formed proofs, as this is something that may help to optimize proof search.

Problem 2. Discovery of proof families. *Given a set of positive and negative examples of well-formed coinductive proof trees belonging to a proof family, classify any new example of a coinductive tree, whether it belongs to the given proof family.*

This problem has practical applications: finding that some unfinished proof belongs to a family of successful proofs may save intermediate derivation steps; and knowing that some unfinished proof belongs to the family of failed proofs, may serve as a hint to abandon any future attempts.

Table 20.1 Summary of the results of classification of coinductive derivation trees for the four main classification problems, performed in neural networks (first four columns), and in SVMs with kernel functions (columns five and six); the latter is only tested for the derivation trees for `Stream`.

	`ListNat` best test	`ListNat` best average	`Stream` best test	`Stream` best average	SVM best test	SVM best average
Problem 1	88.2%	76.4%	85	84.3 %	100 %	89 %
Problem 2	100 %	92.3%	100 %	99.1 %	n/a	88 %
Problem 2′	n/a	n/a	100 %	90.6 %	n/a	88%
Problem 3	100 %	99 %	n/a	n/a	n/a	n/a
Problem 4	n/a	n/a	100 %	85.7 %	n/a	90%

The next problem is discovery of the proof families comprised of coinductive proof trees that may potentially lead to successful proofs — *success families*.

Problem 3. Discovery of potentially successful proofs. *Given a set of positive and negative examples of well-formed coinductive trees belonging to a success family, classify any new example of a coinductive tree, whether it belongs to the given success family.*

Finally, when it comes to coinductive logic programs defining infinite data structures, such as streams, detection of success families is impossible. In such cases, detection of well-typed and ill-typed proofs within a proof family will be an alternative to determining success families.

Problem 4. Discovery of ill-typed proofs. *Given a set of positive and negative examples of ill-typed coinductive trees belonging to a given proof family, classify any new example of a coinductive tree, whether it is ill-typed or well-typed.*

To machine learn classes of proof trees using statistical pattern recognition, we used several well-known tools, such as neural networks and SVMs. All experiments involving neural networks were made in MATLAB Neural Network Toolbox (a pattern-recognition package), with a standard three-layer feed-forward network, with sigmoid hidden and output neurons. The network was trained with scaled conjugate gradient back-propagation. Such networks can classify vectors arbitrarily well, given enough neurons in the hidden layer, we used 40, 50, 60, 70, 90 hidden neurons for various experiments. All experiments involving SVMs were performed in MATLAB Bioinformatics toolbox (an SVM package with Gaussian Radial Basis kernel).

We used datasets of coinductive proof trees of various sizes — from 120 to 400 examples of coinductive derivation trees for various experiments; we tested all four problems stated above using proof trees for two distinct logic programs — `ListNat` defining lists of natural numbers and `Stream` defining infinite streams of bits. Table 20.1 shows the results.

Overall, the success rate of the classification results well exceeded our initial expectations. Only **Problem 1** results were somewhat disconcerting, but we think this problem has less practical impact. The results indicate that well-founded coinductive proof trees possess a number of strongly correlated features that determine the variety of meta-properties of the trees given by **Problems 1–4**, and such properties can be detected by the state-of-the-art pattern-recognition methods.

Bibliography

D. Basin, A. Bundy, D. Hutter and A. Ireland. *Rippling: Meta-level Guidance for Mathematical Reasoning.* Cambridge University Press, Cambridge. 2005.

Y. Bertot and E. Komendantskaya. Inductive and coinductive components of corecursive functions in Coq. *Electr. Notes Theor. Comput. Sci.*, **203(5)**, 25–47. 2008.

C. Bishop. *Pattern Recognition and Machine Learning.* Springer, Berlin. 2006.

P. Chaput, V. Danos, P. Panangaden and G. D. Plotkin. Approximating labelled Markov processes again! *Proceedings of the Third International Conference of Algebra and Coalgebra in Computer Science*, LNCS, vol. 5728. Springer, Berlin, pp. 145–156. 2009.

S. Colton. *Automated Theory Formation in Pure Mathematics.* Springer-Verlag, Berlin. 2002.

T. Coquand. Infinite objects in type theory, types for proofs and programs. In H. Barendregt and T. Nipkow (eds). *Selected Papers from the International Workshop on Types for Proofs and Programs*, LNCS, vol. 806. Springer-Verlag, Berlin 62–78. 1994.

L. De Raedt, *Logical and Relational Learning.* Springer, Berlin. 2008.

R. Duda, P. Hart and D. Stork. *Pattern Classification.* John Wiley, Hoboken, New Jersey. 2001.

T. Gartner, J. Lloyd and P. Flach. Kernels and distances for structured data. *Mach. Learn.*, **57(3)**, 205–232. 2004.

G. Gupta, A. Bansal, R. Min, L. Simon and A. Mallya. Coinductive logic programming and its applications. In V. Dahl and I. Niemelä (eds). *Proceedings of the 23rd International Conference*, LNCS vol. 4670. Springer, Berlin, pp. 27–44. 2007.

A. Ireland, G. Grov and Michael Butler. Reasoned modelling critics: turning failed proofs into modelling guidance, In M. Frappier, U. Glässer, S. Khurshid, R. Laleau and S. Reeves. *Proceedings of the Second International Conference Abstract State Machines, Alloy, B and Z*, LNCS, vol. 5977. Springer, Berlin, pp. 189–202. 2010.

B. Jacobs and J. Rutten. A tutorial on coalgebras and coinduction. *EATCS Bulletin*, **62**, 222–259. 1997.

M. Johansson, L. Dixon and Alan Bundy. Case-analysis for rippling and inductive proof. In M. Kaufmann and L. C. Paulson. *Proceedings of the First International Conference Interactive Theorem Proving*, LNCS, vol. 6172. Springer, Berlin, pp. 291–306. 2010.

E. Komendantskaya and J. Power. Coalgebraic derivations in logic programming. In M. Bezem (ed.). *Proceedings of the 25th International Workshop/20th Annual Conference of the EACSL.* Dagstuhl Publishing, Saarbrücken/Wadern, pp. 352–366. 2011a. Available online at: `http://www.dagstuhl.de/dagpub/978-3-939897-32-3`. Accessed. 13 August 2014.

E. Komendantskaya and J. Power. Coalgebraic semantics for derivations in logic programming. In A. Corradini, B. Klin and C. Cîrstea (eds). *Proceedings of the 4th International Conference on Algebra and Coalgebra in Computer*

Science, LNCS, vol. 6859. Springer, Berlin, pp. 268–282. 2011b.

K. Kersting, L. De Raedt and T. Raiko. Logical Hidden Markov Models. *J. Artif. Intell. Res.*, **25**, 425–456. 2006.

J. W. Lloyd. *Logic for Learning: Learning Comprehensible Theories from Structured Data*, Springer, Berlin. 2003.

R. Milner. *Communication and Concurrency*, Prentice Hall, Upper Saddle River, New Jersey. 1989.

A. Passerini, P. Frasconi and L. De Raedt. Kernels on Prolog proof trees: Statistical learning in the ILP setting. *J. Mach. Learn. Res.*, **7**, 307–342. 2006.

G. D. Plotkin. A structural approach to operational semantics. *J. Log. Algebr. Program.*, **60–61**, 17–139. 2004.

J. A. Robinson. A machine-oriented logic based on resolution principle. *J. ACM*, **12(1)**, 23–41. 1965.

J. J. M. M. Rutten. Universal coalgebra: a theory of systems. *Theor. Comput. Sci.*, **249**, 3–80. 2000.

L. Simon, A. Bansal, A. Mallya and G. Gupta. Co-logic programming: extending logic programming with coinduction. In L. Arge, C. Cachin, T. Jurdziński and A. Tarlecki (eds). *Proceedings of the 34th International Colloquium Automata, Languages and Programming*, LNCS, vol. 4596. Springer, Berlin, pp. 472–483. 2007.

V. Sorge, A. Meier, R. L. McCasland and S. Colton. Automatic construction and verification of isotopy invariants. *J. Autom. Reasoning*, **40(2–3)**, 221–243. 2008.

D. Turi and G. D. Plotkin. Towards a mathematical operational semantics. In E. Merelli and I. Petre (eds). *Proceedings of the 5th International Workshop on Interactions between Computer Science and Biology*, Electronic Notes in Theoretical Computer Science, vol. 306. Elsevier, Amsterdam, pp. 280–291. 1997.

Chapter 21

Can ILP Deal with Incomplete and Vague Structured Knowledge?

Francesca A. Lisi

Dipartimento di Informatica, Università degli Studi di Bari "Aldo Moro", Italy

Umberto Straccia

ISTI — CNR, Pisa, Italy

21.1 Introduction

Ontologies are currently a prominent source of *structured* knowledge. The logical languages known as *Description Logics* (DLs) [Baader *et al.* (2003)] play a key role in the design of ontologies as they are essentially the theoretical counterpart of the Web Ontology Language OWL 2[1] — the current standard language to represent ontologies — and its profiles.[2] For example, DL-Lite [Calvanese *et al.* (2006)] is the DL behind the *OWL 2 QL* profile and is especially aimed at applications that use very large volumes of instance data, and where query answering is the most important reasoning task.

Incompleteness and *vagueness* are inherent properties of knowledge in several real-world domains. DL-based ontology languages were born to address the former. Indeed, the Open World Assumption (OWA) holds in DLs. Fuzzy extensions of DLs have been more recently devised to address the latter (see the survey in [Lukasiewicz and Straccia (2008)]). They include, among others, a fuzzy DL-Lite like DL which has been implemented in the SoftFacts[3] system [Straccia (2010)].

---

[1] http://www.w3.org/TR/2009/REC-owl2-overview-20091027/.

[2] http://www.w3.org/TR/owl2-profiles/.

[3] http://www.straccia.info/software/SoftFacts/SoftFacts.html.

In this chapter, we sketch the results of our preliminary investigation of the issue of whether ILP can deal with incomplete and vague structured knowledge. More precisely, we provide the ingredients for learning fuzzy DL inclusion axioms with ILP. The resulting method adapts known results in ILP concerning the induction of crisp rules, notably FOIL [Quinlan (1990)], to the novel context of ontologies.

The chapter is organized as follows. Section 21.2 introduces fuzzy DLs. Section 21.3 describes our preliminary contribution to the problem in hand, also by means of an illustrative example. Section 21.4 concludes the chapter with final remarks and comparison with related work.

21.2 Fuzzy Description Logics

For computational reasons, the logic we adopt is based on a fuzzy extension of the DL-Lite DL without negation [Straccia (2010)]. It supports at the intentional level unary relations (called *concepts*) and binary relations (called *roles*), while also supporting n-ary relations (relational tables) at the extensional level.

Formally, a *knowledge base* $\mathcal{K} = \langle \mathcal{F}, \mathcal{O}, \mathcal{A} \rangle$ consists of a *facts component* $\mathcal{F}$, an *ontology component* $\mathcal{O}$ and an *abstraction component* $\mathcal{A}$. Information can be retrieved from $\mathcal{K}$ by means of an appropriate *query language.*

In order to deal with vagueness, Gödel logic [Hájek (1998)] is adopted, where

$$a \otimes b = \min(a, b),$$
$$a \oplus b = \max(a, b),$$
$$a \Rightarrow b = \begin{cases} 1 & \text{if } a \leq b \\ b & \text{otherwise} \end{cases}, \quad \text{and} \quad \ominus a = \begin{cases} 1 & \text{if } a = 0 \\ 0 & \text{otherwise} \end{cases}.$$

Facts Component. $\mathcal{F}$ is a finite set of expressions of the form

$$R(c_1, \ldots, c_n)[s], \tag{21.1}$$

where R is an n-ary relation, every c_i is a constant, and s is a degree of truth (or *score*) in $[0, 1]$ indicating to which extent the tuple $\langle c_1, \ldots, c_n \rangle$ is an instance of relation R. We may omit the score component and in such case the value 1 is assumed. Facts are stored in a relational database.

Ontology Component. $\mathcal{O}$ is a finite set of *inclusion axioms* having the form

$$Rl_1 \sqcap \ldots \sqcap Rl_m \sqsubseteq Rr, \tag{21.2}$$

where $m \geq 1$, all Rl_i and Rr have the same arity and each Rl_i is a so-called *left-hand relation* and Rr is a *right-hand relation*. We assume that relations occurring in $\mathcal{F}$ do not occur in inclusion axioms (and so we do not allow that database relation names occur in $\mathcal{O}$). The intuitive semantics is that if a tuple $\mathbf{c}$ is instance of each relation Rl_i to degree s_i then $\mathbf{c}$ is instance of Rr to degree $\min(s_1, \ldots, s_m)$.

The exact syntax of the relations appearing on the left-hand and right-hand side of inclusion axioms is specified below:

$$\begin{array}{lcl} Rl & \longrightarrow & A \mid R[i_1, i_2] \\ Rr & \longrightarrow & A \mid R[i_1, i_2] \mid \exists R.A \end{array} \tag{21.3}$$

where A is an atomic concept and R is a role with $1 \leq i_1, i_2 \leq 2$. Here $R[i_1, i_2]$ is the projection of the relation R on the columns i_1, i_2 (the order of the indexes matters). Hence, $R[i_1, i_2]$ has arity 2. Additionally, $\exists R.A$ is a so-called qualified existential quantification on roles which corresponds to the FOL formula $\exists y.R(x, y) \wedge A(y)$ where $\wedge$ is interpreted as the t-norm $\otimes$ in the Gödel logic.

Abstraction Component. $\mathcal{A}$ is a finite set of *abstraction statements* of the form

$$R \mapsto (c_1, \ldots, c_n)[c_{score}].sql, \tag{21.4}$$

where sql is an SQL statement returning n-ary tuples $\langle c_1, \ldots, c_n \rangle$ $(n \leq 2)$ with score determined by the c_{score} column. The tuples have to be ranked in decreasing order of score and, as for the fact component, we assume that there cannot be two records $\langle \mathbf{c}, s_1 \rangle$ and $\langle \mathbf{c}, s_2 \rangle$ in the result set of sql with $s_1 \neq s_2$ (if there are, then we remove the one with the lower score). The score c_{score} may be omitted and in that case the score 1 is assumed for the tuples. We assume that R occurs in $\mathcal{O}$, while all of the relational tables occurring in the SQL statement occur in $\mathcal{F}$. Finally, we assume that there is at most one abstraction statement for each abstract relational symbol R.

Query Language. The query language enables the formulation of conjunctive queries with a scoring function to rank the answers. More precisely, a *ranking query* is of the form

$$\begin{array}{r} q(\mathbf{x})[s] \leftarrow \exists \mathbf{y}\ R_1(\mathbf{z}_1)[s_1], \ldots, R_l(\mathbf{z}_l)[s_l], \\ \mathsf{OrderBy}(s = f(s_1, \ldots, s_l, p_1(\mathbf{z}'_1), \ldots, p_h(\mathbf{z}'_h)) \end{array} \tag{21.5}$$

where

(1) q is an n-ary relation, every R_i is a n_i-ary relation $(1 \leq n_i \leq 2)$. $R_i(\mathbf{z_i})$ may also be of the form $(z \leq v), (z < v), (z \geq v), (z > v), (z = v)$,

$(z \neq v)$, where z is a variable, v is a value of the appropriate concrete domain;

(2) $\mathbf{x}$ are the *distinguished variables*;

(3) $\mathbf{y}$ are existentially quantified variables called the *non-distinguished variables*. We omit to write $\exists\mathbf{y}$ when $\mathbf{y}$ is clear from the context;

(4) $\mathbf{z_i}, \mathbf{z'_j}$ are tuples of constants or variables in $\mathbf{x}$ or $\mathbf{y}$;

(5) $s, s_1, \ldots, s_l$ are distinct variables and different from those in $\mathbf{x}$ and $\mathbf{y}$;

(6) p_j is an n_j-ary *fuzzy predicate* assigning a score $p_j(\mathbf{c}_j) \in [0, 1]$ to each n_j-ary tuple $\mathbf{c}_j$ of constants;

(7) f is a *scoring function* $f\colon ([0,1])^{l+h} \to [0,1]$, which combines the scores of the l relations $R_i(\mathbf{c}'_i)$ and the n fuzzy predicates $p_j(\mathbf{c}''_j)$ into an overall score s to be assigned to $q(\mathbf{c})$.

We call $q(\mathbf{x})[s]$ its *head*, $\exists\mathbf{y}.R_1(\mathbf{z}_1)[s_1], \ldots, R_l(\mathbf{z}_l)[s_l]$ its *body* and $\mathsf{OrderBy}(s = f(s_1, \ldots, s_l, p_1(\mathbf{z}'_1), \ldots, p_h(\mathbf{z}'_h))$ the *scoring atom*. We also allow the scores $[s], [s_1], \ldots, [s_l]$ and the scoring atom to be omitted. In this case we assume the value 1 for s_i and s instead. The informal meaning of such a query is: if $\mathbf{z}_i$ is an instance of R_i to degree at least or equal to s_i, then $\mathbf{x}$ is an instance of q to degree at least or equal to s, where s has been determined by the scoring atom.

The answer set $ans_{\mathcal{K}}(q)$ over $\mathcal{K}$ of a query q is the set of tuples $\langle \mathbf{t}, s\rangle$ such that $\mathcal{K} \models q(\mathbf{t})[s]$ with $s > 0$ (informally, $\mathbf{t}$ satisfies the query to non-zero degree s) and the score s is as high as possible, *i.e.* if $\langle \mathbf{t}, s\rangle \in ans_{\mathcal{K}}(q)$ then (i) $\mathcal{K} \not\models q(\mathbf{t})[s']$ for any $s' > s$; and (ii) there cannot be another $\langle \mathbf{t}, s'\rangle \in ans_{\mathcal{K}}(q)$ with $s > s'$.

21.3 ILP for Learning Fuzzy DL Inclusion Axioms

In this section we consider a learning problem where:

- the target concept H is a DL-Lite atomic concept;
- the background theory $\mathcal{K}$ is a DL-Lite-like knowledge base $\langle \mathcal{F}, \mathcal{O}, \mathcal{A}\rangle$ of the form described in Section 21.2;
- the training set $\mathcal{E}$ is a collection of fuzzy DL-Lite-like facts of the form (21.1) and labeled as either positive or negative examples for H. We assume that $\mathcal{F} \cap \mathcal{E} = \emptyset$;
- the target theory $\mathcal{H}$ is a set of inclusion axioms of the form

$$B \sqsubseteq H \tag{21.6}$$

where H is an atomic concept, $B = C_1 \sqcap \ldots \sqcap C_m$, and each concept C_i has syntax

$$C \longrightarrow A \mid \exists R.A \mid \exists R.\top. \tag{21.7}$$

We now show how we may learn inclusion axioms of the form (21.6). To this aim, we define for $C \neq H$

$$\mathcal{I}_{ILP} \models C(t) \text{ iff } \mathcal{K} \cup \mathcal{E} \models C(t)[s] \text{ and } s > 0. \tag{21.8}$$

That is, we write $\mathcal{I}_{ILP} \models C(t)$ if it can be inferred from $\mathcal{K}$ and $\mathcal{E}$ that t is an instance of concept C to a non-zero degree.

Now, in order to account for multiple fuzzy instantiations of fuzzy predicates occurring in the inclusion axioms of interest to us, we propose the following formula for computing the *confidence degree* of an inclusion axiom:

$$cf(B \sqsubseteq H) = \frac{\sum_{t \in P} B(t) \Rightarrow H(t)}{|D|} \tag{21.9}$$

where

- $P = \{t \mid \mathcal{I}_{ILP} \models C_i(t) \text{ and } H(t)[s] \in \mathcal{E}^+\}$, i.e. P is the set of instances for which the implication covers a positive example;
- $D = \{t \mid \mathcal{I}_{ILP} \models C_i(t) \text{ and } H(t)[s] \in \mathcal{E}\}$, i.e. D is the set of instances for which the implication covers an example (either positive or negative);
- $B(t) \Rightarrow H(t)$ denotes the degree to which the implication holds for the instance t;
- $B(t) = \min(s_1, \ldots, s_n)$, with $\mathcal{K} \cup \mathcal{E} \models C_i(t)[s_i]$;
- $H(t) = s$ with $H(t)[s] \in \mathcal{E}$.

Clearly, the more positive instances supporting the inclusion axiom, the higher the confidence degree of the axiom.

Note that the confidence score can be determined easily by submitting appropriate queries via the query language described in Section 21.2. More precisely, proving the fuzzy entailment in (21.8) for each C_i is equivalent to answering a unique ranking query whose body is the conjunction of the relations R_l resulting from the transformation of C_is into FOL predicates and whose score s is given by the minimum between s_ls.

HotelTable		
id	rank	noRooms
h1	3	21
h2	5	123
h3	4	95

RoomTable			
id	price	roomType	hotel
r1	60	single	h1
r2	90	double	h1
r3	80	single	h2
r4	120	double	h2
r5	70	single	h3
r6	90	double	h3

Tower
id
t1

Park
id
p1
p2

DistanceTable			
id	from	to	time
d1	h1	t1	10
d2	h2	p1	15
d3	h3	p2	5

For illustrative purposes we consider the case involving the classification of hotels as good ones. We assume to have a background theory $\mathcal{K}$ with a relational database $\mathcal{F}$ storing facts such as an ontology $\mathcal{O}$[4] encompassing the following inclusion axioms

$$Park \sqsubseteq Attraction,\ Tower \sqsubseteq Attraction,\ Attraction \sqsubseteq Site$$

and a set $\mathcal{A}$ of abstraction statements such as:

$Hotel \mapsto (h.id)$.
```
SELECT h.id
FROM HotelTable h
```

$cheapPrice \mapsto (h.id, r.price)[score]$.
```
SELECT h.id, r.price, cheap(r.price) AS score
FROM HotelTable h, RoomTable r
WHERE h.id = r.hotel
ORDER BY score
```

$closeTo \mapsto (from, to)[score]$.
```
SELECT d.from, d.to closedistance(d.time) AS score
FROM DistanceTable d
ORDER BY score
```

where *cheap(p)* is a function determining how cheap a hotel room is given its price, modelled as e.g. a so-called left-shoulder function (defined in Fig. 21.1). We set $cheap(p) = ls(p; 50, 100)$, while $closedistance(d) = ls(d; 5, 25)$.

Assume now that our target concept H is $GoodHotel$, and that

- $\mathcal{E}^+ = \{GoodHotel^+(h1)[0.6], GoodHotel^+(h2)[0.8]\}$, while $\mathcal{E}^- = \{GoodHotel^-(h3)[0.4]\}$;
- $GoodHotel^+ \sqsubseteq GoodHotel$ and $GoodHotel^- \sqsubseteq GoodHotel$ occur in $\mathcal{K}$.

As an illustrative example, we compute the confidence degree of

$$r : Hotel \sqcap \exists cheapPrice.\top \sqcap \exists closeTo.Attraction \sqsubseteq GoodHotel$$

i.e. a good hotel is one having a cheap price and close proximity to an attraction. Now, it can be verified that for $\mathcal{K}' = \mathcal{K} \cup \mathcal{E}$

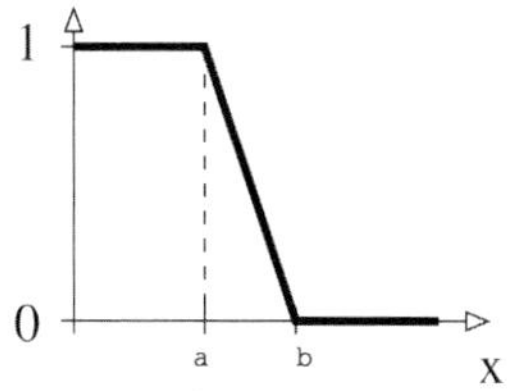

$$ls(x; a, b) = \begin{cases} 1 & \text{if } x \leqslant a \\ 0 & \text{if } x \geqslant b \\ (b - x)/(b - a) & \text{if } x \in [a, b] \end{cases}$$

Fig. 21.1 Left shoulder function $ls(x; a, b)$.

[4]http://donghee.info/research/SHSS/ObjectiveConceptsOntology(OCO).html.

(1) The query

$$q(h)[s] \leftarrow GoodHotel^{+}(h), cheapPrice(h,p)[s_1], closeTo(h,a)[s_2], Attraction(a), s = \min(s_1, s_2)$$

has answer set $ans_{\mathcal{K}'}(q_P) = \{(h1, 0.75), (h2, 0.4)\}$ over $\mathcal{K}'$;

(2) The query

$$q(h)[s] \leftarrow GoodHotel(h), cheapPrice(h,p)[s_1], closeTo(h,a)[s_2], Attraction(a), s = \min(s_1, s_2)$$

has answer set $ans_{\mathcal{K}'}(q_D) = \{(h1, 0.75), (h2, 0.4), (h3, 0.6)\}$ over $\mathcal{K}'$;

(3) Therefore, according to (21.9), $P = \{h1, h2\}$, while $D = \{h1, h2, h3\}$;

(4) As a consequence,

$$cf(r) = \frac{0.75 \Rightarrow 0.6 + 0.4 \Rightarrow 0.8}{3} = \frac{0.6 + 1.0}{3} = 0.5333.$$

21.4 Final Remarks

In this chapter we have briefly presented the core ingredients for inducing ontology inclusion axioms within the KR framework of a fuzzy DL-Lite-like DL. These ingredients can be used to extend FOIL as shown in [Lisi and Straccia (2011)]. Related FOIL-like algorithms [Shibata *et al.* (1999); Drobics *et al.* (2003); Serrurier and Prade (2007)] can only learn fuzzy rules. The formal study of fuzzy ILP contributed by [Horváth and Vojtás (2007)] is also relevant but less promising than our proposal in practice. Closer to our application domain, [Iglesias and Lehmann (2011)] extends an existing ILP system for learning $\mathcal{ALC}$ DL concepts (DL-Learner) with some of the most up-to-date fuzzy ontology tools whereas [Konstantopoulos and Charalambidis (2010)] is based on an ad-hoc translation of fuzzy Łukasiewicz $\mathcal{ALC}$ DL constructs into logic programs.

Bibliography

F. Baader, D. Calvanese, D. McGuinness, D. Nardi and P. F. Patel-Schneider (eds). *The Description Logic Handbook: Theory, Implementation, and Applications.* Cambridge University Press, Cambridge. 2003.

D. Calvanese, G. De Giacomo, D. Lembo, M. Lenzerini and R. Rosati. Data complexity of query answering in description logics. In P. Doherty, J. Mylopoulos and C. A. Welty (eds). *Proceedings of the Tenth International Conference on Principles of Knowledge Representation and Reasoning.* AAAI Press, Boston, Massachusetts, pp. 260–270. 2006.

M. Drobics, U. Bodenhofer and E.-P. Klement. FS-FOIL: an inductive learning method for extracting interpretable fuzzy descriptions. *Int. J. Approximate Reasoning*, **32(2–3)**, 131–152. 2003.

P. Hájek. *Metamathematics of Fuzzy Logic.* Springer, Berlin. 1998.

T. Horváth and P. Vojtás. Induction of fuzzy and annotated logic programs. In S. H. Muggleton, R. P. Otero, and A. Tamaddoni-Nezhad (eds). *Revised Selected Papers from the 16th International Conference on Inductive Logic Programming*, LNCS, vol. 4455. Springer, Berlin, pp. 260–274. 2007.

J. Iglesias and J. Lehmann. Towards Integrating Fuzzy Logic Capabilities into an Ontology-based Inductive Logic Programming Framework. In *Proceedings of the 11th International Conference on Intelligent Systems Design and Applications.* IEEE Press, Piscataway, New Jersey, pp. 1323–1328. 2011.

S. Konstantopoulos and A. Charalambidis. Formulating description logic learning as an inductive logic programming task. In *Proceedings of the IEEE International Conference on Fuzzy Systems.* IEEE Press, Piscataway, New Jersey, pp. 1–7. 2010.

F. A. Lisi and U. Straccia. An inductive logic programming approach to learning inclusion axioms in fuzzy description logics. In F. Fioravanti (ed.). *Proceedings of the 26th Italian Conference on Computational Logic.* CEUR-WS.org, pp. 57–71. 2011.

T. Lukasiewicz and U. Straccia. Managing uncertainty and vagueness in description logics for the semantic web. *J. Web Semant.*, **6**, 291–308. 2008.

J. R. Quinlan. Learning logical definitions from relations. *Mach. Learn.*, **5**, 239–266. 1990.

M. Serrurier and H. Prade. Improving expressivity of inductive logic programming by learning different kinds of fuzzy rules. *Soft Comput.*, **11(5)**, 459–466. 2007.

D. Shibata, N. Inuzuka, S. Kato, T. Matsui and H. Itoh. An induction algorithm based on fuzzy logic programming. In N. Zhong and L. Zhou (eds). *Methodologies for Knowledge Discovery and Data Mining*, LNCS, vol. 1574. Springer, Berlin, pp. 268–273. 1999.

U. Straccia. SoftFacts: A top-k retrieval engine for ontology mediated access to relational databases. In *Proceedings of the IEEE International Conference on Systems, Man and Cybernetics*, pp. 4115–4122. IEEE Press, Piscataway, New Jeresey. 2010.

PART 5

Logical Learning

Chapter 22

Towards Efficient Higher-Order Logic Learning in a First-Order Datalog Framework

Niels Pahlavi and Stephen H. Muggleton

Department of Computing, Imperial College London, UK

Within inductive logic programming (ILP), the concepts to be learned are normally considered as being succinctly representable in first-order logic. In a previous chapter the authors demonstrated that increased predictive accuracy can be achieved by employing higher-order logic (HOL) in the background knowledge. In this chapter, the flexible higher-order Horn clauses (FHOHC) framework is introduced. It is more expressive than the formalism used previously and can be emulated (with the use of "holds" statements and flattening) in a fragment of Datalog. The decidability, compatibility with ILP systems like Progol and positive learnability results of Datalog are then used towards efficient higher-order logic learning (HOLL). We show with experiments that this approach outperforms the HOLL system λProgol and that it can learn concepts in other HOLL settings like learning HOL and using HOL for abduction.

22.1 Introduction

Within ILP, it is usual to assume that all concepts to be learned can be succinctly represented in FOL. However, in [Pahlavi and Muggleton (2010)] the authors demonstrated that in certain learning problems, increased predictive accuracy can be achieved by employing HOL in background knowledge, thus advocating HOLL. In this chapter we explore whether some of the learning advantages provided by a HOL framework can be achieved within FOL. In particular, we introduce and explore a HOL formalism, FHOHC.

Table 22.1 HOLL settings in ILP.

Setting	Background Knowledge	Hypothesis	Examples	Learning
1	HOL, Given	FOL, To be learned	FOL, Given	Induction
2	FOL, Given	HOL, To be learned	FOL, Given	Induction
3	HOL, Given	FOL/HOL, Given	FOL/HOL, To be learned	Abduction

We also show that statements in FHOHC can be emulated in a fragment of Datalog FOL using "holds" statements (as suggested in [McCarthy and Hayes (1969)]) and flattening (as defined in [Rouveirol (1994)]). This fragment of FOL, called flattened holds Datalog programs (FHDP), has the advantage of being decidable and of having positive ILP learnability results. Figure 22.1 presents two examples of such HOL clauses (lines 1 and 3).

Using the power of expressivity of HOL in logic-based machine learning (thus realizing HOLL) to outperform first-order logic learning (FOLL) has been advocated in an ILP context, as in [Pahlavi and Muggleton (2010)] and [Feng and Muggleton (1992)] but also with a different logic in [Lloyd (2003)]. Figure 22.1 summarizes three settings of interest for HOLL in ILP.

In [Pahlavi and Muggleton (2010)], the HOLL system λProgol was introduced. It is based on the ILP system Progol [Muggleton and Bryant (2000)], and its underlying logic is HOL as it is based on Miller and Nadathur's higher-order Horn clauses (HOHC), defined in [Nadathur and Miller (1990)]. The paper experimentally compared λProgol with Progol in Setting 1 (see Figs. 22.1 and 22.2). It was demonstrated that λProgol can achieve considerably higher accuracy in this setting than Progol, however, several issues still need to be addressed. The HOL formalism HOHC was chosen for its supposed expressivity and soundness. Yet, several limitations

$R(X,Y) \leftarrow transitive(R), R(X,Z), R(Z,Y).$ (1)
$holds(R,X,Y) \leftarrow holds(transitive,R), holds(R,X,Z), holds(R,Z,Y).$ (2)
$P(sko\_cst).\ P(X) \leftarrow P(0), P(succ(sko\_cst)).$ (3)
$holds(P,sko\_cst).\ holds(P,X) \leftarrow holds(P,0), holds(succ,sko\_cst,Y), holds(P,Y).$ (4)

Fig. 22.1 Flexible higher-order Horn clauses programs representing transitivity for binary relations and mathematical induction for Peano numbers (lines 1 and 3, respectively) and their corresponding flattened holds Datalog programs (lines 2 and 4, respectively).

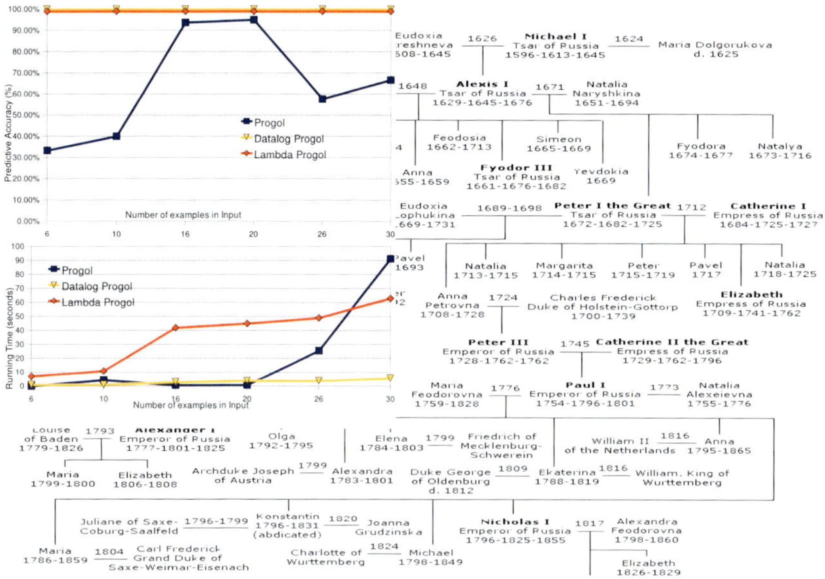

Fig. 22.2 Left: Comparison between Progol, Progol with FHDP and λProgol on the Ancestor example (upper graph: predictive accuracy; lower graph: running times). Right: Part (around one third) of the Romanov dynasty tree used in the experiment.

are intrinsic to it. Clauses with flexible heads (atoms whose predicate is a variable [Nadathur and Miller (1990)]) are not allowed for decidability reasons, which limits the expressivity and may be a problem in Settings 2 and 3. There is an issue with complexity. The system has not yet been adapted to handle abduction as in Progol5 [Muggleton and Bryant (2000)] and the Progol theoretical results remain to be proved for HOHC. We will see how the use of FHOHC and FHDP may overcome these issues.

In Section 22.2, the frameworks FHOHC and FHDP are described. Section 22.3 presents results in three different HOLL settings and develops the experiment detailed in [Pahlavi and Muggleton (2010)]. Finally, Section 22.4 concludes and suggests further work.

22.2 HOLL with First-Order Datalog and Progol

In Definition 22.1, we introduce FHOHC, which is based on first-order Horn clauses and allows for predicate (at least second-order) variables.

Definition 22.1. (FHOHC). A represents atomic formulas (or atoms), G goal formulas and D program formulas (or definite formulas, or clauses). Horn clauses are defined by the following grammar. $G ::= A|G \wedge G$ *and* $D ::= A|G \supset A|\forall x D$. An atomic formula is $P(t_1, \ldots, t_k)$ where P is a either a predicate symbol or higher-order variable of arity k and $t_1, \ldots, t_k$ are terms. A term is either a variable or $f(t_1, \ldots, t_j)$ where f is a functor of arity j and $t_1, \ldots, t_j$ are terms. A functor of arity 0 is a constant.

Compared with HOHC [Nadathur and Miller (1990)], FHOHC allows for flexible heads and therefore for more expressivity. These were prevented in HOHC because of decidability issues but we will now show how FHOHC can be emulated with a fragment of first-order Datalog. Datalog [Ceri *et al.* (1989)] is a restriction of Logic Programming that allows only variables and constants as terms (and hence avoids the use of function symbols). It has the advantage of being decidable. It has a declarative semantics and one can benefit from some positive ILP learnability results within it, as summarized in [Kietz and Dzeroski (1994)] and [Cohen and Page (1995)]. The use of "holds" statements as suggested in [McCarthy and Hayes (1969)] allows us to turn a higher-order atom into a first-order one. Moreover the flattening/unflattening procedures [Rouveirol (1994)] can translate generic Horn clauses into Datalog ones and vice versa, without loss of generality. This is why we introduce FHDP in Definition 22.2 to emulate HOL and FHOHC.

Definition 22.2. (FHDP). An FHDP is a flexible higher-order Horn clause program which has been transformed as follows. First, every atom $P(t_1, \ldots, t_k)$, P being a predicate symbol or a higher-order variable, is replaced by the atom $holds(P, t_1, \ldots, t_k)$ of arity $k+1$. Then the flattening algorithm, defined in [Rouveirol (1994)], is applied to the modified program.

In Fig. 22.1, two examples of such FHDP programs are presented (lines 2 and 4). With such an underlying framework, we can obviously use any of the first-order ILP systems available. Progol [Muggleton and Bryant (2000)] is a popular implementation, which allows us to learn in the HOLL Settings 1 and 2 requiring inductive reasoning but also in Setting 3 requiring abductive reasoning with Progol5 (see Fig. 22.1). Developing HOLL with the Datalog fragment FHDP and Progol enables us to directly use an ILP system like Progol and its results (including Progol5), to benefit from the efficiency of deduction of Datalog and its decidability, and to have more expressivity than HOHC with flexible heads to handle more learning settings. In terms of learnability and predictability, the existing positive results for Datalog can be used but the higher-order nature of the programs may also provide more complex and better choices of features, as analyzed in [Cohen and Page (1995)].

22.3 Experiments

In this section, we show how our Datalog approach can be applied on three examples covering the three HOLL settings defined in Section 22.1. All the corresponding files and experiments can be found at [Pahlavi (2011)]. In Examples 1,2 and 3, (...) corresponds to omitted parts.

HOLL Setting 1: Inductive learning of FOL hypothesis with HOL background. This follows the experiment fully described in [Pahlavi and Muggleton (2010)], about the learning of the predicate *ancestor* given the predicate *parent*. Progol rarely finds the definition (either returning incorrect recursive definitions, non-recursive definitions or not being able to induce clauses that compress the data). On the other hand, λProgol learns the correct definition in all the cases, which is non-recursive and can be learned from any given positive example. This is due to the presence of the higher-order predicate *trans_closure*, which represents the transitive closure of any binary relation. Here we use our FHDP approach in the comparison. The λProgol files (see Example 22.1) are totally emulated (with the exception of the addition of a prune statement to prevent higher-order tautologies in Progol). Hence the same learned hypothesis and the same predicative accuracy results (see Fig. 22.2). In Fig. 22.2, the running times are also added, which show that the FHDP approach is considerably faster compared to standard Progol and λProgol (both being similar), which illustrates the efficiency of the Datalog framework. This type of learning can be used with multiple higher-order predicates and with non-IID problems.

Example 22.1. Setting 1: Input file for learning ancestor.

```
:- modeh(*,holds(ancestor,+person,+person))?
:- modeb(*,holds(#predso,#predpp,+person,+person))?
predso(trans_clos). predpp(parent). predpp(married).
person(X) :- male(X). person(X) :- female(X).
holds(trans_clos,R,X,Y) :- holds(R,X,Y).
holds(trans_clos,R,X,Z) :- holds(R,X,Y), holds(trans_clos,R,Y,Z).
```

prune(holds(P,A,B),Body) :- in(holds(trans_clos,P,A,B),Body).
holds(married,michael_I,eudoxia_stresh). (...) holds(parent,michael_I,alexis_I). (...)
:-holds(ancestor,maria_1,nat_narysh). (...) holds(ancestor,alex_II,maria_6). (...)
Learned clause: holds(ancestor,X,Y) :- holds(trans_clos,parent,X,Y).

HOLL Setting 2: Inductive learning of HOL hypothesis with FOL background knowledge. In Example 22.2, a higher-order clause representing the transitivity of any binary relation (as in Fig. 22.1) is learned from examples of two binary relations (one being transitive, the other not). The running time is under a second. This learning could not be done with λProgol, as it involves a clause with a flexible head. This type of learning can be used for transfer learning.

Example 22.2. Setting 2: Input file for learning transitivity.
:- modeh(*,holds(+predicate,+argument,+argument))?
:- modeb(*,holds(#predicate,+predicate))?
:- modeb(*,holds(+predicate,+argument,+argument))?
predicate(trans). predicate(cause). predicate(pred). argument(a). (...)
holds(trans,cause). :- holds(trans,pred).
holds(cause,a,b). (...) holds(pred,c,d). (...)
:- holds(cause,b,a). (...) :- holds(pred,a,c). (...)
Learned clause: holds(R,X,Y) :- holds(trans,R),holds(R,X,Z),holds(R,Z,Y).

HOLL Setting 3: Abductive learning of FOL hypothesis with HOL background knowledge. In Example 22.3, we follow the approach in [Darlington (1968)], to formulate and adapt the general (second-order) concept of mathematical induction for Peano numbers $(f(0) \wedge (f(x) \rightarrow f(Sx)) \rightarrow f(y))$ in the FHOHC and FHDP frameworks (as in Fig. 22.1). It is included with the *less_than* predicate and is used to abduce the "base case" of a particular (first-order) predicate f. We also have to include the Clark completion of the "step case" of the definition of f for mathematical induction to be utilized. The running time is under five seconds. This learning can be adapted to structural induction, to predicate invention and to abduce higher-order hypothesis.

Example 22.3. Setting 3: Input file for abduction with mathematical induction.
:-modeh(*,holds(lt,#peano_int,+peano_int))?
:-modeb(*,holds(s,+peano_int,+peano_int))? :-observable(holds/2)?
peano_int(0). peano_int(s(X)) :- peano_int(X). holds(s,W,s(W)).
holds(F,sko_x). holds(F,X) :- holds(F,0),holds(s,sko_x,Y),holds(F,Y).

holds(lt,U,V) :- holds(s,X,U),holds(s,Y,V),holds(lt,X,Y).
holds(f,X) :- holds(s,X,Y),holds(lt,X,Y). holds(lt,X,Y) :- holds(s,X,Y),holds(f,X).
holds(f,s(s(s(s(0))))). (...) :- holds(lt,s(0),0). (...)
Learned clause: holds(lt,0,Y) :- holds(s,X,Y).

22.4 Conclusion and Further Work

In this chapter, the HOL framework FHOHC is introduced, which is more expressive than HOHC and can be emulated (with the use of "holds" statements and flattening) in the FHDP fragment of Datalog, which is decidable, efficient, can be directly used by ILP systems like Progol and has positive learnability results. We have showed on concrete experiments that this approach learns as well as λProgol (based on HOHC) on HOLL Setting1 (learning of FOL with HOL background) but with better running times. Moreover, it can learn examples in HOLL Settings 2 (learning of HOL with FOL background) and 3 (abduction of FOL with HOL background), in which λProgol cannot be used or has not yet been implemented to learn. We are currently finishing more experiments in order to have more insight on the performance of this new approach (including one about the learning of the move of a bishop in chess involving multiple HOLL settings). We are also completing the formalization of the emulation of FHOHC in FHDP with respect to the semantics of the considered clauses, the inferences involved and the learning algorithm. We think that this approach could be used further, including in more complex situations, to abduce HOL, for predicate invention and for transfer learning.

Bibliography

S. Ceri, G. Gottlob and L. Tanca, What you always wanted to know about datalog (and never dared to ask). IEEE T. Knowl. Data En., 1, 146–166. 1989.

W. Cohen and C. D. Page. Polynomial learnability and Inductive Logic Programming: methods and results. *New Generat. Comput.*, **13**, 369–409. 1995.

J.L. Darlington. Automatic Theorem Proving with Equality Substitutions and Mathematical Induction. *Mach. Intell.*, **3**, 113–127. 1968.

C. Feng and S. H. Muggleton. Towards inductive generalisation in higher order logic. In D. Sleeman and P. Edwards (eds). Proceedings of the Ninth International Workshop on Machine Learning. Morgan Kauffman, San Francisco, California, pp. 154–162. 1992.

J. -U. Kietz and S. Dzeroski. Inductive Logic Programming and Learnability. *SIGART Bull.*, **5(1)**, 22–32. 1994.

J. W. Lloyd. *Logic for Learning.* Springer, Berlin. 2003.

J. McCarthy and P. J. Hayes. Some philosophical problems from the standpoint of artificial intelligence. *Mach. Intell.*, **4**., 463–504. 1969.

S. H. Muggleton and C. Bryant. Theory completion using inverse entailment. In J. Cussens and A. Frisch (eds). *Proceedings of the 10th International Workshop on Inductive Logic Programming*, LNCS, vol. 1866. Springer-Verlag, Berlin, pp. 130–146. 2000.

G. Nadathur and D. Miller. Higher-order horn clauses. *J. ACM.*, **37(4)**, 777–814. 1990.

N. Pahlavi. ILP11 Experiments. Available online: `http://www.doc.ic.ac.uk/namdp05/ILP11`. Accessed 13 August 2014.

N. Pahlavi and S. H. Muggleton. Can HOLL Outperform FOLL? In P. Frasconi and F. A. Lisi (eds). *Proceedings of the 20th International Conference on Inductive Logic Programming*, LNCS, vol. 6489. Springer-Verlag, Berlin, pp. 198–205. 2010.

C. Rouveirol. Flattening and saturation: two representation changes for generalization. *Mach. Learn.*, **14(1)**, 219–232. 1994.

Chapter 23

Automatic Invention of Functional Abstractions

Robert J. Henderson and Stephen H. Muggleton

Department of Computing, Imperial College London, UK

We investigate how new elements of background knowledge can be abstracted automatically from patterns in programs. The approach is implemented in the *KANDINSKY* system using an algorithm that searches for common subterms over sets of functional programs. We demonstrate that KANDINSKY can invent higher-order functions such as *map*, *fold*, and *sumBy* from small sets of input programs. An experiment shows that KANDINSKY can find high-compression abstractions efficiently, with low settings of its input parameters. Finally, we compare our approach with related work in the inductive logic programming and functional programming literature, and suggest directions for further work.

23.1 Introduction

Can background knowledge be learned automatically through problem-solving experience? This would be a form of *meta-learning* [Vilalta and Drissi (2002)], distinct from *base learning* which is concerned simply with solving problem instances. We propose that a general strategy for acquiring new background knowledge can be found in the *abstraction principle* of software engineering. *Abstractions* [Abelson and Sussman (1996)] are re-usable units obtained by separating out and encapsulating patterns in programs. We define *abstraction invention* as the process of formulating useful abstractions in an inductive programming context, and when these abstractions take the form of functions, *functional abstraction invention* (FAI). Some forms of *predicate invention* may be regarded as FAI (since predicates are functions).

```
incElems([],[]).                      doubleElems([],[]).
incElems([H|T],[H1|T1]) :-            doubleElems([H|T],[H1|T1]) :-
    inc(H,H1), incElems(T,T1).            times(2,H,H1), doubleElems(T,T1).
```

Fig. 23.1 To abstract over the commonality manifest in the above two programs requires quantification over predicate symbols, which is impossible in first-order logic.

We have implemented KANDINSKY[1], a system which performs FAI over sets of functional (λ-calculus) programs by *Inverse β-Reduction* (IβR), an analogue of inverse resolution [Muggleton (1987); Muggleton and Buntine (1988)]. This move from first-order logic to λ-calculus is crucial because it allows our system to invent *higher-order* functional abstractions, an ability that is necessary in order to generalise on arbitrary patterns in programs. See Fig. 23.1 for an example where first-order methods fail.

KANDINSKY is set within a larger inductive programming framework called *compression-based learning* (CBL). CBL takes advantage of the general correspondence that exists between learning and compression (*minimum description length* [Grünwald (2005)]), to allow both base learning and meta-learning to be understood in a unified manner in terms of transformation operators. See Fig. 23.2 for an illustration of CBL. We shall leave further discussion of CBL for a future chapter; the rest of this chapter is concerned only with the FAI meta-learning technique.

23.2 KANDINSKY's Abstraction Invention Algorithm

Given a set of k λ-calculus terms, each with at most n subterms, the number of possible combinations of two or more subterms with at most one subterm taken per term is of the order of $(n+1)^k$. Any of these combinations can potentially be *anti-unified* by IβR to form an abstraction, but enumerating all of them by brute force is intractable for even moderately large values of k and n. To cope with this, we have designed a heuristic search procedure *auSearch* (anti-unification search) whose running time is polynomial in both k and n.

To prepare a set of terms for *auSearch*, all their subterms are generated, converted to a tree representation (Defn. 23.1), and each subterm paired with a 'tag' (Defn. 23.2) marking its origin. *auSearch* itself (Fig. 23.3) searches the space of 'common parts' (Defn. 23.1) that are obtainable

[1]Source code available at: `http://ilp.doc.ic.ac.uk/kandinsky`

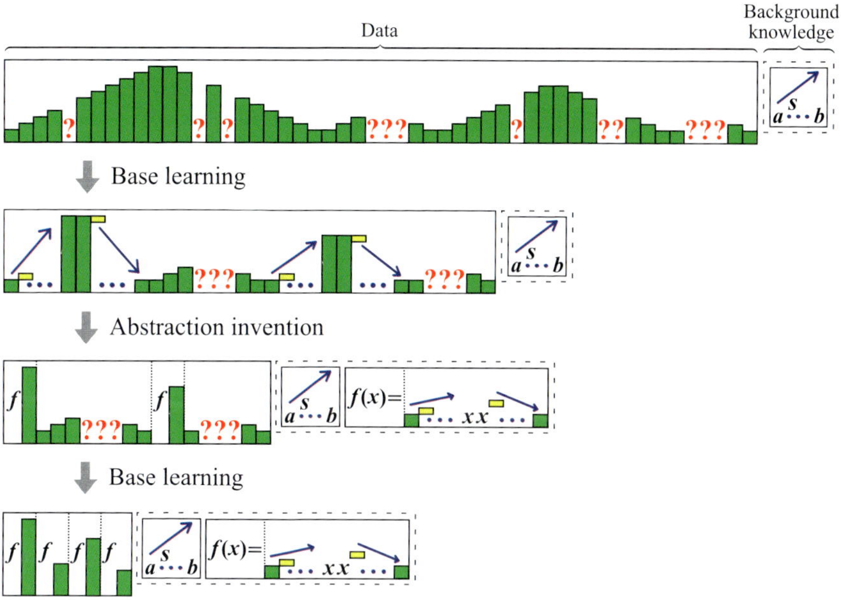

Fig. 23.2 An illustration of CBL. The top line represents the input in a learning problem: there is numerical data with some values missing, and there is background knowledge consisting here of an 'arithmetic progression' operator. From top to bottom, the learner performs a succession of transformations, each of which involves compression (reducing the width of the entire horizontal block), and some of which also involve generalisation (prediction of the missing data values).

Input: $\sigma, \tau \in \mathbb{N}$; I, a set of $\langle \text{tag}, \text{tree} \rangle$ pairs.
Output: a set of *auSearch* results.

1. **proc** $auSearch(\sigma, \tau, I)$:
2. Let $R = bagof(findOne(\sigma, \tau, I))$.
3. Divide R into disjoint subsets by tag-set. For each of these subsets, extract the top σ elements by score. Place all of the extracted elements into a new set R'.
4. Return the top τ elements by score of R'.

Fig. 23.3 The *auSearch* algorithm. *findOne* is a non-deterministic procedure that returns many *auSearch* results on backtracking. *findOne* and *auSearch* are mutually recursive. Owing to lack of space we defer a specification of *findOne* to a longer paper.

by anti-unifying combinations of two or more subterms. It makes use of a heuristic 'score' function (Defn. 23.3) in order to guide the search. Each *auSearch* result represents one candidate abstraction, which can be constructed from the subterms marked by the result's tag-set.

Definition 23.1 (tree, node, common part, mismatch point, size). A *tree* is a pair $\langle h, B\rangle$ where h is a *node* and B is a list of trees. In the representation of λ-terms as trees, each node is a symbol representing either a variable, a function application, or an anonymous function (λ-abstraction). A *common part* is either a *mismatch point* $\bullet$, or a pair $\langle h, B\rangle$ where h is a node and B is a list of common parts. The *size* of a tree or common part is equal to the number of nodes it contains. A mismatch point has zero size.

Definition 23.2 (tag, term index, subterm index). A *tag* consists of a pair of integers called the *term index* and the *subterm index*. It represents a reference to a particular subterm within a particular term, given a list of terms.

Definition 23.3 (*auSearch* result, score). An *auSearch result* is a pair of the form $\langle \gamma, T\rangle$, where γ is a common part and T is a tag-set (set of tags). Its *score*, an approximation to the degree of compression that can be obtained by deriving an abstraction from this result, is given by $(n-1)c - (n+2)m - n$, where n is the number of unique term indices contained in T, c is the size of γ, and m is the number of mismatch points contained in γ.

auSearch has two *beam-size* parameters σ and τ which limit how many intermediate results are stored during the search. When these parameters are both infinite, the search is complete but has exponential time complexity in the size of the input; when they are finite, the search is incomplete but the time complexity is polynomial.

Equipped with *auSearch*, KANDINSKY can perform a process called *exhaustive greedy abstraction invention*. Here, a set of programs is provided as input, and KANDINSKY constructs the most compressive abstraction that it can find, adds it to the set, and re-expresses the other programs in terms of it. This process repeats continually, halting only when no further compression is possible. A demonstration on two (hand-constructed) datasets *Map-Fold* (MF) and *Sum-Means-Squares* (SMS) is shown in Fig. 23.4.

(a)

Map-Fold dataset (size = 71)

```
incElems    = fix (\ r lst -> if (null lst) nil (cons
                (inc (head lst)) (r (tail lst))))
doubleElems = fix (\ r lst -> if (null lst) nil (cons
                (times two (head lst)) (r (tail lst))))
length      = fix (\ r lst -> if (null lst) zero (inc
                (r (tail lst))))
```

↓

After 1 stage (size = 53, compression = 25.4%)

```
g1          = \ a1 -> fix (\ a2 a3 -> if (null a3) nil
                (cons (a1 (head a3)) (a2 (tail a3))))
incElems    = g1 inc
doubleElems = g1 (times two)
length      = fix (\ a4 a5 -> if (null a5) zero (inc
                (a4 (tail a5))))
```

↓

After 2 stages (size = 50, compression = 29.6%)

```
g2          = \ a1 a2 -> fix (\ a3 a4 -> if (null a4)
                a1 (a2 a4 (a3 (tail a4))))
g1          = \ a5 -> g2 nil (\ a6 -> cons (a5 (head
                a6)))
incElems    = g1 inc
doubleElems = g1 (times two)
length      = g2 zero (\ a7 -> inc)
```

(b)

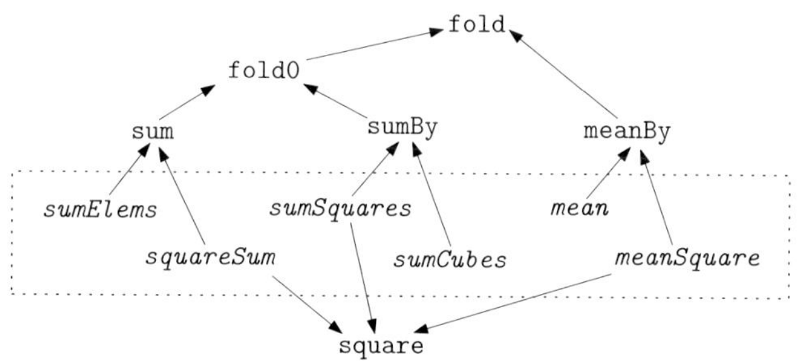

Fig. 23.4 (a) KANDINSKY's output trace on the MF dataset, which consists of three list-processing programs. In stage 1, KANDINSKY antiunifies `incElems` with `doubleElems` to produce an abstraction `g1` which we may recognise as *map*, a higher-order function which maps an arbitrary unary operation over the elements of a list. In stage 2, KANDINSKY antiunifies `length` with a subterm of `g1` to produce `g2`, a form of *fold* which accumulates over a list using a binary operation. (b) Summary of results for the SMS dataset. The input programs (inside dashed rectangle) express various actions over the elements of a list. KANDINSKY succeeded in finding six abstractions, which we inspected and assigned suitable names. `sumBy` is a higher-order analogue of `sum` which maps an arbitrary function over a list before summing its elements; `meanBy` is a generalisation of `mean` along similar lines. `fold0` is a specialisation of `fold`.

23.3 Experiment

In this section we ask: in practice, can we expect KANDINSKY to find near-optimally compressive abstractions in polynomial time? As discussed in Section 23.2, *auSearch* can always find an optimally compressive abstraction when the beam-size parameters σ and τ are infinite, because under those conditions it generates every abstraction in the entire search space. However, finite values of the beam-size parameters are necessary for a tractable polynomial-time search. By studying the effect on compression of varying these parameters, we wish to determine if one can expect to achieve near-optimal compression even when using relatively small finite values.

We ran exhaustive greedy abstraction invention on the MF and SMS datasets, at values of σ of 1, 2, 3, 5, 10, and 50, for all values of τ between 0 and 50, and recorded the overall compression for each run (Fig. 23.5a). We also measured the time taken at the same values of σ and for values of τ at $0, 5, 10 \ldots 50$ (Fig. 23.5b). To reduce the effects of measurement error,

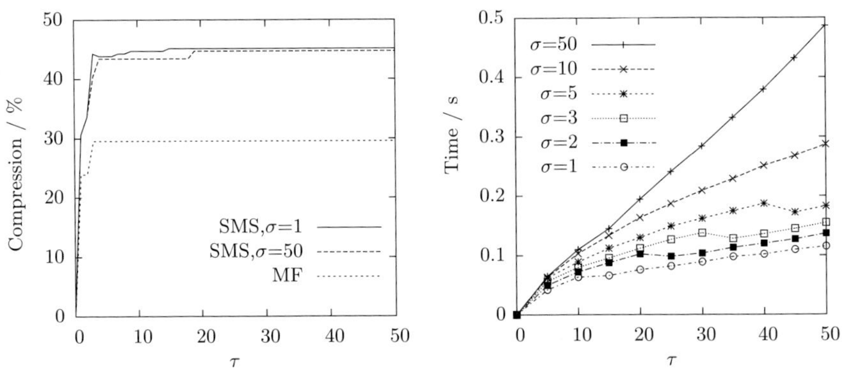

(a) Effect of τ on compression, for both datasets.

(b) Effect of τ and σ on time taken, for SMS.

σ	1	2	3	5	10	50
τ	15	24	32	44	–	–

(c) Effect of σ on the smallest value of τ at which the compression plateau of 45.1% was reached, for SMS.

Fig. 23.5 Experimental results. The two datasets are MF and SMS. σ and τ are the beam-size parameters of KANDINSKY's search algorithm. In (a), the compression-τ curves for MF are all identical for the six values of σ that were tested; for SMS they are all different but lie very close together, so we have only plotted those for the lowest and highest σ values. In (b), we have plotted the curves for SMS only; the curves for MF show a somewhat similar pattern. The experiment was run on a 2.8 GHz desktop PC with 4 GB of RAM.

each timing measurement was averaged over 200 identical runs for MF and 20 identical runs for SMS.

From the results, we see that as tau increases, compression increases. However, the vast majority of compression is achieved for both datasets by $\tau = 4$: the compression curves reach a 'plateau' very rapidly. For larger values of σ, a larger value of τ tends to be needed to reach the maximum achievable level of compression (Fig. 23.5c). Time taken increases with both τ and σ.

The 'plateau' phenomenon that we observe supports the hypothesis that low beam-size parameters are adequate for achieving near-optimal compression. For the datasets studied here, it seems unlikely that the plateau is a 'false-summit', because the invented abstractions capture almost all of the obvious commonality manifest in the input programs. However, whether this plateau effect will occur for arbitrary input programs is an open question; ultimately it would be worth trying to obtain a theoretical justification.

23.4 Related/Further Work and Conclusion

Our FAI technique is inspired by a standard 'recipe' which human programmers use to derive functional abstractions from patterns in programs, described by, for example, Abelson and Sussman [Abelson and Sussman (1996)]. One previous attempt to automate this kind of recipe is due to Bakewell and Runciman [Bakewell and Runciman (1999)]; they implemented an abstraction construction algorithm for Haskell programs, however they did not address the problem of searching for a compressive abstraction. In inductive logic programming, the Duce [Muggleton (1987)] and CIGOL [Muggleton and Buntine (1988)] systems use inverse resolution to perform FAI in propositional and first-order logic, respectively; KANDINKSY shares a lot with these systems, both its inverse deduction approach (IβR), as well as its use of a compression-guided search algorithm.

For further work, we hope shortly to combine KANDINSKY with a base learning system so as to realise a full CBL framework. Many improvements can also be made to KANDINSKY itself; most significantly it is currently limited to deriving abstractions from *syntactic* commonality in programs, whereas a more powerful system could search the space of all *semantic* equivalences via β-η-δ transformations.

To conclude, we have defined the term *abstraction invention* to mean the derivation of new knowledge from patterns in programs. We have demonstrated and experimentally justified an efficient algorithm for *functional* abstraction invention over λ-calculus programs in the KANDINSKY system. KANDINSKY invented, without any prior knowledge of such concepts, higher-order functions such `map`, `fold`, `sumBy`, and `meanBy`. Some of these functions are strikingly similar to ones in the Haskell standard library [Peyton Jones (1987)], so KANDINSKY is clearly able to invent abstractions that are natural from a human perspective.

Acknowledgments

Thank you to Dianhuan Lin, Alireza Tamaddoni-Nezhad, and Jianzhong Chen, for their helpful comments on an earlier draft of this chapter.

Bibliography

H. Abelson and G. J. Sussman. *Structure and Interpretation of Computer Programs.* MIT Press, Cambridge, Massachusetts. 1996.

A. Bakewell and C. Runciman. Automated Generalisation of Function Definitions. In A. Middeldorp, T. Sato (eds). *Proceedings of the 4th Fuji International Symposium on Functional and Logic Programming*, LNCS, vol. 1722. Springer-Verlag, Berlin, pp. 225–240. 1999.

P. Grünwald. *Minimum Description Length Tutorial. Advances in Minimum Description Length: Theory and Applications.* MIT Press, Cambridge, Massachusetts, pp. 23–79. 2005.

S. H. Muggleton. Duce, an oracle based approach to constructive induction. *Proceedings of the 10th International Joint Conference on Artificial Intelligence*, pp. 287–292. Morgan Kauffman, San Francisco, California. 1987.

S. H. Muggleton and W. Buntine. Machine invention of first-order predicates by inverting resolution. *Proceedings of the 5th International Conference on Machine Learning*, 339–352. Morgan Kaufmann, San Francisco, California. 1988.

S. L. Peyton Jones. *The Implementation of Functional Programming Languages.* Prentice Hall, Upper Saddle River, New Jersey. 1987.

R. Vilalta and Y. Drissi. A perspective view and survey of meta-learning. *Artif. Intell. Rev.*, **2(18)**, 77–95. 2002.

PART 6

Constraints

Chapter 24

Using Machine-Generated Soft Constraints for Roster Problems

Yoshihisa Shiina and Hayato Ohwada

Faculty of Science and Technology,
Tokyo University of Science, Japan

This chapter describes a method for generating rules that classify good rosters and bad rosters using Inductive Logic Programming (ILP). The obtained rules can be regarded as general conditions of good rosters in which preferred shifts are assigned for workers, and thus are converted into soft constraints in Constraint Logic Programming (CLP). The proposed method automatically generates such constraints from past good rosters, providing a new solution to optimization problems such as scheduling and layout. In this chapter, we demonstrate how to generate and apply classification rules (soft constraints) based on ILP through a simple roster example.

24.1 Introduction

Constraint Logic Programming (CLP) provides a solution to combinatorial problems (e.g. scheduling and layout) in Operations Research [Jaffar (1987)]. CLP uses hard constraints that must be satisfied and soft constraints specifying preferred solutions, and finds a best solution by minimizing the number of soft constraints violated. Owing to the declarative nature of CLP, such constraints can be easily put into a CLP program. However, soft constraints are usually situation-oriented, and thus it is hard to set up soft constraints manually.

This chapter describes a method for generating rules that classify good rosters and bad rosters using ILP. The obtained rules can be regarded as general conditions of good rosters in which preferred shifts are assigned for workers. In this sense, these conditions can be viewed as soft constraints that may be satisfied to find preferred solutions.

The chapter is organized as follows. Section 24.2 describes a simple roster example and how to specify the example using CLP. Section 24.3 presents how to learn rules that classify good and bad rosters in ILP. Section 24.3 also provides how learned rules are converted into soft constraints that can be solved in CLP. Section 24.4 describes an initial experiment result, and the final section provides concluding remarks.

24.2 A Simple Roster Problem

A simple roster program for a single worker is taken from [Wallace *et al.* (2004)]. A 5×7 matrix is employed when there are five weeks and seven days per week. There are five possible shift patterns to be assigned for each day:

```
1 Day-off shift     2 Morning shift     3 Evening shift
4 Mid-day shift     5 Supplementary shift
```

Each number indicates a shift pattern.

Constraints are usually categorized into hard constraints and soft constraints in CLP. Hard constraints must be satisfied to obtain feasible solutions. Soft constraints are desirable but not obligatory, and thus may be violated. In this sense, soft constraints are used to present preferences for the workplace and worker in the roster problem.

The problem has the following four hard constraints:

HC-1 This is a constraint for indicating the times of each shift pattern for each day and is described as follows:

```
1: week(2,0,2,2,1,2,5), % Day-off shift
```

where the function `week` has seven arguments that indicate the day-off times for each day. In this case, there are two day-off Mondays (first argument).

HC-2 A day-off shift must be assigned at least once within consecutive seven days.

HC-3 A day-off shift must not be assigned more than once every three days.

HC-4 A supplementary shift must not be assigned more than once every two days.

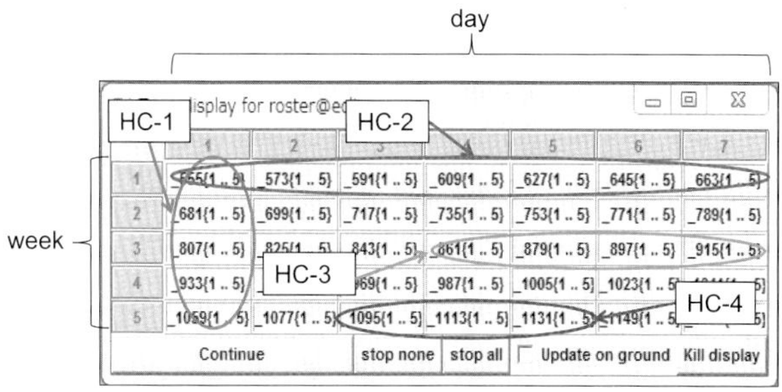

HC-1: Two variables of 5 must be assigned to 1(day-off) .
HC-2: At least one variable of 7 must be assigned to 1(day-off).
HC-3: No more than three consecutive variables must be assigned to 1(day-off) .
HC-4: No more than two consecutive variables must be assigned to 5(supplementary) .

Fig. 24.1 Hard constraints.

Figure 24.1 illustrates typical hard constraints, where each cell is a logical variable to be instantiated in a shift pattern.

The problem also has the following soft constraints.

SC-1 A morning shift (shift:2) should not follow an evening shift (shift:3).
SC-2 A day-off shift (shift:1) should not be isolated.
SC-3 A supplementary shift (shift:5) should be isolated.

These soft constraints can be described as follows using CLP:

```
Viol1 #= (SomeDay #= 3 and NextDay #= 2)
Viol2 #= (Someday #= 1 and Before #\= 1 and After #\= 1)
Viol3 #= (SomeDay #= 5 and NextDay #= 5)
```

where the variables `Viol1`, `Viol2` and `Viol3` are Boolean variables indicating whether the corresponding constraints on the right-hand side can be satisfied or not. The infix notation `#=` (`#\=`) on the right-hand side denotes equality (inequality).

Given a set of soft constraints, CLP minimizes the number of soft constraints violated using a branch-and-bound search. Figure 24.2 depicts the solution of the simple roster problem where a worker's shift entry is satisfied under given hard and soft constraints.

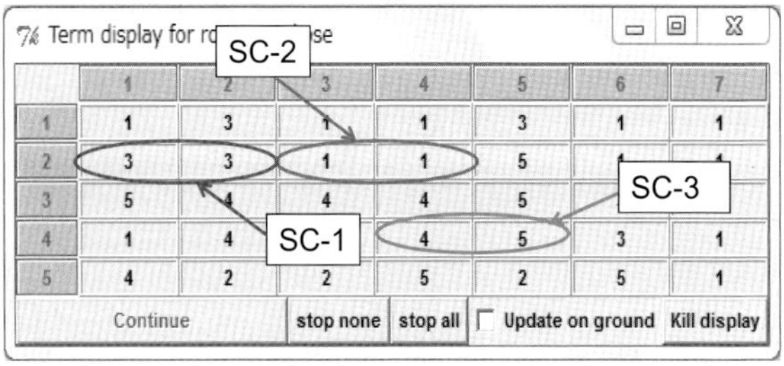

1: week(2,0,2,2,1,2,5), % Day-off shift
2: week(0,1,1,0,1,0,0), % Morning shift
3: week(1,2,1,0,0,2,0), % Evening shift
4: week(1,2,1,2,0,0,0), % Mid-day shift
5: week(1,0,0,1,3,1,0) % Supplementary shift

Fig. 24.2 Soft constraints.

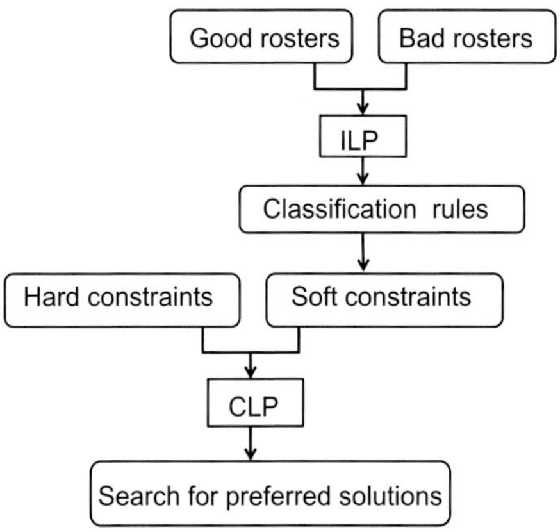

Fig. 24.3 The proposed method.

24.3 Proposed Method

The proposed method consists of the following two processes:

(1) ILP generates rules that classify good rosters and bad rosters.
(2) Learned rules are converted into soft constraints that are added to the soft constraint set in CLP.

Figure 24.3 illustrates these processes.

24.3.1 *Rule generation*

Suppose that we have the following positive examples:

```
+good(r1). +good(r7). +good(r8). +good(r9). +good(r10).
```

where `+good(r1)` means that roster `r1` is a good roster.

We also have the following negative examples:

```
-good(r2). -good(r3). -good(r4). -good(r5).
        -good(r6). -good(r11).
```

We set up the background knowledge as follows:

```
week1(r1,Monday,1).       week1(r1,Tuesday,3).
week1(r1,Wednesday,1).    week1(r1,Thursday,1).
week1(r1,Friday,3).       week1(r1,Saturday,1).
week1(r1,Sunday,1).
```

where `week1` indicates the first week in the roster, and this predicate means a shift pattern of a specific day in the first week with respect to a specific roster.

Mode declarations that are the same as Progol [Muggleton (1995)] are given as follows:

```
:- modeh(*,good(+roster)).
:- modeb(*,week1(+roster,#day,#shift)).
```

Here, the first declaration is the target hypothesis, and the second is for background knowledge.

Given such information, we obtained the following rules:

```
good(A) :- week1(A,Saturday,1), week5(A,Monday,1).
good(A) :- week1(A,Thursday,5).
```

The first rule means that the shift on Saturday of the first week is a day-off shift(1), and the shift on Monday of the fifth week is a day-off shift(1). The second rule means that the shift on Thursday of the first week is a supplementary shift(5). These two rules represent a general condition of good rosters due to the ILP facility classifying good and bad rosters.

24.3.2 *Applying learned rules*

In order to apply learned rules, we automatically generate soft constraints from them. The notation `R[week,day]` is introduced to specify a logical

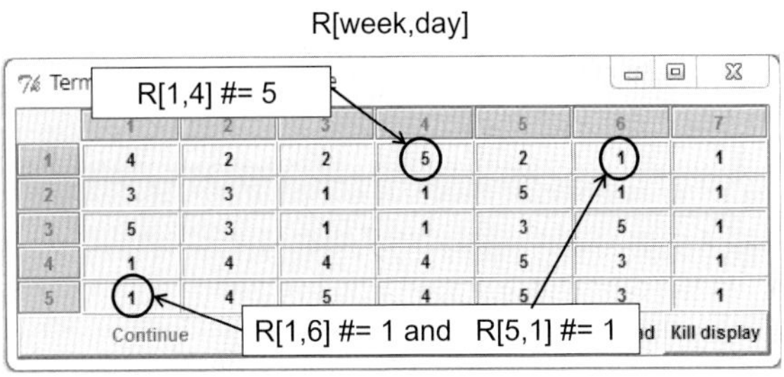

Fig. 24.4 Roster obtained using the learned rules.

variable in the roster matrix. The condition `week1(A,Saturday,1)` in the first rule above can be denoted as the equality `R[1,6] #= 1`. The conjunctive condition on the right-hand side of the first rule is negated because soft constraints should be added to the constraint set as the negation of the conjunctive condition. Therefore, the above rules are converted into the following expressions:

```
Viol4 #= (R[1,6] #\= 1 or R[5,1] #\= 1)
Viol5 #= (R[1,4] #\= 5)
```

The roster obtained using the learned rules is depicted in Fig. 24.4.

24.4 Experiment

We conducted an experiment by overlaying 50 good rosters and 50 bad rosters using our ILP system (GKS) [Mizoguchi and Ohwada (1995)] on top of the CLP system (ECLiPSe) [Wallace *et al.* (1997)]. Seventeen rules were produced. Typical rules are as follows:

(1) good(A) :- week1(A,Friday,3), week1(A,Sunday,1), week3(A, Saturday,5).
(2) good(A) :- week1(A,Tuesday,1), week2(A,Saturday,1), week4(A, Friday,1).

These rules were converted into the following soft-constraint expressions:

```
Viol8 #= (R[1,5] #\= 3 or R[1,7] #\= 1 or R[3,6] #\= 5)
Viol15 #= (R[1,2] #\= 1 or R[2,6] #\= 1 or R[4,5] #\= 1])
```

These soft constraints were used to obtain a preferable solution for the roster problem. In contrast, soft constraints derived from residual rules were violated under the given hard constraints. This means that a hard constraint checking component is needed for the learning procedure.

24.5 Concluding Remarks

We used ILP to generate rules that classify good rosters and bad rosters. The learned rule represents the preference for workers in a roster. The generated rule is converted into soft constraints that are added to a soft constraint set in CLP. A newly obtained roster is constrained by the converted soft constraints. We demonstrated a proposed method through a simple roster problem.

In future work, we will apply our proposed method to a practical nurse scheduling problem that demonstrates the usefulness of combining CLP and ILP.

Bibliography

J. Jaffar and J. -L Lassez. Constraint logic programming. In *Proceedings of the 14th ACM Symposium on Principles of Programming Languages.* ACM, New York, pp. 111–119. 1987. POPL 1987: Munich, 21–23 January 1987.

F. Mizoguchi and H. Ohwada. Using inductive logic programming for constraint acquisition in constraint-based problem solving. In D. Page (ed.). *Proceeding of the 15th International Workshop on Inductive Logic Programming,* LNAI, vol. 1446. Springer-Verlag, Berlin, pp. 297–332. 1995.

S. H. Muggleton. Inverse entailment and progol. *New Generat. Comput.*, **13(3–4)**, 245–286. 1995.

M. Wallace, J. Schimpf, K. Shen and W. Harvey. On Benchmarking constraint logic programming platforms. Response to Fernandez and Hill's "A Comparative Study of Eight Constraint Programming Languages over the Boolean and Finite Domains", *Constraints*, **9**, 5–34. 2004.

M. Wallace, S. Novello and J. Schimpf: ECLiPSe: A platform for constraint logic programming. *ICL Syst. J.*, **12**, 159–200. 1997.

PART 7

Spacial and Temporal

Chapter 25

Relational Learning for Football-Related Predictions

Jan Van Haaren and Guy Van den Broeck
Department of Computer Science
Katholieke Universiteit Leuven, Belgium

Association football recently undersaw some radical changes, leading to higher financial stakes, further professionalization and technical advances. This gave rise to overwhelming amounts of data becoming available for analysis. Therefore, we propose football-related predictions as an interesting application for relational learning. We argue that football data are highly structured and naturally represented in a relational way. Furthermore, we identify interesting learning tasks that require a relational approach, such as link prediction and structured output learning. Early experiments show that this relational approach is competitive with a propositionalized approach for the prediction of individual football matches' goal difference.

25.1 Introduction

Association football is becoming increasingly competitive and the financial stakes of football clubs have dramatically increased. Over the past 25 years club budgets have grown enormously due to gate sale revenues, broadcasting revenues, merchandising and prize money [Lago *et al.* (2006)]. As a result, football clubs and football leagues have become more professional. Football clubs have to adopt a well-thought out selling and buying policy, and their managers have to exploit the capabilities of their players in the best possible manner. Recently introduced player tracking systems produce overwhelming amounts of data, which are being used by experts to analyze matches and players' performance [Xu *et al.* (2005)].

Current approaches to football-related predictions do not use the rich structured data that are available nowadays. We will show that machine learning techniques can be applied to this data. The techniques applied until now come from statistical modeling, not machine learning. We will argue that football-related data are relational and that relational learning is particularly suited for football-related predictions. The rise of the Internet has made football betting increasingly popular. Therefore, the prediction of football match results is an interesting learning task. However, despite the simplicity of both rules and objectives, football match results are highly uncertain and difficult to predict. Typically, football matches are low-scoring, which makes it hard to identify events that have an immediate impact on the final result. We report on early experiments with kLog [Frasconi *et al.* (2011)] that show that our relational approach is competitive with a propositionalized approach for the prediction of the goal difference for individual matches in a domestic football league.

25.2 Related Work

Football analytics has been given little attention in academic literature due to the limited availability of publicly available match statistics. Nevertheless, a number of descriptive and predictive models for football match results have been proposed over the years. The first generation of football-related models was mainly concerned with the distribution of the number of goals scored in a football match. Moroney [Moroney (1956)] shows that both the Poisson distribution and the negative binomial distribution provide an appropriate fit to football match results. Maher [Maher (1982)] presents a technique for modeling outcomes of football matches between two specific teams. This technique represents each team's individual score by means of an independent Poisson variable. As a consequence, the resulting model is able to take each team's strength into account. Dixon and Coles [Dixon and Coles (1997)] propose a number of adaptations to Maher's model. They show that there exists a strong dependency between the individual scores in low-scoring football matches, which an independent Poisson distribution is not able to account for. Therefore, Dixon and Coles suggest directly modifying the marginal Poisson distributions for low-scoring football matches. Baio and Blangiardo [Baio and Blangiardo (2010)] propose a Bayesian hierarchical model for each team's individual score. They show that there is no need for bivariate Poisson variables to capture the correlation between individual scores. This correlation is automatically taken into account when assuming two conditionally independent Poisson variables for the number of goals scored. This is the case because the observable variables influence each other at a higher level.

25.3 Current Limitations and Challenges

Most of the available techniques for predicting football match results are applications and extensions of well-known statistical methods. These techniques learn models that have limited expressivity and they do not leverage the full range of rich data that are currently available. Typically, these techniques are limited to learning from match results of previously played football matches. We can distinguish two clear reasons for this limitation:

(1) **Until recently, match statistics were usually not publicly available.** In contrast, for popular American sports (e.g., basketball and baseball) it is common that detailed match statistics are available both in print and online. Consequently, there has been an explosion in interest for analytics in these sports by academic researchers and fans alike.
(2) **It is not obvious how to derive meaningful measures and statistics from football matches.** Football has a very complex structure, which cannot easily be captured by a fixed set of parameters. Football teams have a lot of freedom in the tactics they use and football players are nearly unrestricted in their movement on the pitch. Therefore, it was not until the late 1990s that the large-scale registration of match statistics became possible. Nowadays, modern camera-based tracking systems are used for high-accuracy measurements of player and ball movements. These measurements enable the calculation of detailed match statistics for both football players and football teams.

However, the discussion in the previous section shows that the current approaches for modeling football matches are unable to handle the huge amounts of data made available by camera-based tracking systems. Despite the immense popularity of football, little research has been conducted on more sophisticated models. These models have to deal with two major challenges:

(1) **A model should account for the numerous aspects that influence the result of a football match.** Match statistics are not limited to final scores, but also hold interesting details on the way these

final scores came about. For example, knowing that the referee in a particular football match pulled a red card for the home team might help explain an unexpected win for the away team.

(2) **A model should account for time-dependent and positional information.** Player forms are one example of time-dependent information that is worth keeping track of because football players are rarely able to maintain the same level of performance throughout an extended period of time. At a lower level, the passes and tackles performed during a football match are another example of time-dependent information.

25.4 Relational Representation

Relational models have many interesting properties that allow them to address the challenges outlined in the previous section in a straightforward way. A relational model's most important asset is the **flexibility** with which it can represent data. The parameter set of such a model is not fixed beforehand but can vary according to the events that occur during a football match. As a result, special events such as a red card or an own goal can be stressed. Furthermore, the definition of relations among objects (e.g., football players and football teams) can represent complexly structured data such as team lineups and player transfers between football clubs. All of this is less obvious or even impossible in a propositional structure such as the attribute-value format.

Current approaches for modeling football matches keep their knowledge in a limited set of model parameters. Consequently, these approaches have difficulties taking **time-dependent and positional information** into account. The resulting models implicitly assume that football teams and football players constantly maintain the same level of performance, but football players rarely perform at the same level over an extended period of time. Furthermore, a team's current form may help explain an apparently anomalous result. Therefore, the ability to represent each player, team and match explicitly is an important asset of a relational model. The definition of relations between pairs of matches preserves the order in which these matches have been played. Hence, the model can easily capture a team's performance gaps and form fluctuations.

Furthermore, relational models also allow for **learning from interpretations**, which is a key concept in many machine learning techniques. An interpretation comprises a set of objects and the relations that exist among these objects. A typical learning approach is to represent each individual football match as a single interpretation. A more sophisticated learning approach is to represent all football matches in one football season as one large interpretation. An important advantage of the latter approach is its support for the definition of relations between pairs of football matches.

25.5 Learning Tasks

Relational models can tackle both descriptive and predictive learning tasks. Descriptive learning tasks focus on assessing past performances (e.g., to identify who was the most efficient player in a football match), whereas predictive learning tasks are mainly concerned with analyzing past performances to predict future behavior (e.g., to predict how many goals a team will score in its next match). Traditional learning tasks include:

- **Regression:** e.g., to predict the number of yellow or red cards a referee will pull during a football match;
- **Classification:** e.g., to classify a football match as a win for the home team, a win for the away team or a draw.

Besides these traditional learning tasks, relational models also allow for more complex learning tasks that require rich structured data representations. Moreover, relational models support structured output learning tasks, which are very common in football. Entities and relations provide an intuitive way to represent the output of these learning tasks. Some interesting learning tasks made possible by relational models include:

- **Collective regression:** e.g., to jointly predict the individual statistics of players in a football match;
- **Collective classification:** e.g., to identify which players will be selected in a team's starting lineup;
- **Link prediction:** e.g., to predict who will pass the ball to whom during a football match.

25.6 Learning Example

In this section, we will illustrate the applicability of relational models for football-related predictions by means of a simple learning task of predicting individual football matches' goal difference. The goal difference for a football match is given as the difference between the number of goals scored by the home team and the number of goals scored by the away team.

Football has a very complex structure, which allows for a large number of possible relational topologies. The relational model that we discuss here represents each football match explicitly by means of its goal difference as well as a set of 26 performance measures, which are derived from match statistics. We consider 13 performance measures that cover relevant aspects such as ball possession, discipline, defending, crossing and passing for both football teams involved in a match. A performance measure can take five different values (very low, low, average, high or very high) to indicate a football team's level of performance in this particular aspect of football.

We use kLog [Frasconi *et al.* (2011)] to implement this relational model. kLog is a language for kernel-based relational learning that builds upon several simple but powerful concepts such as learning from interpretations, data modelling through entities and relationships, deductive databases and graph kernels. Unlike other models based on probabilistic logic, kLog derives features from a ground entity-relationship diagram and is therefore not directly concerned with the representation of probability distributions. An extensive series of statistical techniques is available to fit the model parameters.

Since no comparable models exist, we use two propositionalizations of our relational model to assess the model's performance in predicting goal differences for football matches. The first model represents each football match by means of its goal difference and its 26 performance measures (Weka 1). The second model extends this model with the performance measures and goal differences for each team's previous two matches (Weka 2). We make use of Weka [Holmes *et al.* (1994)] to conduct experiments with these two models. We use the match statistics for the 2010–2011 English Premier League that are available at *The Guardian's* website.[1]

Figure 25.1 shows a comparison of the mean absolute error values for the relational model and the propositionalized models, which have been obtained with support vector regression and tenfold cross validation. Experiments with both a linear kernel function and a sigmoid kernel function have been performed. The comparison shows that the kernel function has no impact on the error values for the kLog model and that the sigmoid function clearly outperforms the linear function for the Weka models.

These preliminary experiments show that the relational approach that we propose is competitive with a propositional approach for our learning task. However, we expect the relational approach to outperform

[1] `http://www.guardian.co.uk/football/chalkboards`

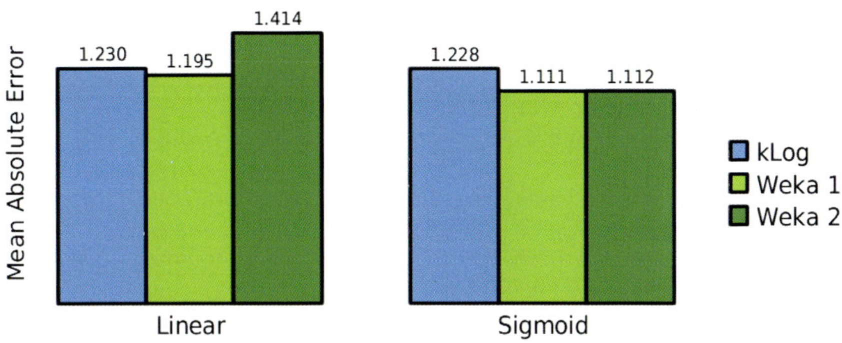

Fig. 25.1 Comparison of the mean absolute error values obtained for the relational kLog model (blue) and the propositionalized Weka models (light and dark green).

propositional learners once more structured data, such as team formations and individual player statistics, are added to the model.

25.7 Conclusion

We have proposed football-related predictions as an interesting application for relational learning. We have argued that football data are highly structured and naturally represented in a relational way. We have identified interesting learning tasks that require a relational approach such as link prediction and structured output learning. Experiments with a relational model yield competitive results.

Acknowledgments

Guy Van den Broeck is supported by the Research Foundation-Flanders (FWO-Vlaanderen). The authors wish to thank Vinicius Tragante do Ó, Hendrik Blockeel and Jesse Davis for their valuable feedback.

Bibliography

G. Baio and M. Blangiardo. Bayesian hierarchical model for the prediction of football results. *J. Appl. Stat.*, **32**, 253–264. 2010.

M. Dixon and S. Coles. Modelling association football scores and inefficiencies in the football betting market. *J. Roy. Stat. Soc. C-App.*, **46(2)**, 265–280. 1997.

P. Frasconi, F. Costa, L. De Raedt and K. De Grave. kLog — A Language for Logic-Based Relational Learning with Kernels. Technical report. 2011. Available online: `http://www.dsi.unifi.it/~paolo/ps/klog.pdf`. Accessed 13 August 2014.

G. Holmes, A. Donkin and I. Witten. Weka: A machine learning workbench. *Proceedings of the 1994 Second Australian and New Zealand Conference on Intelligent Information Systems*, pp. 357–361. 1994. ANZIIS 1994: Brisbane 29 November–2 December 1994.

U. Lago, R. Simmons and S. Szymanski. The financial crisis in European football. *J. Sport. Econ.*, **7(1)**, 3–12. 2006.

M. Maher. Modelling association football scores. *Statistica Neerlandica*, **36(3)**, 109–118. 1982.

M. Moroney. *Facts from Figures.* Penguin, London. 1956.

M. Xu, J. Orwell, L. Lowey, and D. Thirde. Architecture and algorithms for tracking football players with multiple cameras. *IEE P-Vis. Image Sign.*, **152**, 232–241. 2005.

Index